IMAGES
of America

UMATILLA

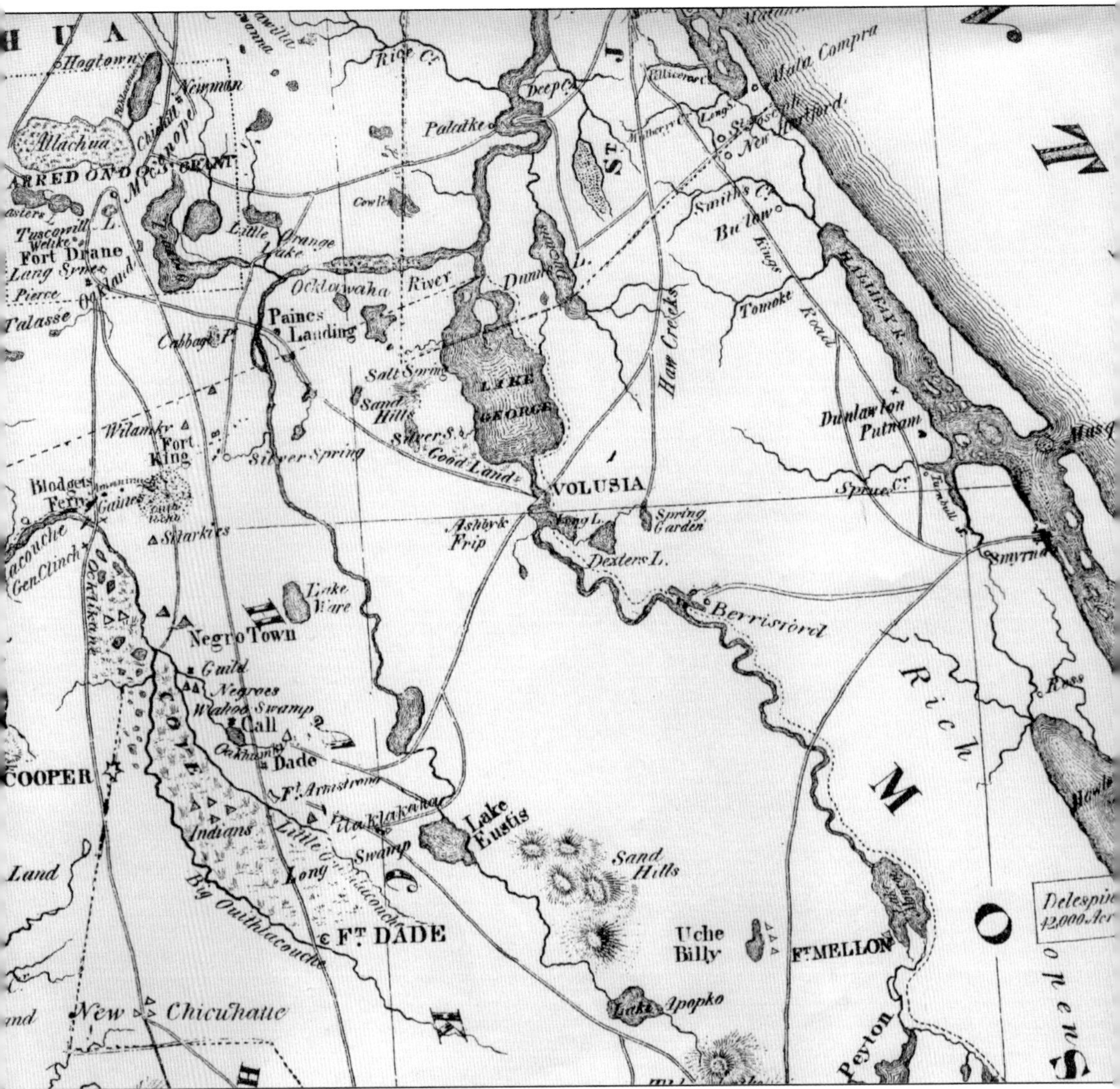

A map drawn during the Seminole Wars of the early 1800s shows Florida's Lake Region and the path of the St. Johns River into the highlands. Forts and natural landmarks were the only interior points, and Umatilla was yet to be settled. Fort Mellon, which was the closest point of delivery by water travel on the St. Johns, is clearly visible and early wagon trails are clearly marked. (Courtesy of Dan Smith.)

ON THE COVER: Pictured left to right in this 1923 photograph are an unidentified woman with Collins family members Harry Jr., Mary, Carolyn, and Bobby as they enjoy an afternoon on Lake Umatilla in a rowboat. Lake Umatilla is over 2 miles long. Boasting over 40 lakes within a 2 mile radius, Umatilla counts boating and fishing among its favorite pastimes. (Courtesy of Rebecca Bryan Dreisbach.)

IMAGES
of America

UMATILLA

Rebecca Bryan Dreisbach

ARCADIA
PUBLISHING

ISBN 978-0-7385-6612-2

Published by Arcadia Publishing
Charleston, South Carolina

Printed in the United States of America

Library of Congress Control Number: 2009924692

For all general information contact Arcadia Publishing at:
Telephone 843-853-2070
Fax 843-853-0044
E-mail sales@arcadiapublishing.com
For customer service and orders:
Toll-Free 1-888-313-2665

Visit us on the Internet at www.arcadiapublishing.com

To my Mother, Virginia Dickinson Collins Bryan, from whose roots a ninth generation grows in Florida sunshine

CONTENTS

ACKNOWLEDGMENTS

Inspiration from a pictured past, coupled with Umatilla's storied history, were the catalysts for writing this book. I hope this collection will inspire pride in Umatilla's past and hope for the future by connecting readers with those whose dreams were realized in a Florida wilderness.

It was the wise counsel of many and generous gifts of time, treasured photographs, maps, and memorabilia that made this book possible. Images in the book appear courtesy of Evelyn "Sis" Allen Sebree, Betty Jo Ramsey Moorhead, Daniel Smith, Eugene "Mike" Graham, Clayton Bishop, Dixie Royal, Lawrence Bains, Dr. Thomas Carr, Russell Bryan, Susie Austin, Jean Collins Gastfield, Ike Vaughn, Bob Skinner, Jimmy Scobie, Warren Smith Jr., The Greater Umatilla Historical Society, The Lake County Historical Society, or the author. I am grateful for the time Dan Smith and Sis Sebree spent reviewing this manuscript. I thank my editor, Lindsay Harris, for her guidance and endless patience.

Unexpected blessings came in the persons of Bertha Carroll, Loretta Cunningham, and Robert Dobson, who were raised in "Southside," Umatilla's historically black community. They kindly opened their home and memories so I could understand more than my experience, and their history deserves its own book.

I especially wish to thank my cousins Sis and Betty Jo, who always were available to make introductions and whose collective history I am happy and proud I share. Thank you for listening to and with me and keeping my room open at The Palms. And, to my friend and Florida citizen-at-large Leslie Kemp Poole, who inspires, encourages, educates, and who planted this book in my mind, thank you.

Tremendous gratitude for my family and friends comes with this book. These photographs—whispers from the past—will now be heard well into the future.

KEY TO PHOTOGRAPH COURTESIES

Evelyn "Sis" Allen Sebree (EAS)
Betty Jo Ramsey Moorhead (BJM)
Daniel Smith (DS)
Eugene "Mike" Graham (MG)
Clayton Bishop (CB)
Dixie Royal (DR)
Lawrence Bains (LB)
Dr. Thomas Carr (TC)
Russell Bryan (RB)
Susie Turner Austin (SA)
Jean Collins Gatsfield (JG)
Ike Vaughn (IV)
The Greater Umatilla Historical Society (UHS)
The Lake County Historical Society (LCHS)

INTRODUCTION

As the gateway to the Ocala National Forest where deer, turkey, wild hog, quail, and dove provide challenge to hunters, Umatilla most naturally lays claim to the title of "Sportsman's Town." Fishing is nearly as common as breathing, with 40 fish-rich lakes within 2 miles of the city limits and several hundred more within a half hour's drive. Bass, bream, catfish, and speckled perch are favorite catches. The beautiful crystal waters and white sands of the nearby Alexander, Juniper, and de Leon Springs have provided recreation and relaxation for centuries. Archeological sites date Timucua Indians to this region between 1,000 and 1,500 AD, hundreds of years before European colonists arrived.

During the British colonial period various southern tribes, including the Yamasees, Creeks, and Miccosukees began migrating into Florida. These tribes, though separate, were collectively called "Cimarrones," which in Spanish meant "wild ones," or "runaways," and is the origin of the name *Seminole*.

When Florida became a U.S. territory in 1821, efforts to encourage new settlement brought federal troops into Florida to relocate the Seminoles. The Florida Wars, also known as the Seminole Wars, dominated Florida's early territorial history. Forts were built throughout the region, known then as Mosquito County, to provide ammunition and supplies for troops. In March 1836, troops camped near present day Umatilla while a bridge was constructed over the Ocklawaha River to the west. A fortified stockade was built and named Fort Mason, most likely to honor Lt. Col. Pierce Mason Butler, the leader of the expedition and after whom Fort Butler in nearby Astor also was named.

Early 1842 brought an end to the war, with authorization to leave the remaining Seminoles on an informal reservation in southwestern Florida. In August 1842, Congress passed the Armed Occupation Act, which offered 160 acres in Florida free to settlers who improved the land and were armed and prepared to defend themselves against Native Americans. Fort Mason became a supply base to support and encourage settlement in the area.

The earliest days of Umatilla are lost to history, but it is known that Nathan Johnston Trowell and his wife, Rebecca Louisa Minors, left South Carolina in 1852 and built a log cabin near present day Lake Umatilla, where their only neighbors were roaming Seminoles and runaway slaves. After Rebecca's death in July 1861, which left Nathan with four motherless young boys, he married Sevenah Hart of Alachua County, Florida. Their honeymoon included a trip through the Ocala scrub on an ox-driven wagon. Nathan and Sevenah had nine more children and today fifth-generation descendants live on a portion of their original homestead.

A notable trader, Trowell kept cattle, planted Sea Island cotton and rice, and built a gristmill and cotton gin. Later, he opened a general store, west of his home, to serve the growing community. Raising cattle became the first industry in Umatilla and was an important supply of cattle for troops during the Seminole, Civil, and Spanish-American wars.

By 1860, the Smith brothers (Wesley, Warren, Kennerly, Henry, Edwin, and Fletcher) and Joshua Turner and family were settled and living nearby. These pioneers planted green vegetables, watermelon, corn, potatoes, sugar cane, cotton, and later citrus. All were recorded in the 1860 census as owning land in what was then Sumter County. It was not until 1887 that Lake County was created from portions of Orange and Sumter Counties.

The James Marion Owens family arrived in 1870, and other early settlers included George and Will Devault, Dr. Hannah and family, Walter Elias Stoops, David McCredie, John Mitchener, Benjamin McLin, Alton Epps, Rev. Edward Guerrant, Robert Lee Collins, John Traub, and the Faw, Bracy, and Whitley families.

Umatilla's mail and supplies were carried by oxcart to and from Mellonville on the St. Johns River, where riverboats traveled to Jacksonville. But in order to receive mail, the settlement needed a name. It was William Whitcomb who suggested the name Umatilla for the growing community. Trowell rode on horseback to the U.S. land grant office in Gainesville and on April 26, 1878, registered the settlement's name as Umatilla.

Trowell was granted permission to establish a post office as part of his general store and became Umatilla's first postmaster. Once Umatilla had an official post, Trowell successfully campaigned for a stop on the new train coming south from Jacksonville. Riders on Umatilla's first train could proudly claim to be on the second rail line in Florida. The narrow-gauge train backed into town, as there was no turnaround, and was slow by today's standards, but was by far the most dependable means of transportation of the day. Anyone could hail the train to catch a ride. Hunters in the scrub often used the train to ride out to hunt and return home. Getting crops and citrus quickly to market brought tremendous change and was a marvelous improvement for backwoods settlers.

Benjamin and Lucy Yancey arrived in Umatilla in 1881. Dalton Huger Yancey joined his brother in 1884. Benjamin Yancey and Nathan Trowell agreed that subdividing lots would encourage close settling in the growing community. Yancey bought property from Trowell and David McCredie, and lots were laid for the Trowell subdivision on the east side of the tracks, and the Yancey subdivision on the west. Benjamin Yancey became Lake County's first judge, and a state senator in the late 1880s. Today the fifth generation of Yanceys live in Umatilla.

In 1894, an inventory of economic and social progress listed four business houses carrying large stocks of general merchandise, a drug store, a bank, a jeweler, a meat market, two well-kept hotels, a wagon and blacksmith shop, three churches (Methodist, Baptist, and Presbyterian), a public school with about 100 pupils enrolled, two large and well-equipped packinghouses, a lumber yard, a printing office issuing a local paper, and a registered voting population of 125. Two days after Christmas, a devastating freeze arrived, followed by a second on February 7, 1895—together historically known as the Big Freeze. According to the old-timers, it "busted the bark from top to bottom" and virtually destroyed every grove and crop. The gravest of times followed and train officials offered free rides out of Florida to those who wanted to leave. Nearby settlements simply disappeared. Hunger and poverty naturally followed, leaving their mark on many.

Those who remained managed to eke a living from lumber, cattle, and vegetable farming. Hardy citrus pioneers replanted and within fifteen years groves so densely carpeted the countryside that the vista through Umatilla was nicknamed "the velvet highway." Citrus production prospered in Florida for decades following World War II, and Umatilla was at its heart. At one time, there was more land in groves than in the city limits. That would change with nature's whim when, despite warnings and protection efforts, the devastating "Hundred Year" freezes in the 1980s forever changed the economic and natural landscapes of Umatilla.

Look just below the town's exteriors and Umatilla's past can be seen. The old train depot hides in the library, the first post office in the Masonic Temple, and an unforgettable school in the Umatilla Historic Museum. Historic homes, churches, and schools give evidence of Umatilla's proud past, which laid a firm foundation for future generations.

One

Early Settlers

The 1830 census showed nearly half (15,500) of the territory of Florida's population of 34,730 was made up of slaves living on plantations. Colonial settlements were mostly in northern and coastal Florida. The area remained a natural wilderness inhabited by roaming Seminoles and runaway former slaves who found central Florida an ideal hiding place. Some runaways lived free and were farmers in the area. Others found sanctuary with the Seminoles, sometimes becoming slaves of the Seminoles and sometimes marrying into the local village.

Disagreements between Seminoles and settlers fueled years of conflict and drew troops into Florida to relocate the Seminoles. Though never numerous, the determined Seminoles fought in diminishing numbers. Peace came early in 1842, with a treaty providing protection for the Seminoles who remained on an informal reservation in southwest Florida. Settlers eagerly awaited an end to the Seminole issue in Florida. In August 1843, Congress passed the Armed Occupation Act, providing 160 acres in Florida to settlers who improved the land and were armed and prepared to defend it from any remaining Seminoles. Early settlers raised cattle and planted corn, vegetables, rice, cotton, and indigo. Homes were built with indigenous materials.

Following the Civil War, another homesteading act offered land in Florida. Many families eager for a new beginning began settling the area. *The Umatilla Progress* wrote, "The families living here [in 1875] could have easily been counted on the fingers, but a kindlier, more hospitable, cheerful and contented people was never seen anywhere—helpful to one another, regardful of one another's feelings and comfort to a degree that was astonishing."

Umatilla history is the story of memories, its successes and failures, and is common to many settlements in Florida following the Seminole and Civil Wars. Early settlers required faith and perseverance to remain through freezes, famine, fire, and economic cycles. Memories recall with good humor the creative ways settlers often made do with little. Today's industries—citrus groves, cattle and horse ranches, watermelon, vegetable farms, beekeeping and honey producers, and emerging ecotourism—are the inheritors of Umatilla's time-honored traditions.

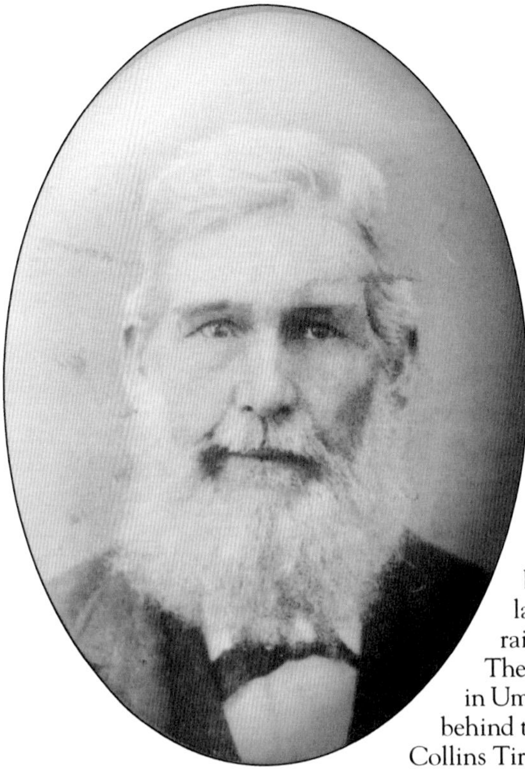

Sevenah and Nathan Trowell were Umatilla's founding family. Trowell, born in 1826, was the pioneer merchant, grower, and owner of the land on which Umatilla was built. He was Umatilla's first postmaster, and for some years was agent for the St. Johns and Lake Eustis Railroad. Trowell and his first wife, Rebecca, homesteaded along the shore of what would be known as Lake Umatilla and built a log home in which to raise their four boys. Tragically, Rebecca died in 1861. Trowell later married Sevenah Hart, and together they raised his four boys and had nine more children. Their child Mary Ann was the first white child born in Umatilla. Trowell built a grist mill and cotton gin behind the present city hall and a general store where Collins Tire stands today. (Both photographs EAS.)

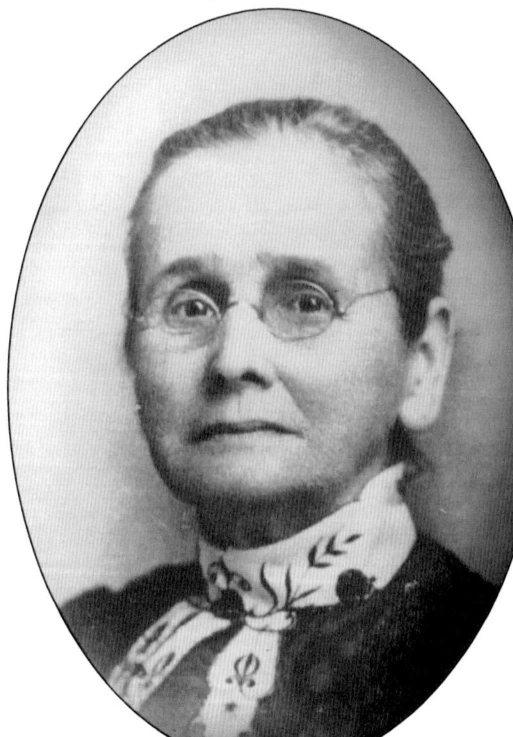

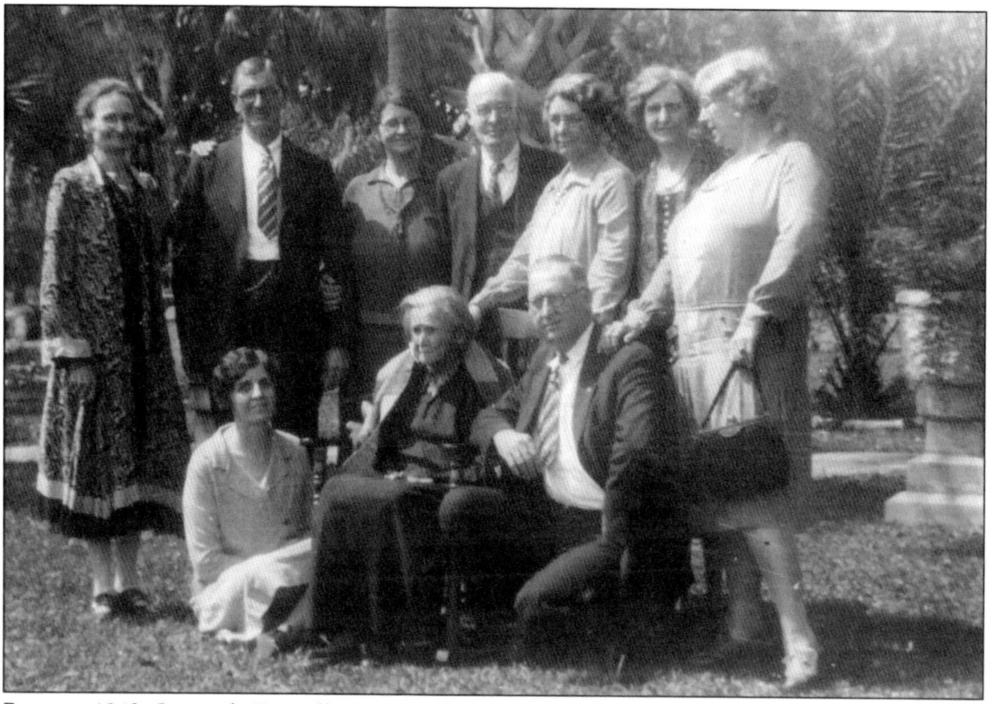

Born in 1843, Sevenah Trowell is pictured above with her children in 1915. Sevenah Trowell lived until 1928. She was fortunate to see the little settlement she and Nathan founded grow into a prosperous town and to know and love her great-grandchildren. Her children are, from left to right, as follows: (standing) Mary Ann, James, Rebecca Louise, William, Drucilla, Bena, and Grace; (kneeling) Romania and John. Pictured below is the home where Sevenah and Nathan Trowell raised their 13 children. After the original log home burned to the ground, Trowell built this home, the first frame house in the area, for his family. Their daughter, Romania, recalled the days when quilting bees were held in the large central hall to catch the cross breeze, and that her responsibility was to fan her grandmother Mary Ann Higginbotham Hart. (EAS.)

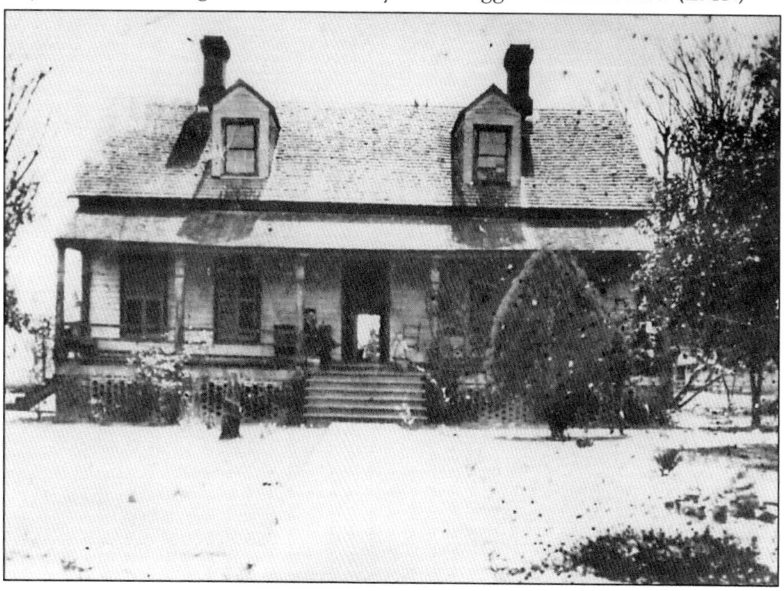

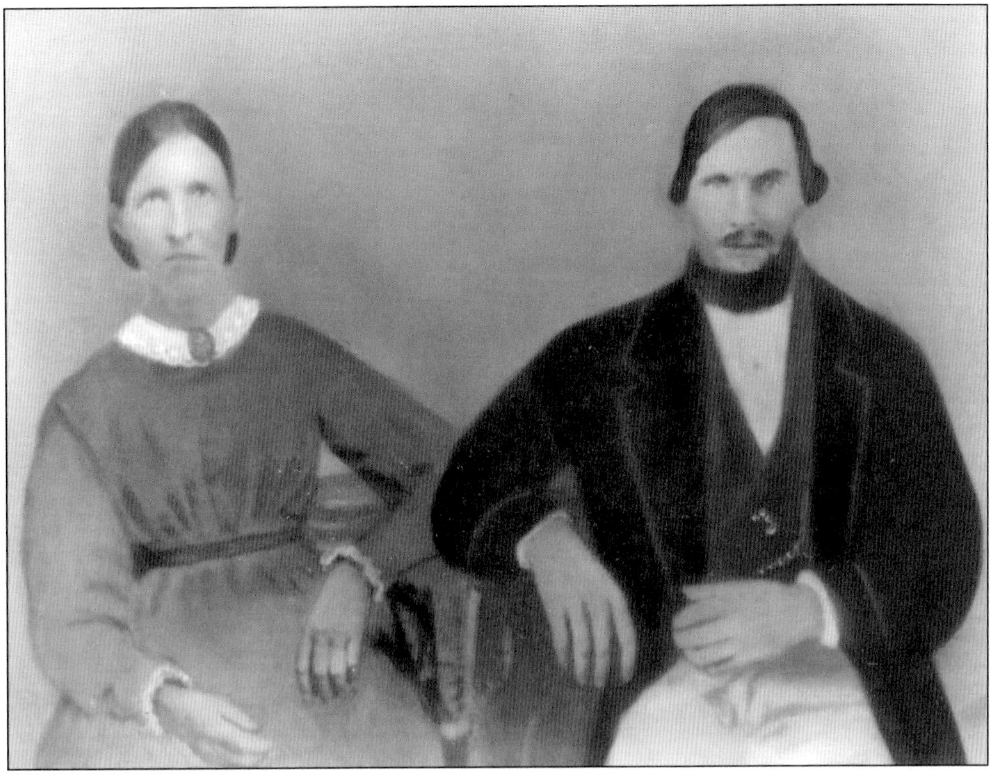

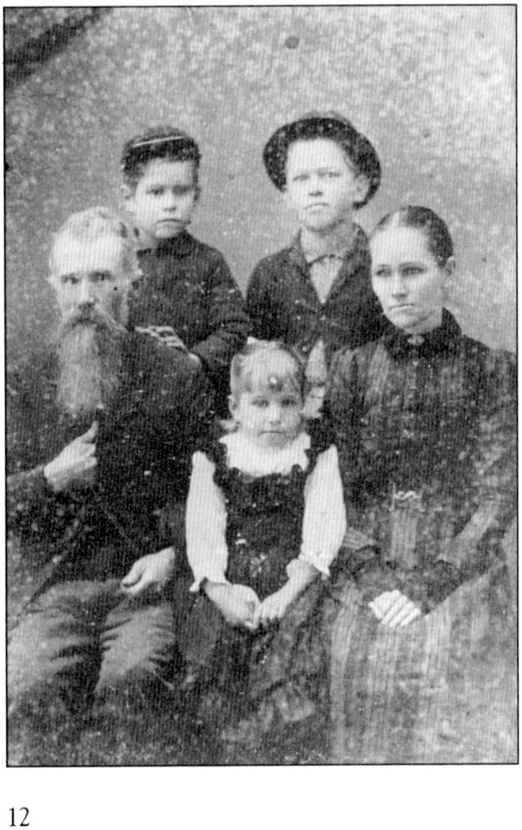

Anne and John Turner are pictured in the mid-1800s. The Turners filed claim to land in 1855 in the area that would become Umatilla, and were one of a handful of families living in the wilds. The Turners had five children: Josh, Ellen, Luraney, Lucretia, and Hulda. Turner grew corn and later concentrated his efforts on growing citrus. He died at age 42, shortly after returning from the Civil War. A portion of the homestead remains in the family today, 150 years later. The old home was built entirely by James Drawdy, even splitting the cypress shingles. During restoration of the home, carpenters said many of the 150-year-old shingles were in perfect condition. The Turners' son Joshua and his wife, California, are pictured on the left with their children Perry Caleb, Gertrude, and Charles John. (Above LB, Left SA.)

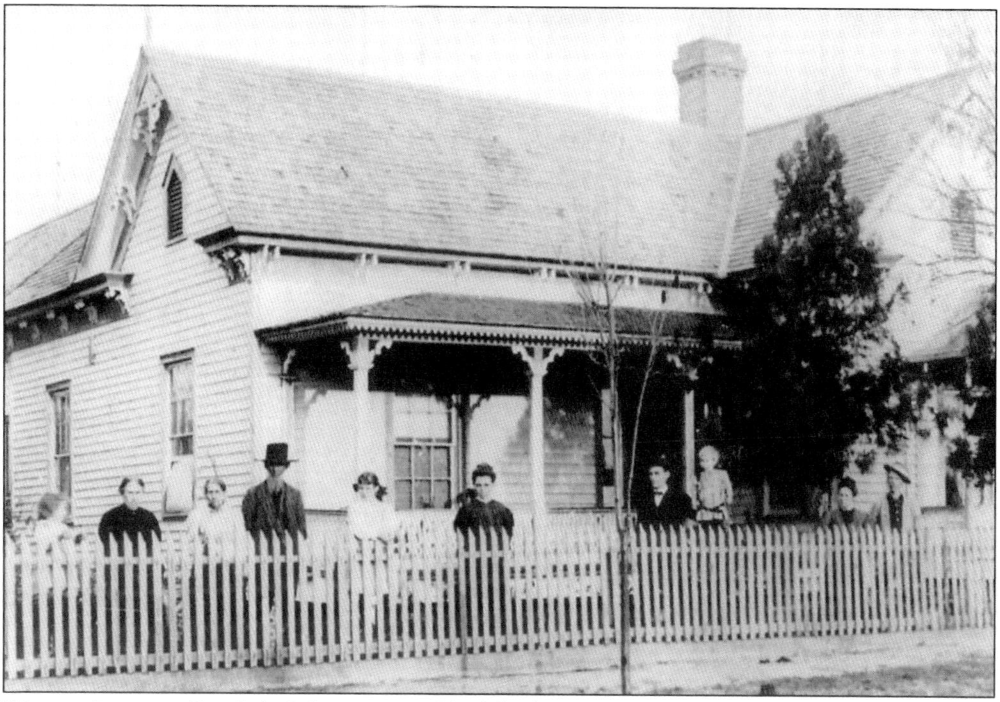

Warren Augustus Smith (at left, wearing a black hat) is pictured at home in the 1890s. Along with five brothers, Warren was living in the area in 1860. All of the Smith brothers, except Fletcher (who was too young), served in the Civil War and miraculously all survived. The entire family moved for a short while during the war to Micanopy, Florida, where Warren's wife, Lucy Caroline Dominey, had family who provided security for the wives while the men were off fighting. Following the war, Warren, Kennerly, Wesley and Fletcher returned to Umatilla in 1868. Lucy and Warren Smith had five children, Ida Iola, Theodore Augustus, William Wesley, Andrew Jackson, and Mary Elizabeth. Pictured below in 1915, Andrew Jackson Smith's home was built entirely of pine logs cut and milled nearby. The home still stands on Church Street. (Both photographs DS.)

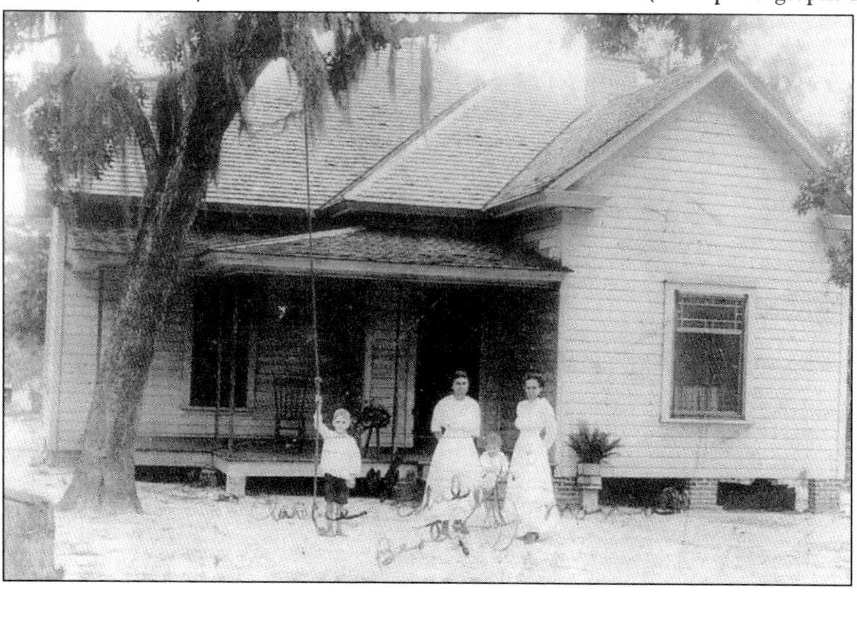

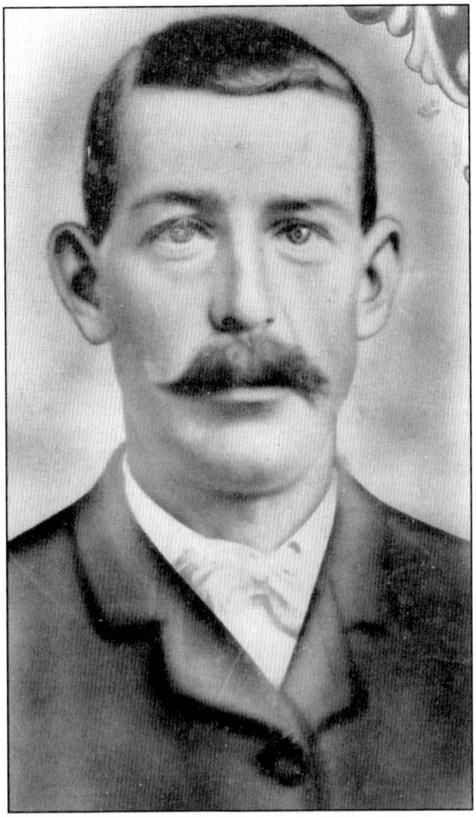

Pioneer Andrew Smith (no relation to the former) married Nettie Hawkins, whose family was one of the earliest settlers. Their daughter Ella married C. A. Vaughn Sr., who served as mayor of Umatilla. Below, members of the Hawkins and Smith families are gathered. Shown, not in order, are Reuben J. Hawkins, Lizzie Hawkins Dowell, Mr. Dowell, Margaret Hawkins Baylor, Ellen Turner Hawkins (whose father, John Turner, came to the area in 1848), Pearl Hawkins, Harry Hawkins, Paul Hawkins, and Mabel Hawkins Stout. The woman seated on the left is Victoria Wiley Hawkins. (Both photographs IV.)

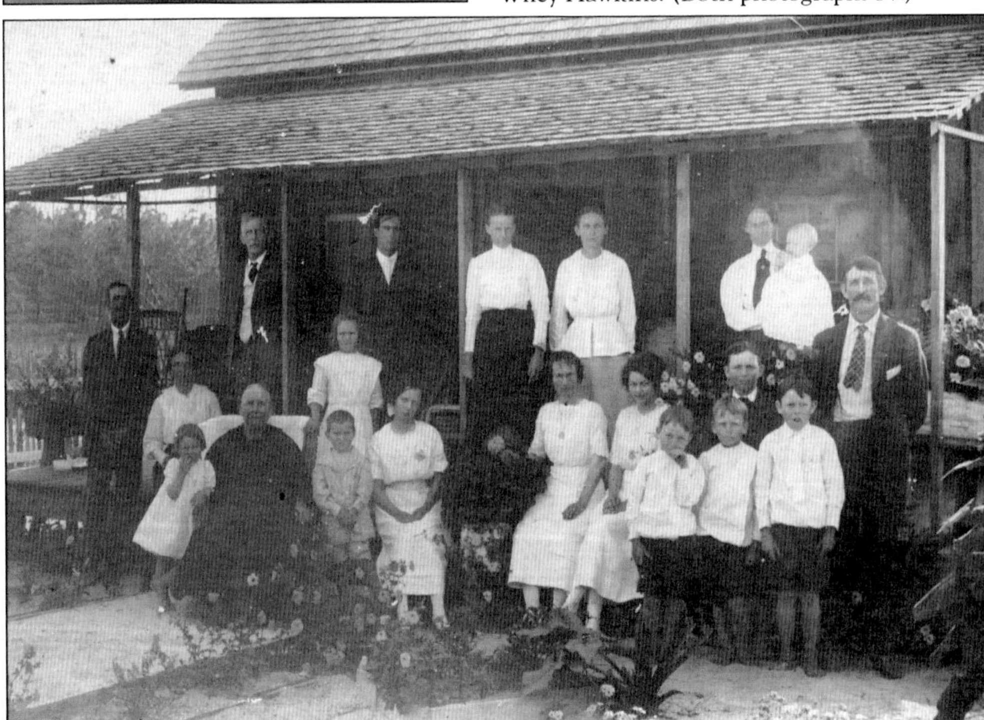

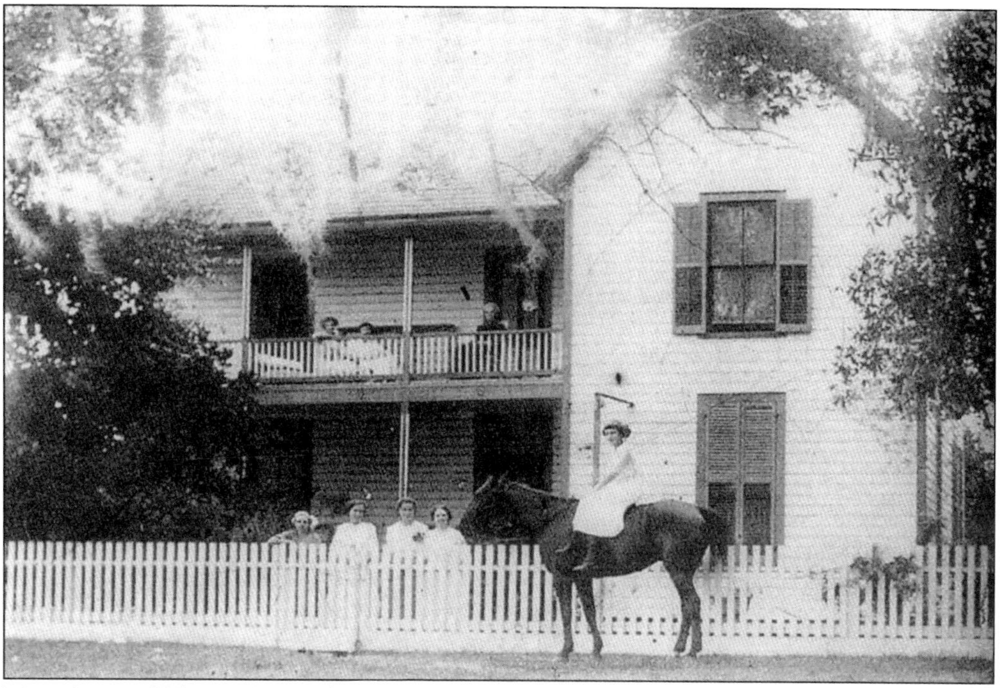

Mary Ann and Thomas J. Woodward's home was built in 1890 and is located at 46 South Central Avenue in Umatilla, catty-corner to the city hall. Mary Ann is seen in this picture on the porch upstairs. Below, the W. M. Strobel House is pictured in 1903. This was the first house Strobel bought when he brought his family to Umatilla. The Strobels had two children, Pearl and Millard (known as Mitt). Mitt was a member of the popular Umatilla marching band in the early 1900s, and Pearl married Ted Epps, whose father had a general merchandise store in Umatilla. Shown in no particular order are Jake, Mrs. Strobel, Pearl, Dick, Kelly, Henry, Maggie, and Mr. Strobel. On the balcony is Mitt. (Above DS, below BJM.)

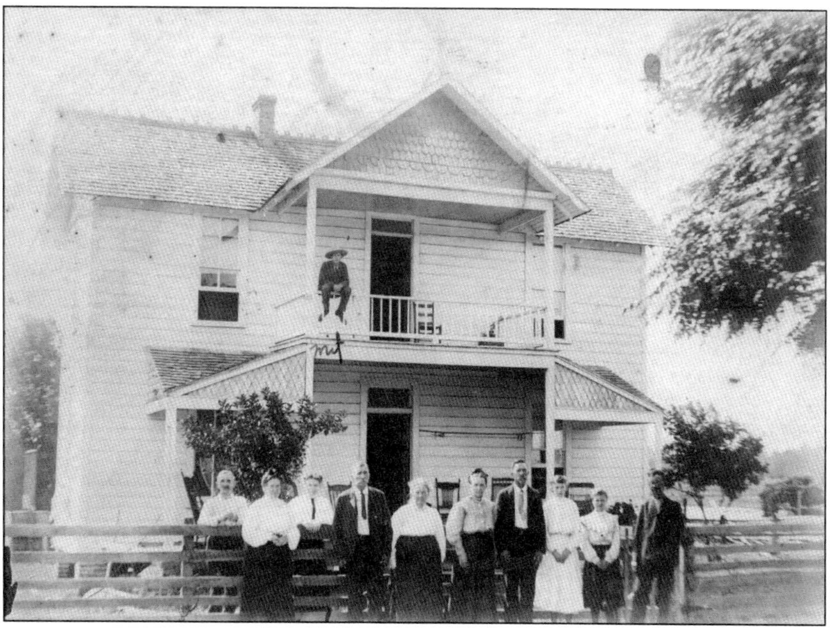

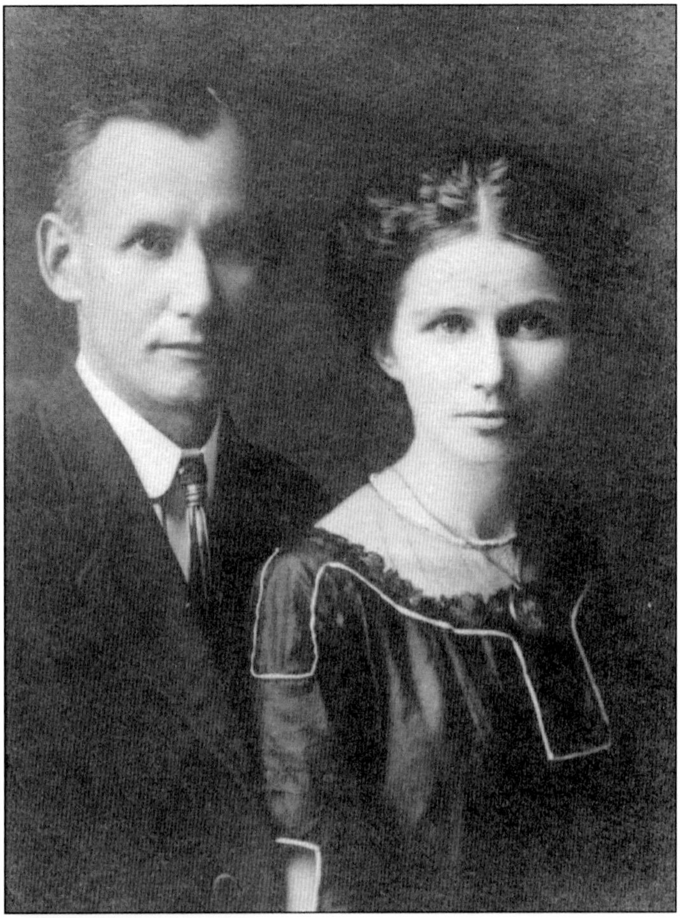

Theodore Augustus Smith, a grandson of pioneer Warren Smith, is pictured with his wife, Gertrude Turner Smith. The Smiths were owners of T. A. Smith Mercantile in Umatilla. Their store was the first block building constructed in Umatilla and included a barber chair, a confectionary, and a soda fountain that was a popular gathering place in Umatilla's early days. Upstairs was the dentist office of Dr. Broyles and later a beauty parlor. Seen below is the home of Smith and his wife, which was on the corner of Pine Street and Rose Street. (Left SA, below DS.)

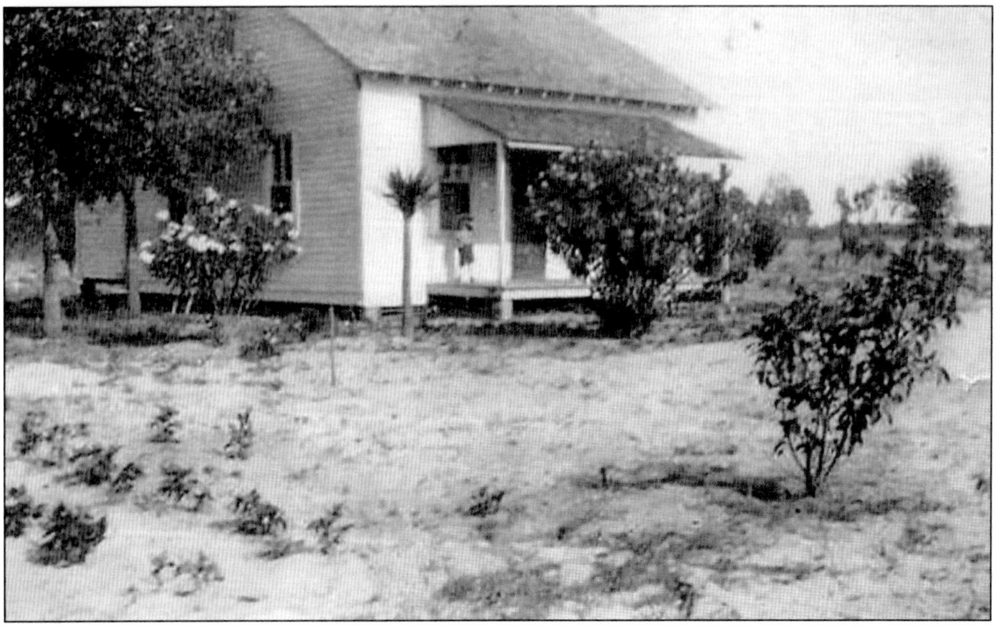

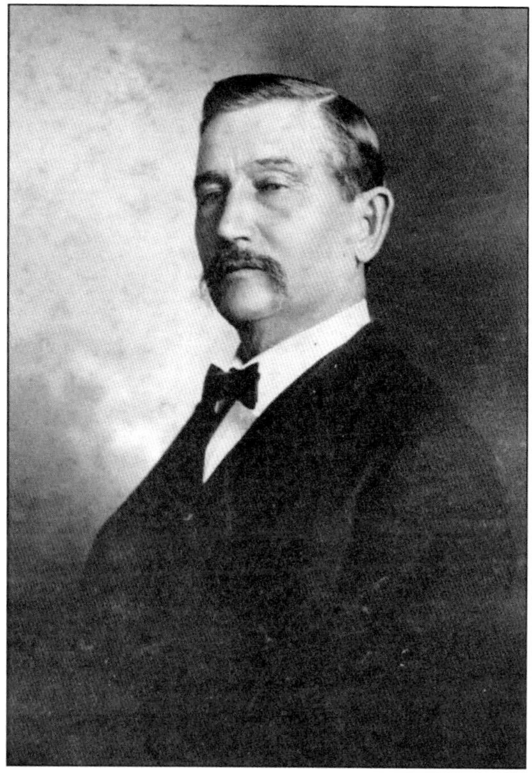

Portraits of Kennerly Smith and his wife, Caroline Higginbotham, are shown here. Kennerly was one of the five Smith brothers who came to the area in the 1850s. Kennerly was a private in Company G, Capt. Stewart's 8th Florida Regiment, CSA during the Civil War. Kennerly served as a shoemaker and leather worker, repairing saddles, bridles, and tack. Kennerly and Caroline had eight children: Mitalena, Maude, Hugh, Lelia, Leon, Herbert, Mattie, and Alvin. (Both photographs LB.)

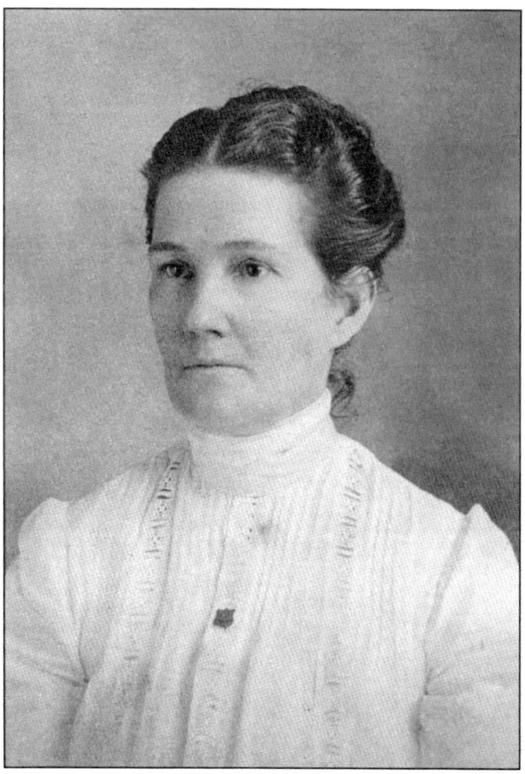

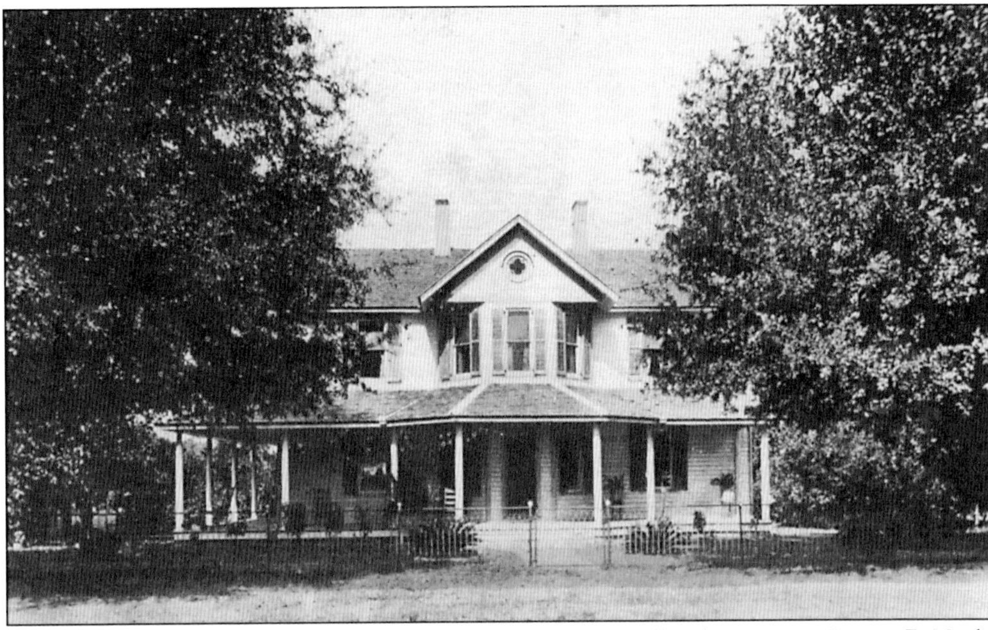

This beautiful home was built by in the early 1900s by Umatilla's first mayor, George DeVault. DeVault, along with Robert Lee Collins and Fletcher Smith, served on the committee that recommended the city boundary lines when Umatilla was incorporated in 1904. The DeVaults were orange growers and operated the first commercial packinghouse in Umatilla. George's brother, Will DeVault, was a partner in the mercantile Faw and DeVault General Store in the 1880s. (EAS.)

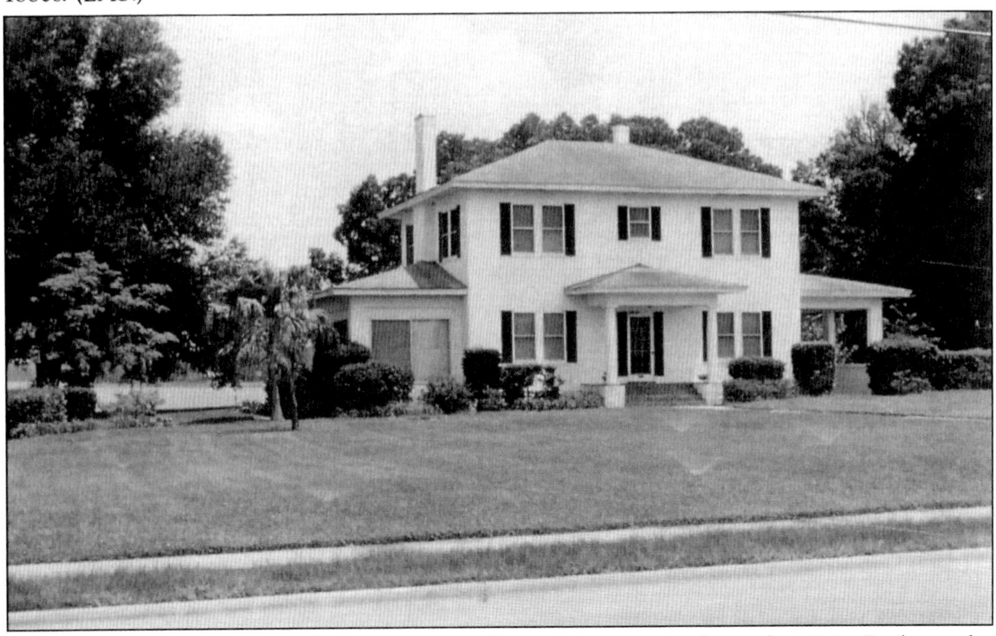

Cleo and Brunt Calhoun built this home on Central Avenue in the early 1930s. Built on the site of the historic Buena Vista hotel, the home sits on the west shore of Lake Umatilla. When the hotel was torn down, materials salvaged were used in the construction of their home. Cleo's father, Charles Turner, was born in 1879 in Umatilla and served as mayor in 1917. (BJM.)

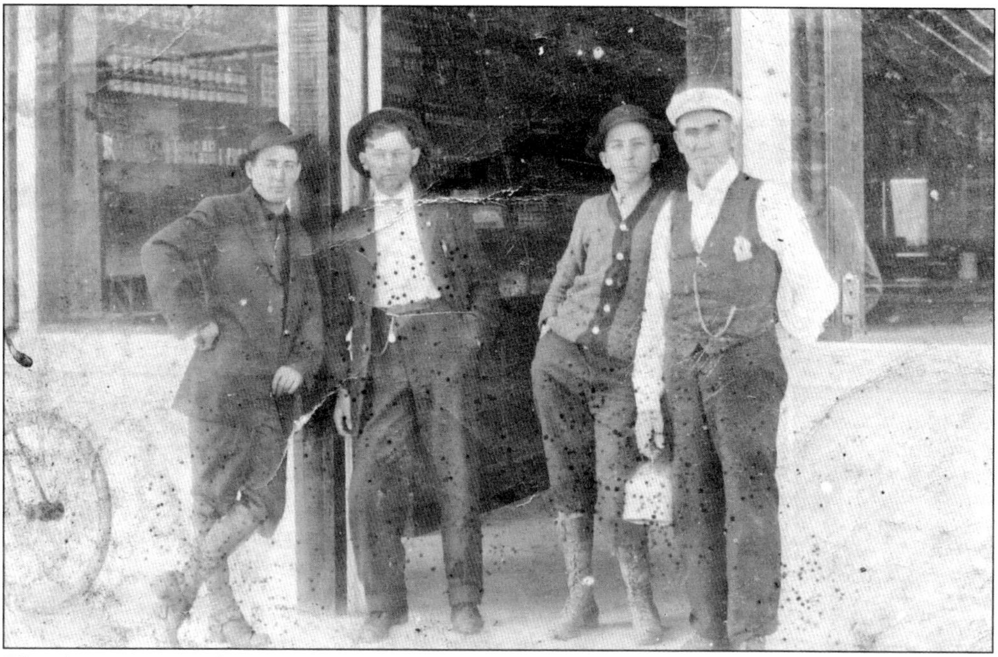

This dapper group of young men posing for the photographer are, from left to right, J. A. Morrell, Carlie Avant "C. A." Vaughn Sr., Norman Collins, and an unidentified gentleman. The men are pictured in front of OK Grocery in 1916. The grocery anchored the Collins Building on the north corner. At right, this portrait of C. A. Vaughn Sr. was taken shortly upon his arrival in Umatilla in 1900. Family legend has it that Vaughn arrived with a change of clothes, a bottle of liquor, and a .45 pistol. Less than 15 years later, he was elected mayor of Umatilla. (Both photographs IV.)

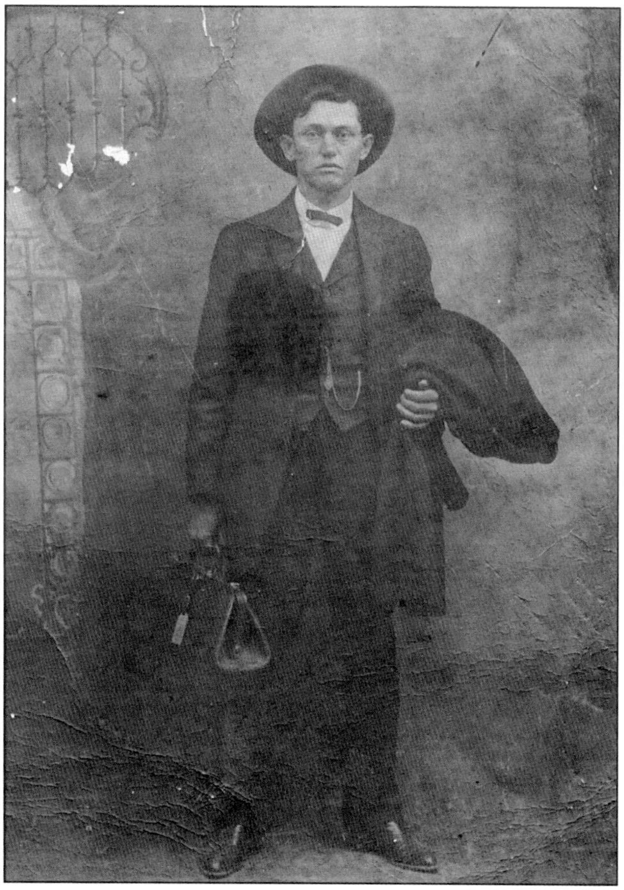

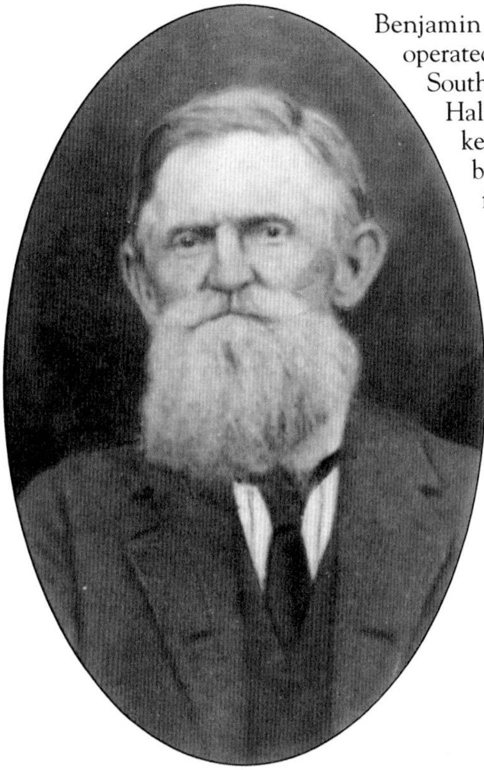

Benjamin Cunningham Yancey was a citrus grower and operated a syrup mill. Yancey had been living in Brazil, South America, where he met and married Lucy Caines Hall, before his arrival in 1881. The Yancey family was key to the early development of Umatilla. Yancey's brother Dalton Huger Yancey became Lake County's first judge and a state senator in the late 1880's. Yancey's son William Lowndes Yancey was Umatilla's first clerk and served as a Lake County commissioner from 1927 to 1935. (LCHS.)

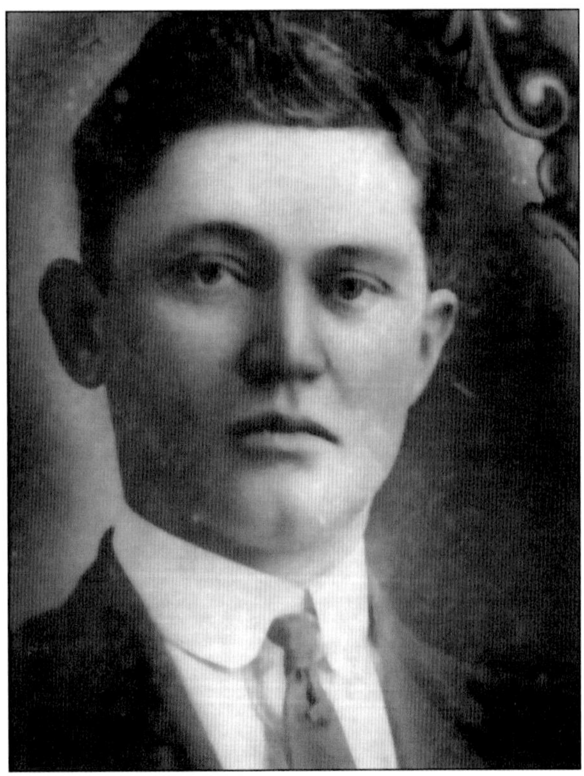

Carlie Avant Vaughn Sr. served as mayor of Umatilla in 1914, and again for two terms, from 1922 until 1926. During his tenure, Umatilla sold its electric plant to the Florida Public Service Company and the rail line between Astor and Umatilla was closed as affordable automobiles and ever-improving roadways replaced passenger train travel. (IV.)

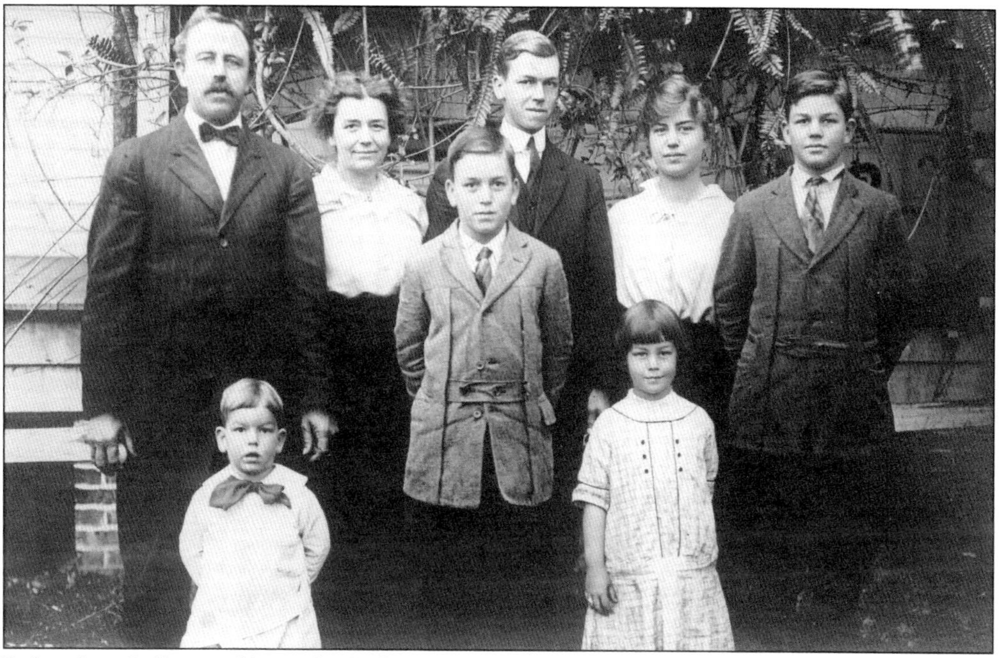

Robert Lee Collins and his wife, Catherine Drucilla Trowell Collins, pose with their children in this 1914 photograph. Pictured are, from left to right, the following: (first row) William Devault, Robert Trowell, and Evelyn Louise; (second row) Robert Lee, Catherine Drucilla Trowell, Harry Lee, Bena Bertha, and Paul Eugene. Collins arrived in Umatilla in 1884 with only a suit of clothes and $10.00 to his name. By the 1920s, his citrus empire had made him the second-largest taxpayer in Lake County. Below is the oft-photographed Collins home, sometimes nicknamed "the White House," which was built in 1904. All the materials were milled on-site and a home was built next door for the workers during construction. The original posts for the wraparound porches were made from palm trunks, which the children remembered for their abundant splinters. Four generations have called the big white house home. One of Collins's great-grandchildren lives in the restored workers' house. (Both photographs EAS.)

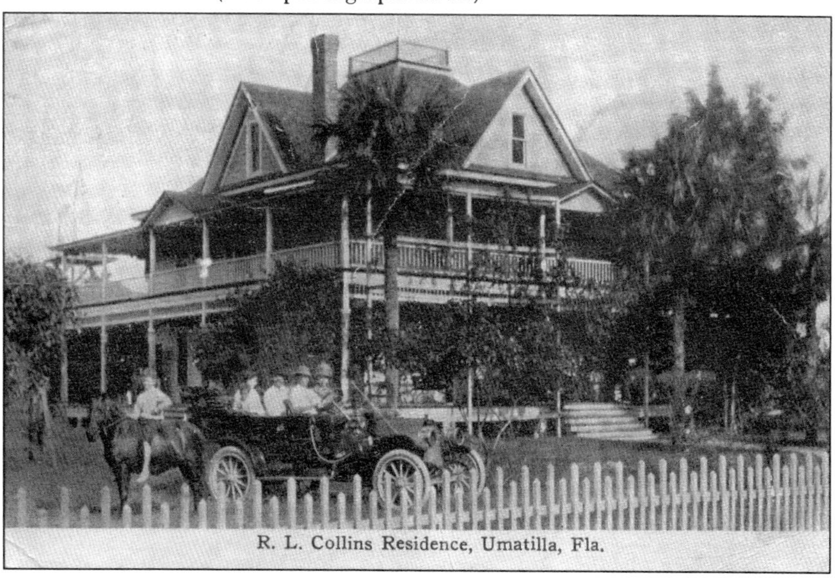

R. L. Collins Residence, Umatilla, Fla.

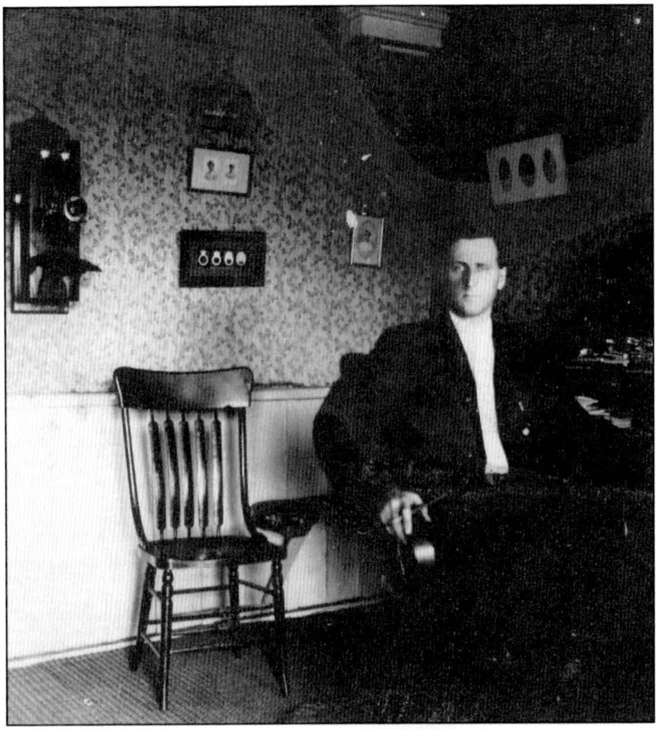

Dr. Charles Roberts is photographed in his office at the turn of the century. The wall phone was one of the first telephone lines in town, though Tibbals Drug Store could proudly claim the phone number "1." Dr. Roberts, however, could likewise claim to have owned the first car in Umatilla. He is pictured below with his 1904 Buick Runaround. Dressed in his driving coat and gloves, Roberts is ready to take his passengers out for a drive. Notice the steering wheel on the right, the crank start, and the tube tires that no doubt found themselves stuck in the sandy roads around town at least a time or two. (Left EAS, below UHS.)

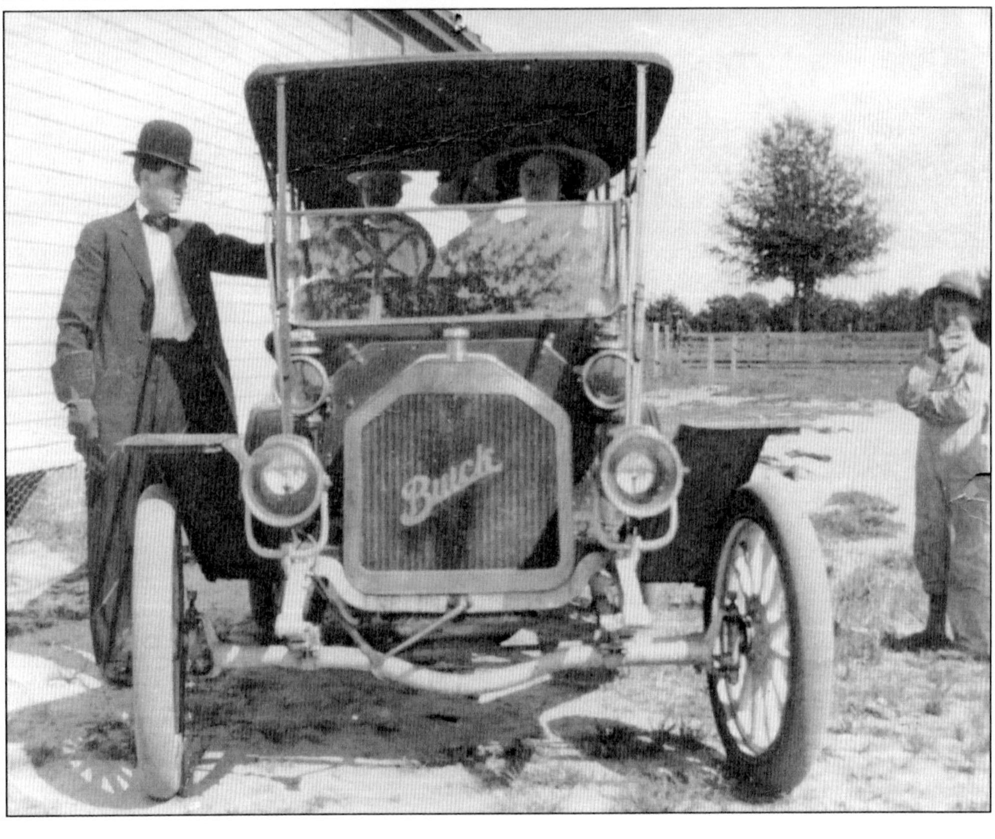

Clyde Vaughn, one of mayor Vaughn's sons, served as Umatilla's city clerk for many years. Vaughn also sold firewood from a location on north Central Avenue and kept a cabbage patch, from which his daughter, Sally Seabrook, recalls eating so much that, to this day, she has little desire for cabbage. Vaughn is pictured with his grandmother Nettie Hawkins Smith. (IV.)

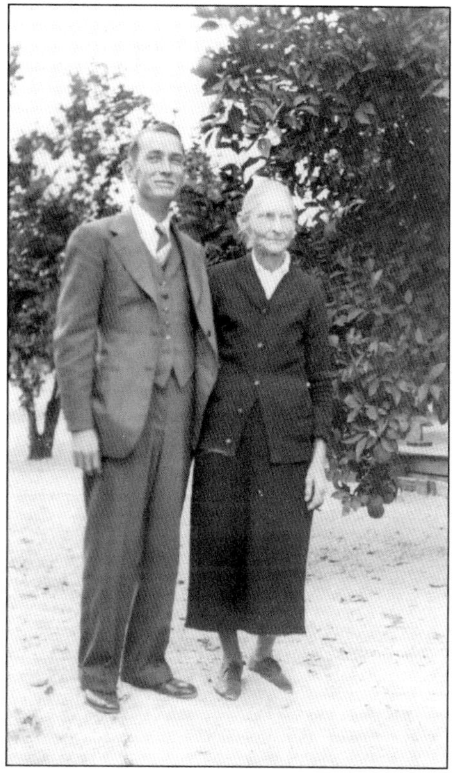

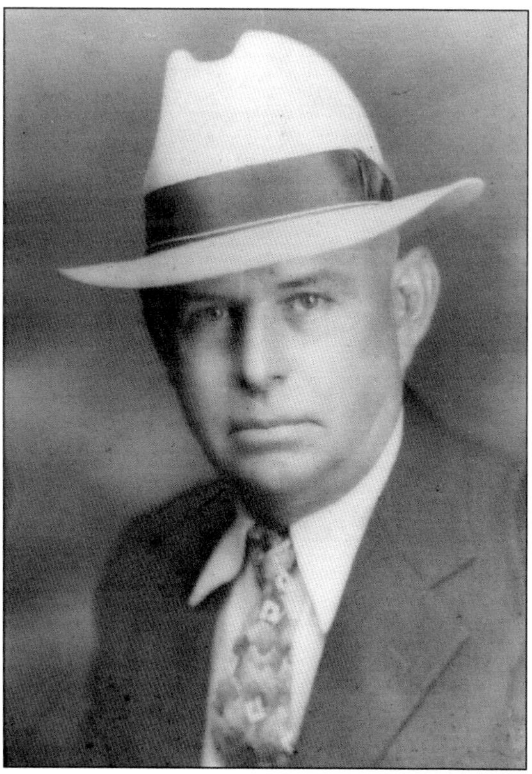

This portrait of Perry Caleb Turner was taken in the 1940s. Turner was the son of Joshua Turner and was the grandson of Umatilla pioneer Charles John Turner. Perry Caleb followed the family tradition and was a successful cattleman and citrus grower in Umatilla. (SA.)

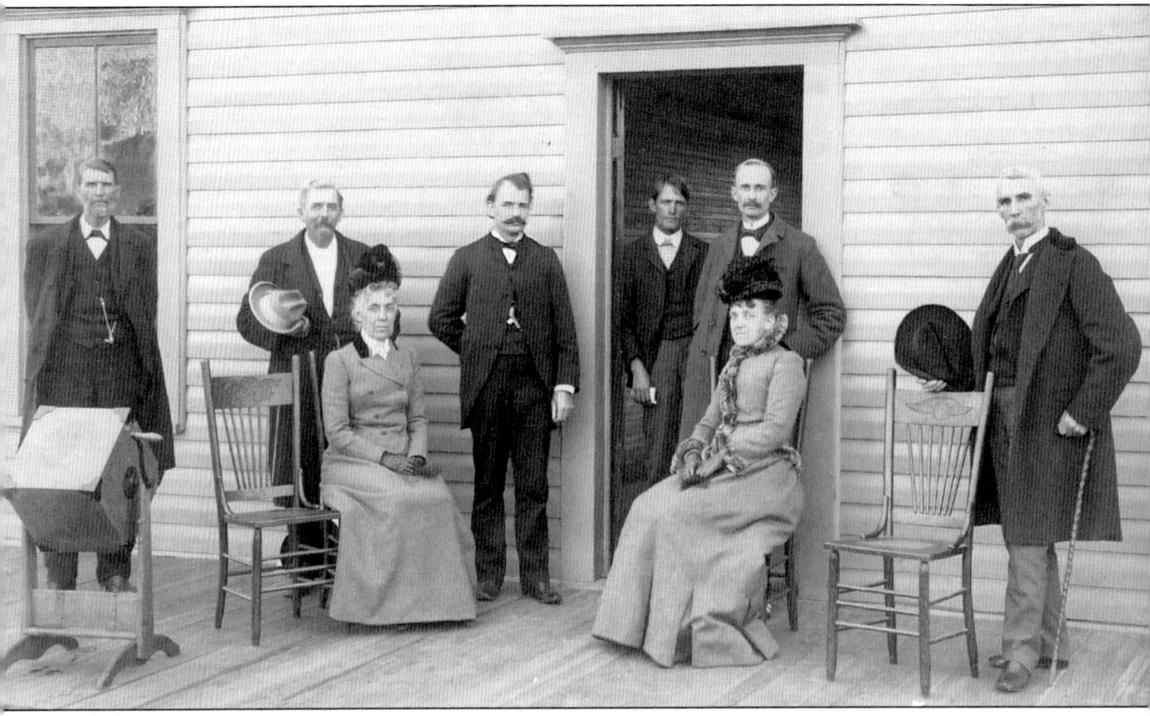

Benjamin E. McLin (far right), of Umatilla, is pictured with Gov. William Sherman Jennings (fourth from left) and members of his cabinet following the 1901 inauguration. Benjamin McLin owned a saw and planing mill in Umatilla, and served as state senator from 1895 to 1897 and again in 1899. McLin was named secretary of agriculture of the state of Florida in 1901 and served until his death in 1912. During his tenure, under governors Jennings and Broward, the drainage of the Florida Everglades project began, with the hope of turning more than 3 million acres of glades into productive agricultural land. Upon his death, Secretary McLin lay in state at the foot of the grand staircase of the Florida capitol. A photograph of McLin lying in state was later used in the restoration of the historic capitol building in Tallahassee. (LCHS.)

Two

A Light Shines through the Cracks

In 1874, before Umatilla was even named, a little log schoolhouse was built on the west side of Lake Enola. Nathan Trowell, David McCredie, and Warren Smith, heads of the first families to settle in Umatilla, provided for the building. It was about 12 by 14 feet, with one door and no windows. The cracks between the logs allowed sufficient lighting and the children sat on hewn log benches, which were arranged so they could lean against the wall. The first teacher was Jasper Roberts, who taught one term of three months and received $15 per month. There were 10 pupils and four patrons.

After the second term, the patrons built a frame building at Bay Springs on the Ocala-Orlando Road, the only established road at the time. In 1876, the new school was in session for nine months with 25 registered pupils. Grace Trowell Davis recalled that, while she was a student, recreation included riding hogs around the schoolhouse. The traditional long hewn bench was remembered for its use during student recitation. William Thomas Kennedy, Alma Bryson, and Mrs. Hansel Williams were teaching in 1895. In 1902, Professor Kennedy began conducting a normal school during the summer months to train future teachers. Kennedy later became Lake County school superintendent and in 1929 wrote the definitive *History of Lake County, Florida.*

In 1887, a new school was built at Osceola Park after the Bay Springs schoolhouse was destroyed by a storm. That building burned to the ground in 1907, and students had to travel to Eustis for schooling. It was not until 1910–1912 that a new $5,000 building was constructed. No longer in use as a school, this building is named the Paul W. Bryan Historic Schoolhouse, in recognition of Bryan's 28 years of membership on the Lake County School Board. It currently houses the Umatilla Museum.

By the 1950s, the single Umatilla school had grown to a campus including an agriculture building, gymnasium, cafeteria, and individual buildings for first through third grades, fourth through eighth grades, and a high school. Pioneer families would be proud of Umatilla's many generations of students and their accomplishments.

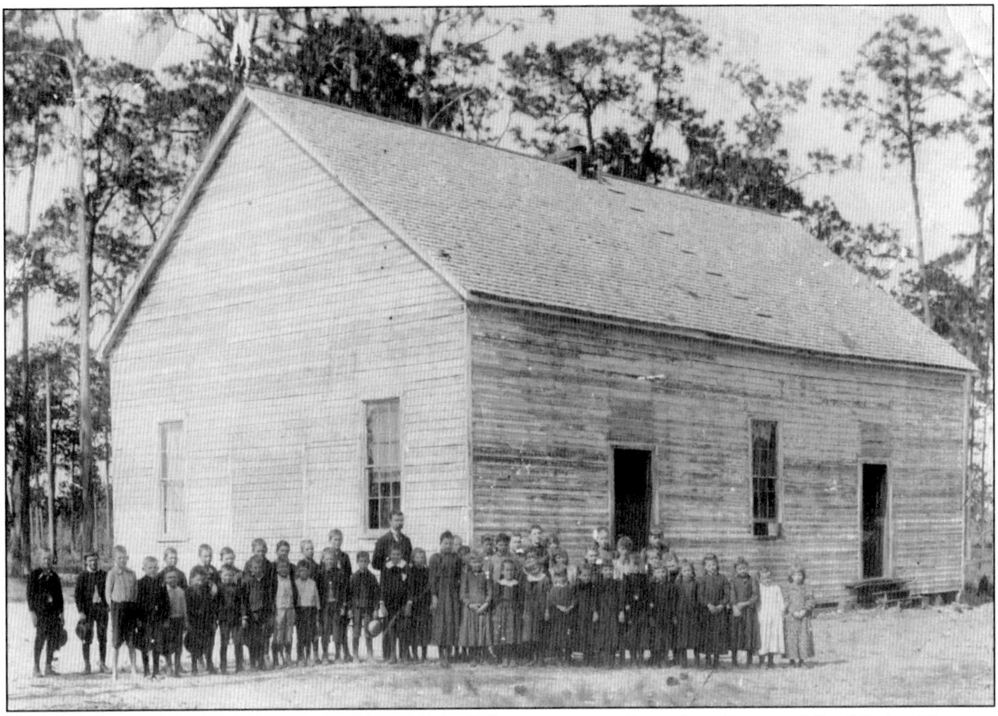

The Bay Springs school, built in 1876, replaced the outgrown log schoolhouse. Until Lake County was formed in 1887, Umatilla was still part of Orange County, which was reflected in the official name of the Bay Springs school—"School No. 16, in the County of Orange." In the 1877 class, the teacher's daily register recorded 40 students, grades 1–12. Capt. Grier was the first teacher, with a salary of $22.50 per month plus board. Three sessions of school were held per year, each 12 weeks long. This schoolhouse was destroyed by a storm in 1880. For a while, students took private instruction until the Osceola Park schoolhouse, seen below, was built on Trowell Avenue. Students met in this schoolhouse from 1887 until it was destroyed by fire in 1907. After the fire, students met in the Masonic lodge or other nearby schools until 1910. (Above UHS, below EAS.)

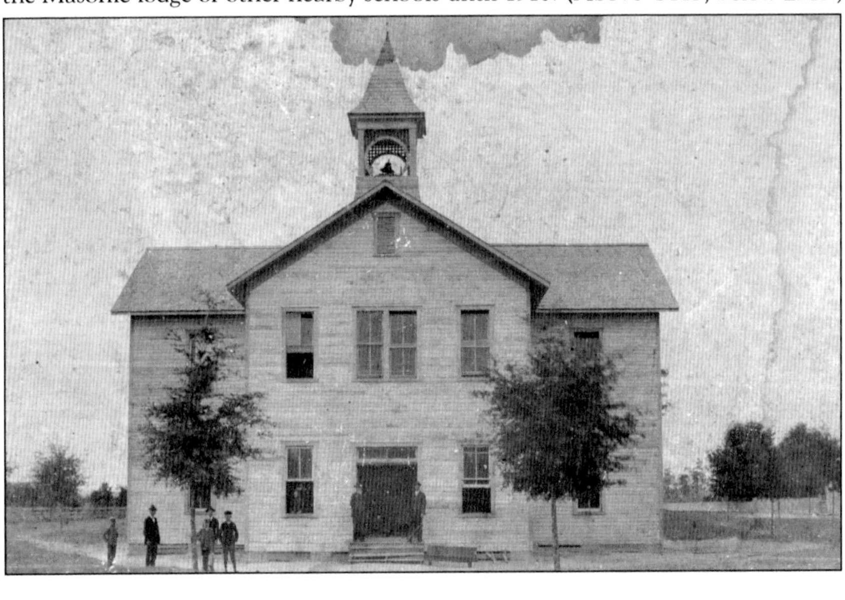

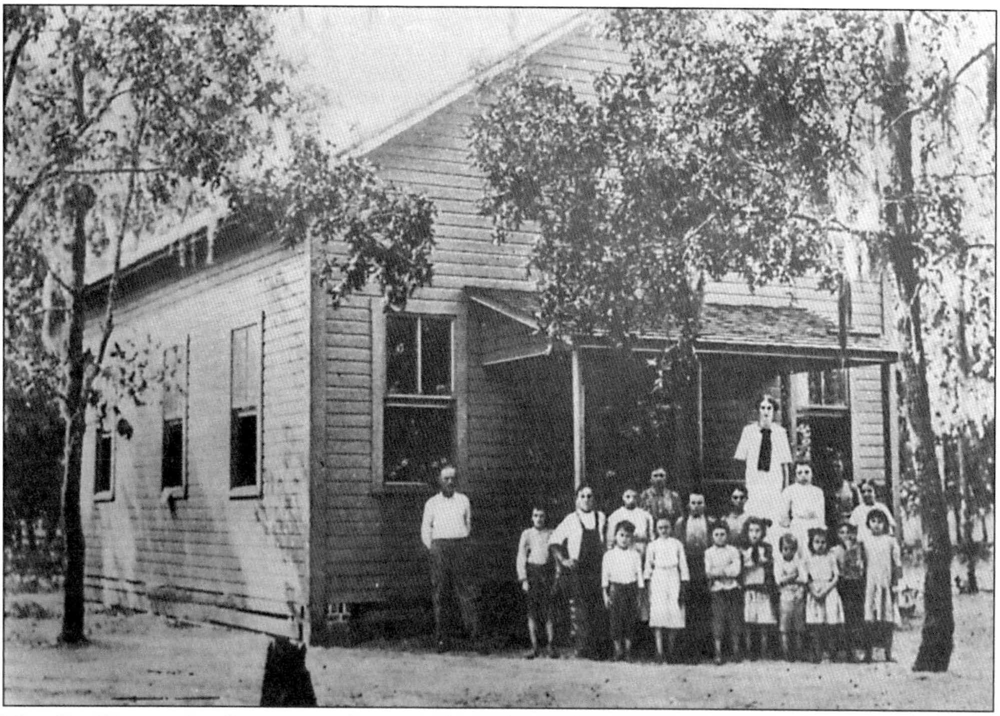

The St. Claire schoolhouse was located about five miles from Umatilla in the Rosedale area. Education was highly valued by the early settlers, and many country communities had their own schoolhouses because travelling even several miles took a great deal of time and did not encourage regular attendance. During the years 1907–1910, when no schoolhouse was in Umatilla, students went to school in the larger towns of St. Claire, Altoona, or Glendale. The photograph below shows the transformation of the St. Claire schoolhouse into a barn. It was used as such until recently, when it was torn down. (Above MG/EAS, below MG.)

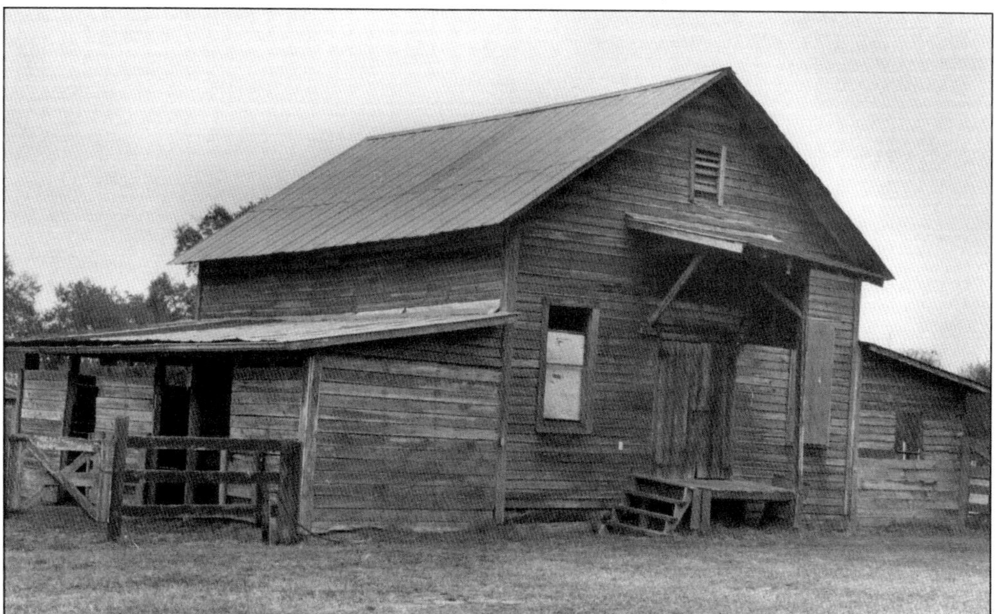

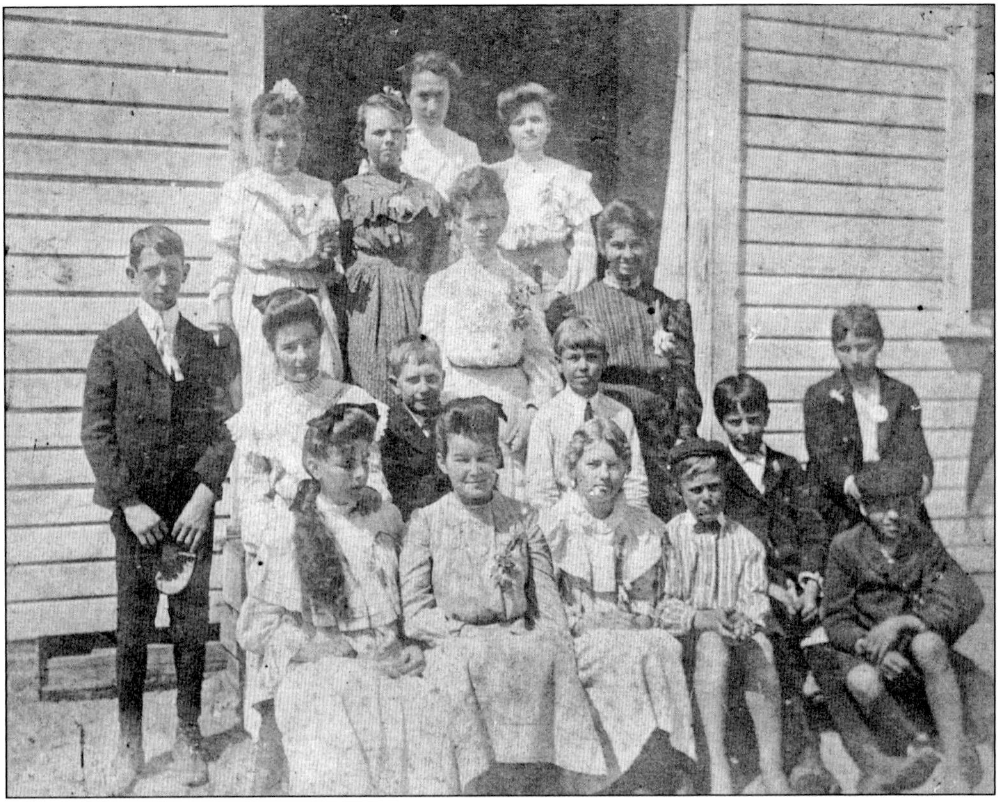

Two classes of students, including several future city leaders, pose on the steps of the Osceola schoolhouse. Taken in 1900, students identified in the above photo are, Harry Collins (small boy, right center, with bangs), "Red" Kennedy (left, hat in hand), and future county commissioner Frank Owens (right, striped shirt, bow tie). Miss Ezell was the teacher. From the class of 1905, identified below, are (not in order) Barnett Guerrant, Professor Kennedy, Fannie Shelton, and Pearl Stroebel. Others, identified but not in order, include Bessie Rushin, Bessie Baylis, Winnie Nutt, Nell Whitcomb, Fred Whitcomb, Fred Yancey, and Herbert Smith. (Above LCHS, below EAS.)

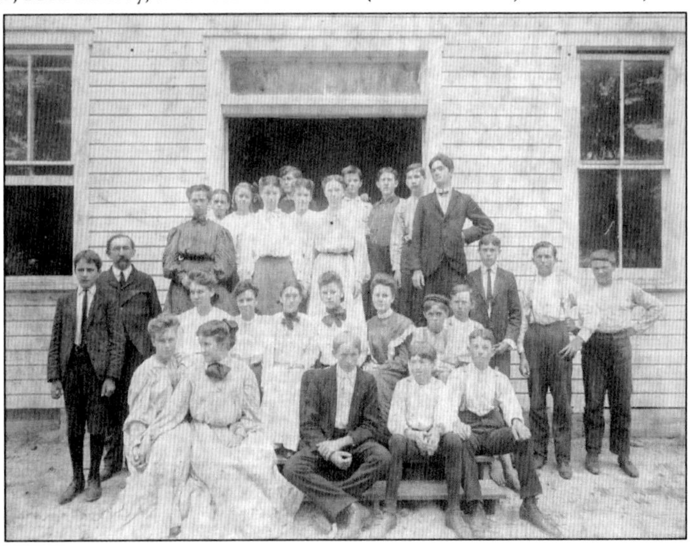

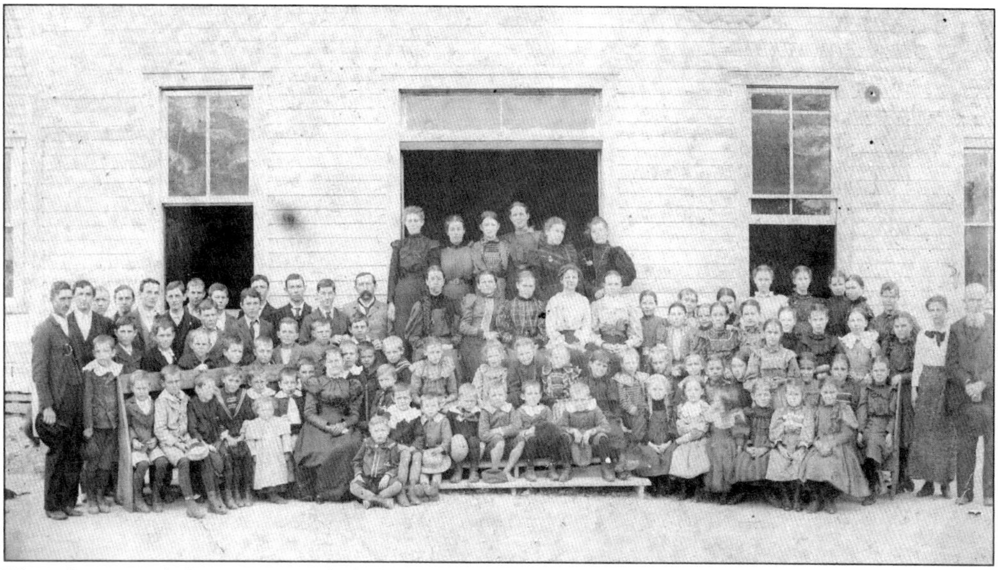

This photograph from 1905 included grades 1–12. Prof. William Kennedy was principal and later became superintendent of Lake County schools. Kennedy, who held summer normal schools for the purpose of training future teachers, is pictured centered left. In the back row, identified from left to right are, Mrs. Frank Whitcomb, Rosa Owens, Patsy Epps, Lucy ?, unidentified, Pearl McCall, and on the far right are Annie Shelton and Dr. Shelton and front center is Frank Owens. This picture of elementary students, below, was taken before 1907. Identified, but in no particular order, are Naomi Shelton, Lucille ?, Ethel Newman Verde, teacher, Annie Kennedy, Bena Collins, Sally R?, Dot Trisler, Pearl McCall, Clyde Vaughn, Radford Collins, Dill Bishop, Margaret ?, Ernest ?, LeRoy Smith, and Paul Guerrant. (Both photographs EAS.)

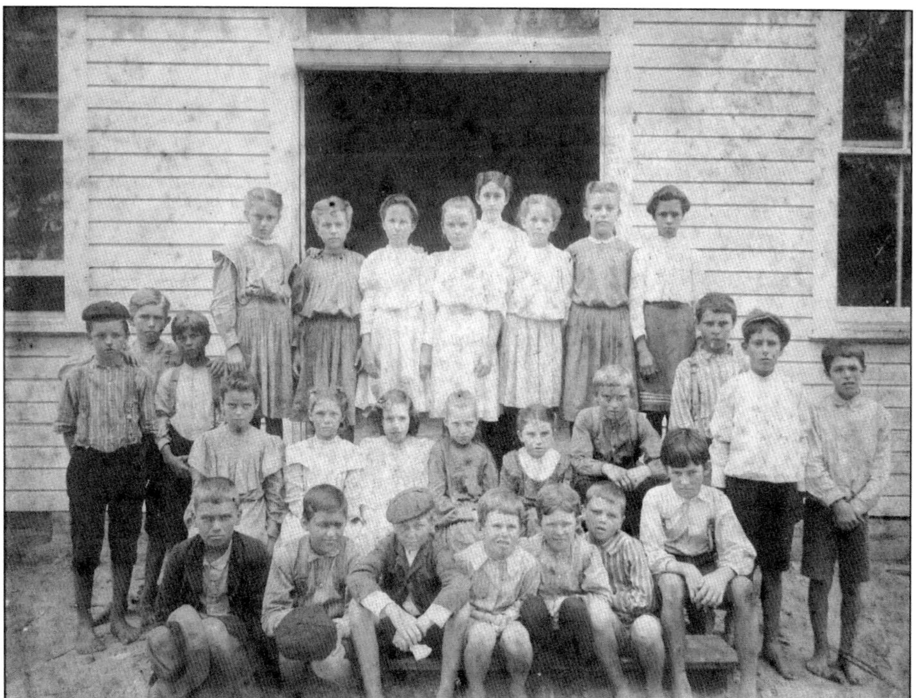

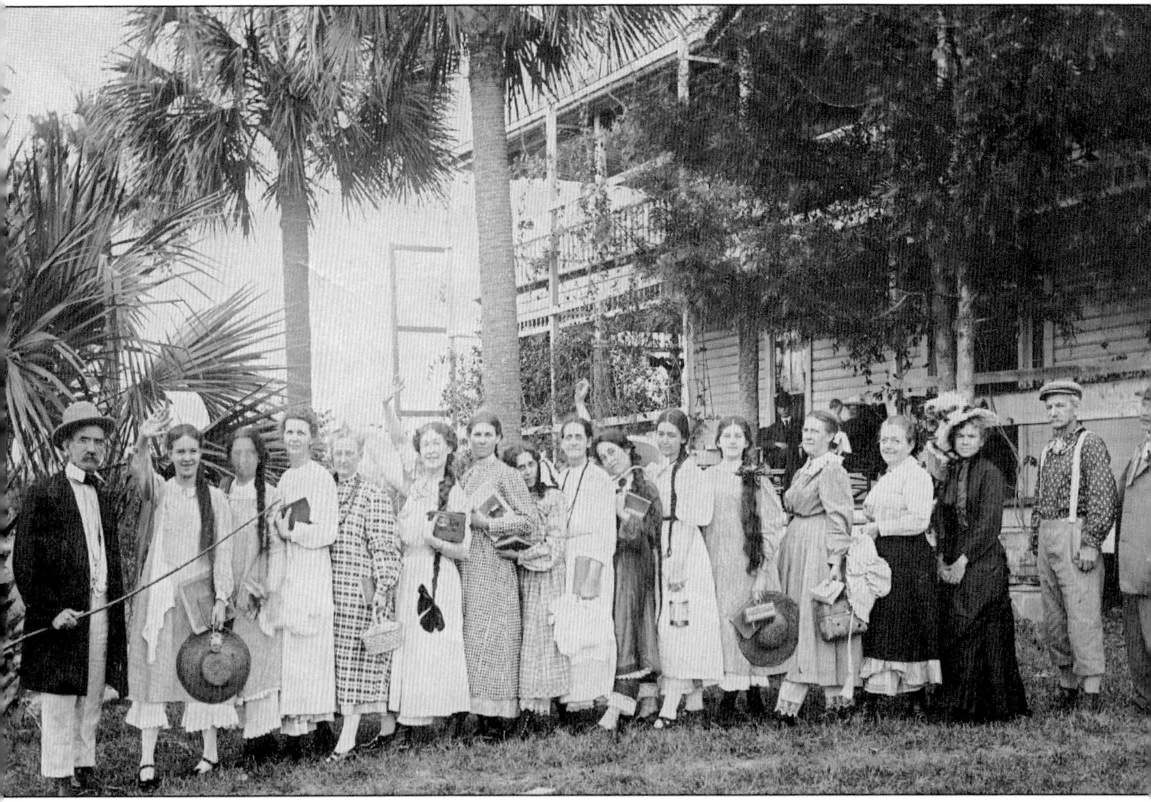

In what looks like a "come as you are" party, these party-goers are dressed in some type of costume and are being "led" by Professor Kennedy (far left) holding some sort of rod, or perhaps a cane fishing pole. All the women have literally let their hair down, are carrying books, baskets, and showing their pantaloons. Everyone appears to have a sense of humor. Posing with the group, in the yard of her own home, Drucilla Collins is identified as the 10th lady from the left. (EAS.)

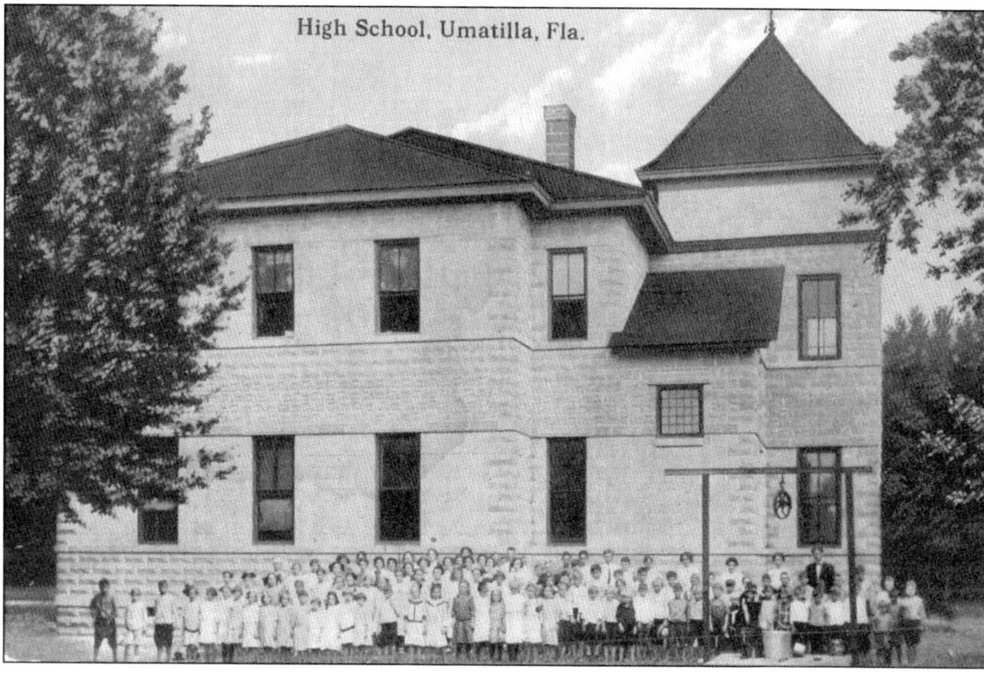

After the Osceola schoolhouse fire in 1907, students waited until 1910 for the city of Umatilla to choose a new site and build a schoolhouse, pictured here with the entire student body out front. Fetching water was part of each school day's activities, and the school well is visible in the schoolyard. The block building cost $5,000 to build, served grades 1–12, and was soon crowded with boom-time growth in Florida. A new brick junior high school building was added to the campus and opened in 1915. Pictured below is the 1923 Umatilla High School, also built to accommodate the growth of Umatilla's student population. This building served Umatilla until the early 1960s. (Above CB, below LCHS.)

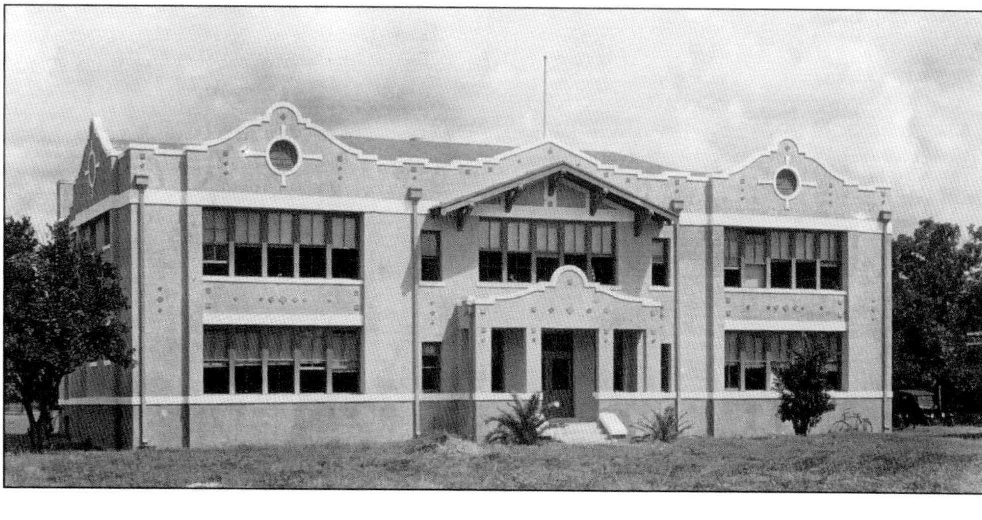

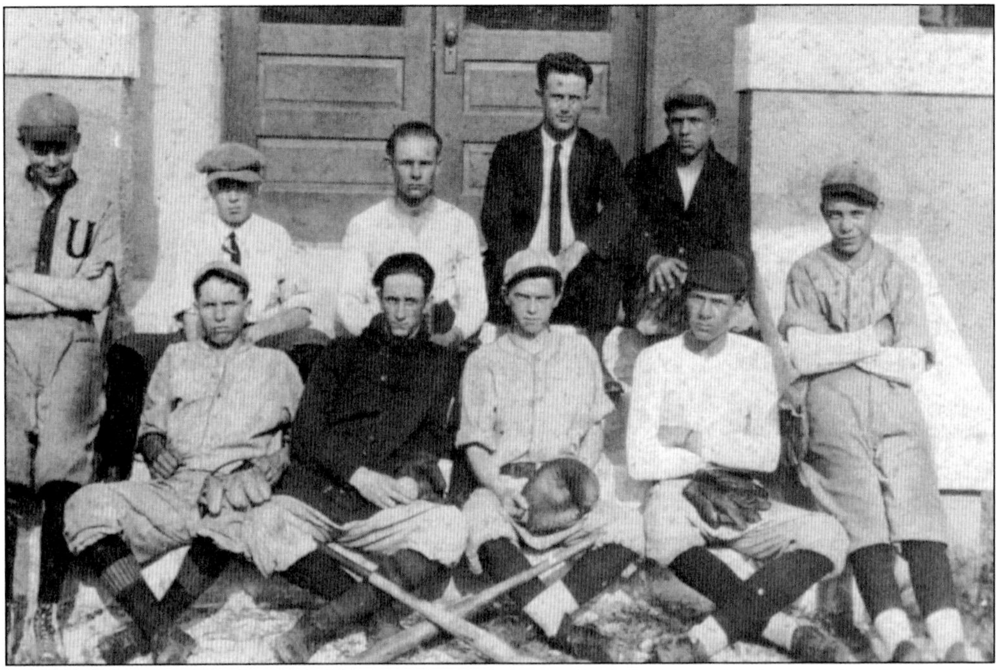

Ellis Moore poses with two teams he coached while teaching at Umatilla High School. The 1925 Umatilla High School baseball team is pictured on the school steps. Baseball was a favorite pastime in Umatilla for the first half of the 1900s, and many towns, including Umatilla, also sponsored city teams. Teams traveled by train to play in nearby towns, and benches were set on open rail cars so fans could travel to games with the team. By the 1940s, the Umatilla Baseball Association had its own lighted and fenced ballpark with grandstands drawing large crowds into town about twice a week for games. Below, Moore, holding the ball, poses with the 1927 Umatilla High School soccer team. Bill Collins is in the back, fourth from left. (Above BJM, below CB.)

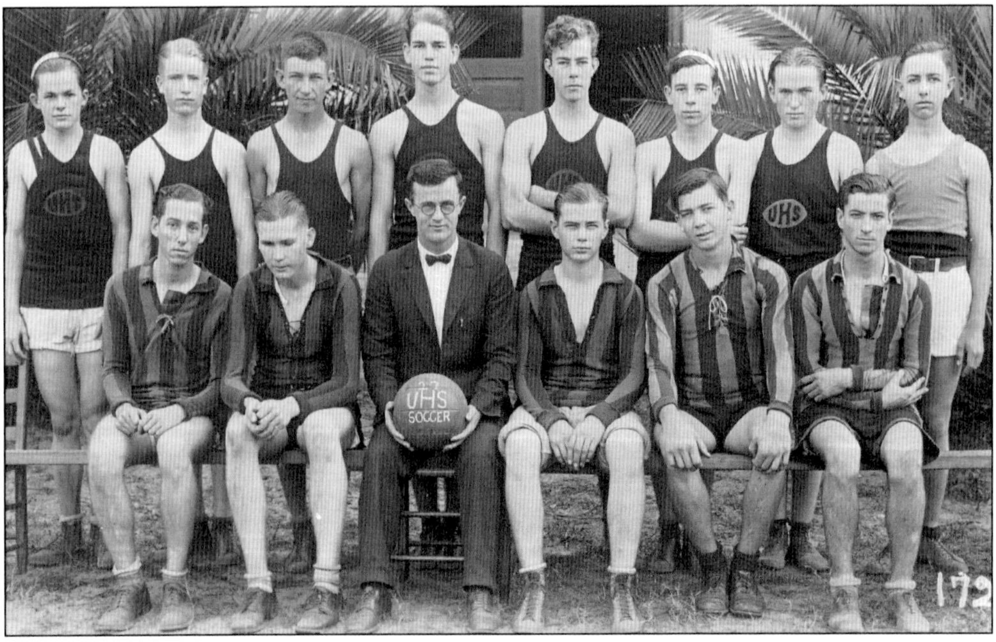

The 1929–1930 junior high basketball team is photographed on the courts. Pictured, from left to right, are the following: (kneeling) Bill Austin, Pat Keel, Bobby Collins; (standing) Bob Vaughn, Earl Powers, Joe Morrell, and Coach W. B. Calhoun. (IV.)

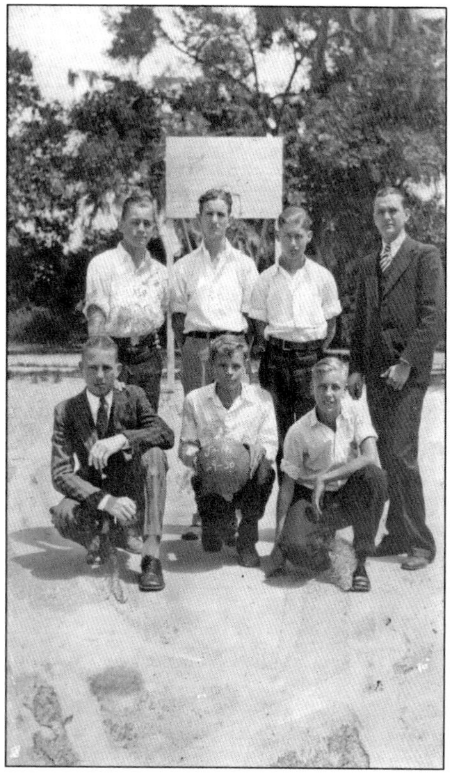

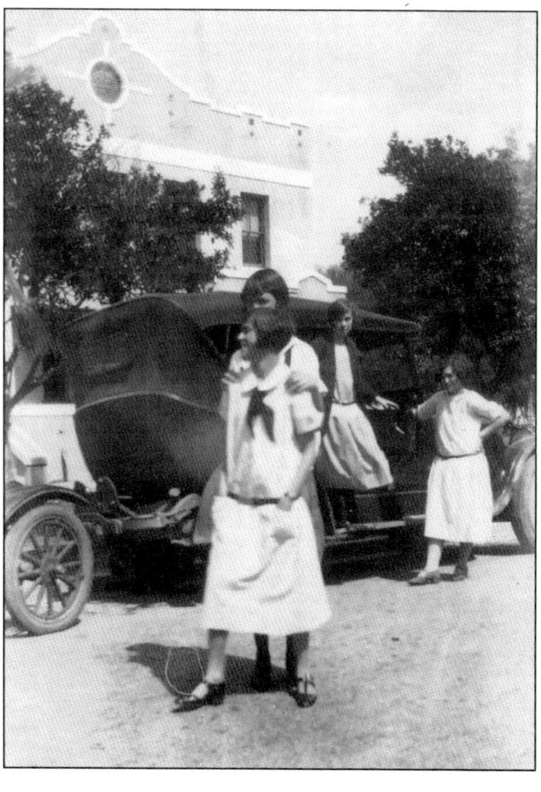

Louise Vaughn and Helen Austin arrive at Umatilla High School in the 1920s, where teachers greet their students in the carpool line before classes begin. The days of "walking five miles uphill, both ways" came to an end with the advent of automobile transportation. (IV.)

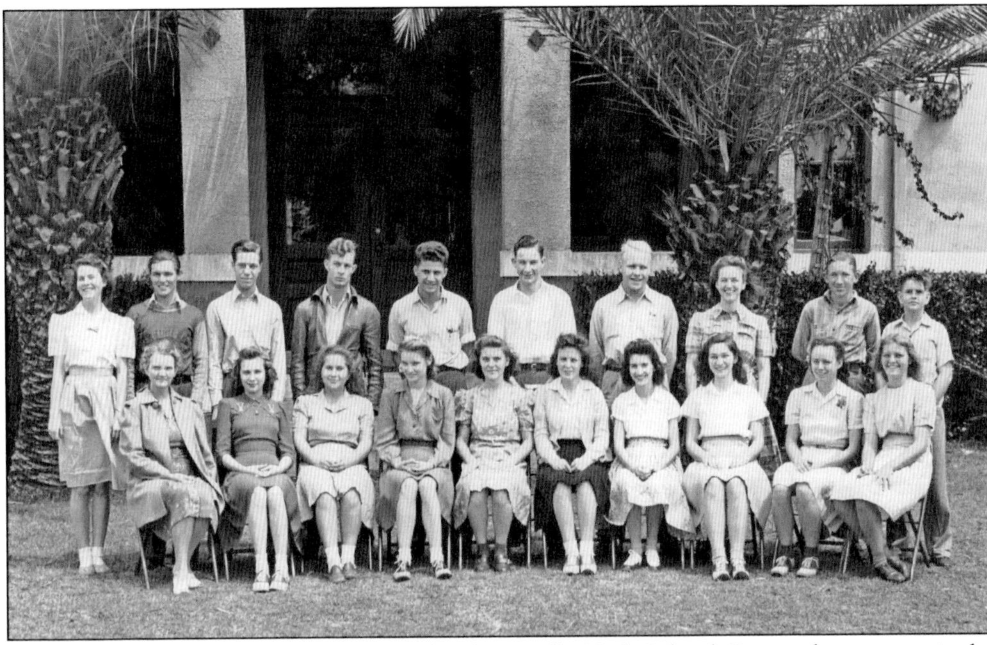

The graduating class of 1942 poses outside of Umatilla High School. Pictured, in no particular order, are Elizabeth Allison, Lois Bates, Mildred Cadwell, Virginia Collins, Sara Finney, Alice Gagner, George Gagner, Fred Getch, Lonnie Green, Gus Hobich, Ralph Lucas, Laurita Orr, Bess Patrick, Robert Penley, Bobbie Player, Pledger Rigdon, Charles Short, Wilma Vaughn, Martha Louise Wilson, and Grable Parks. Pictured below, students enjoy the spring dance in 1942. (Above UHS, below RBD.)

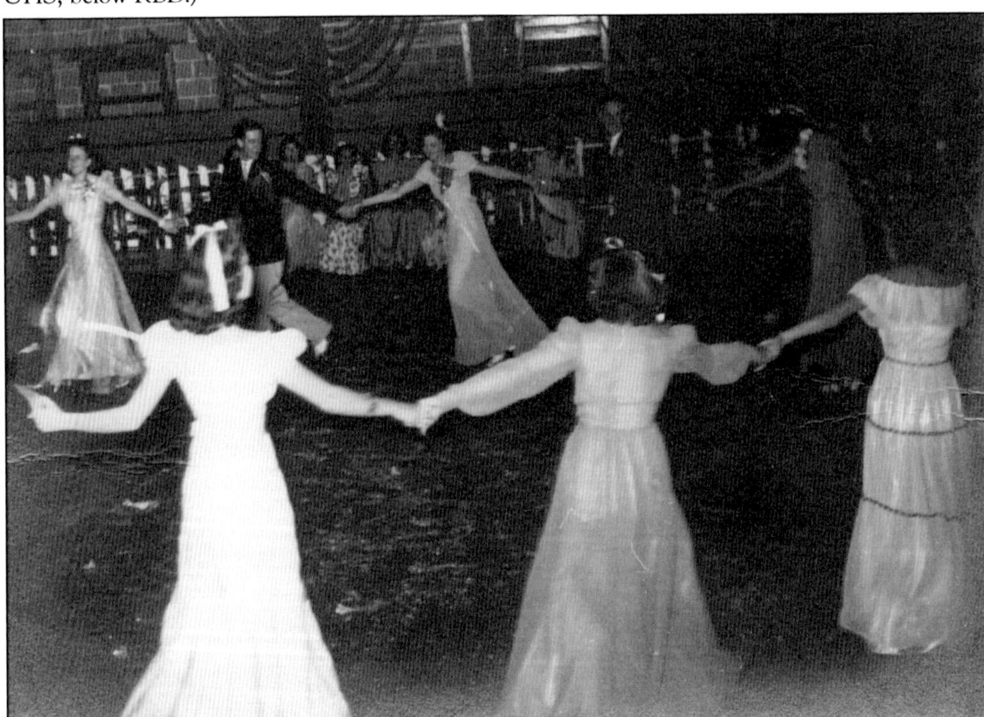

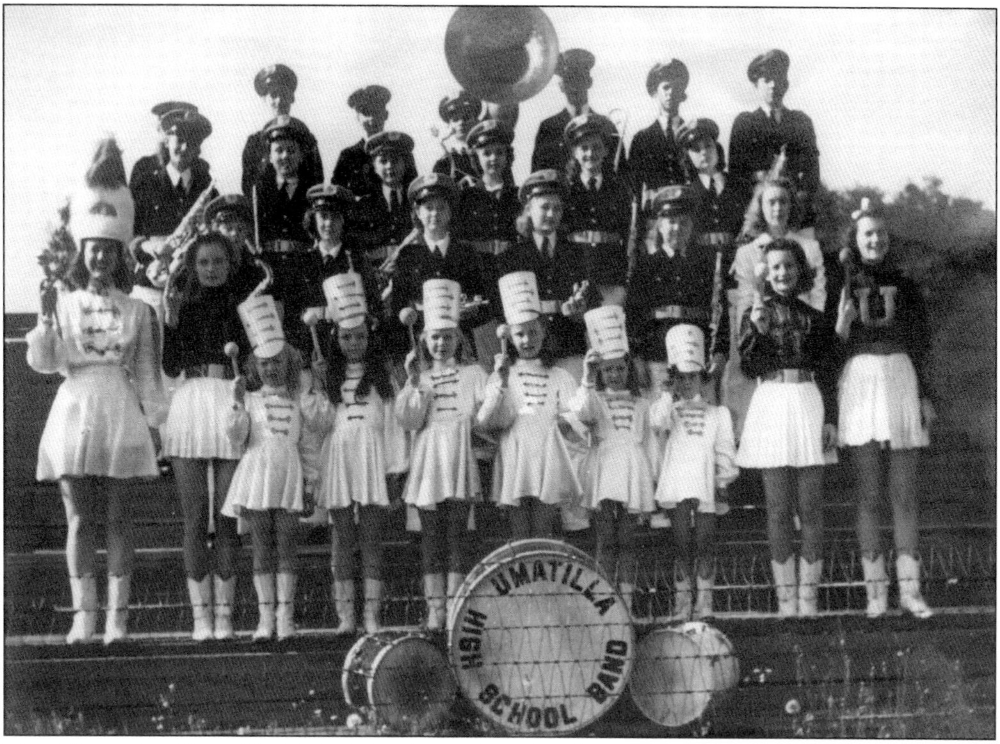

The 18-member Umatilla High School marching band poses on the school bleachers in 1942, complete with six precious little majorettes. The school band performed in many community and area celebrations. Below, drum major Virginia Collins leads the Umatilla High School Band in 1942 parading through downtown on their way to a rally in the park. Two of the signs being carried read "The Road to Happiness Leads This Way" and "Don't Make Excuses Make Good." (Both photographs RBD.)

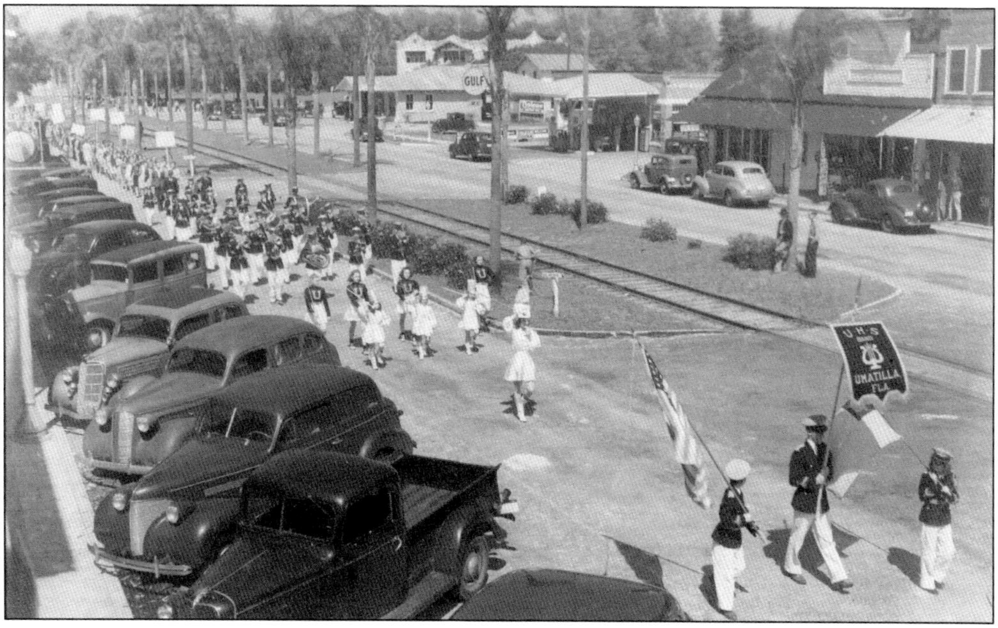

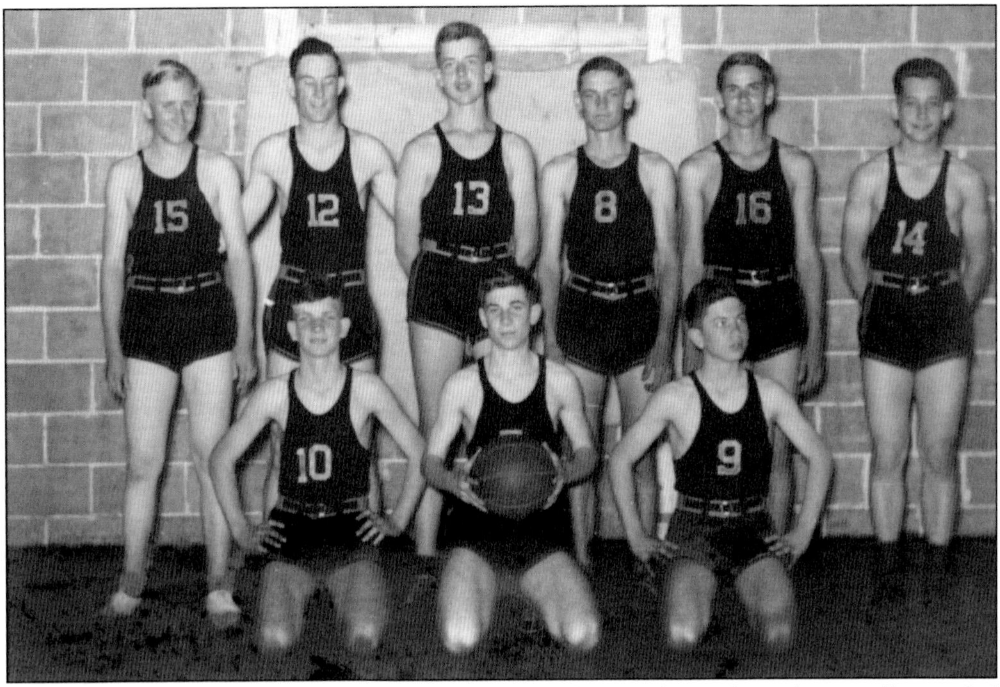

Umatilla High School offered many team sports, and games have always been well-attended community events. The high school boys' basketball team poses in the mid-1940s. Pictured from left to right are the following team members: (first row) unidentified, Jack McCown, Buddy Marshall; (second row) Eph Wiygul, unidentified, Jack Allen, unidentified, Harold Straker, and Davis Parker. Below, the football team takes position in front of the school in the late 1940s. Pictured from left to right are the following: (first row) John Westervelt, Everett Smith, unidentified, Martin Stephens, Jack Nelson, Joe Cooper, unidentified; (center) Tommie Powers; (second row) Billy Merrill, Gerald Lucas, and James Hall. (Above EAS, below UHS.)

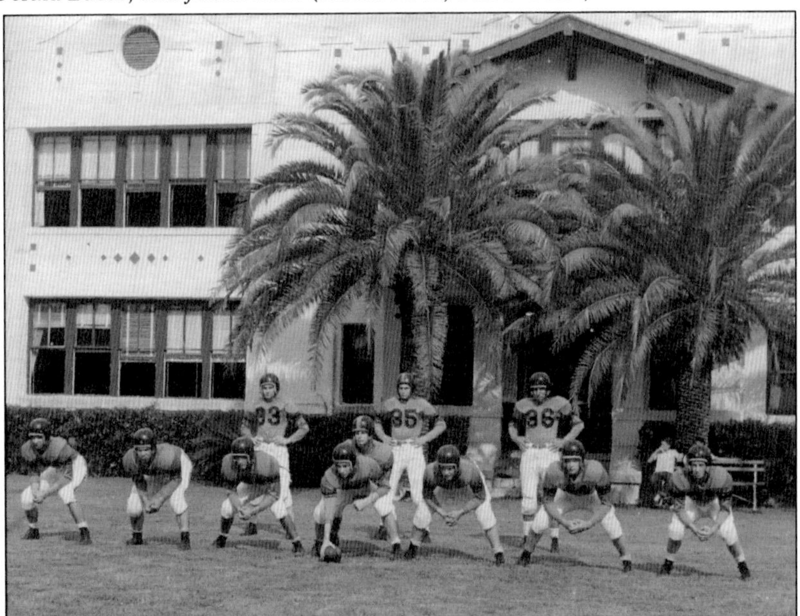

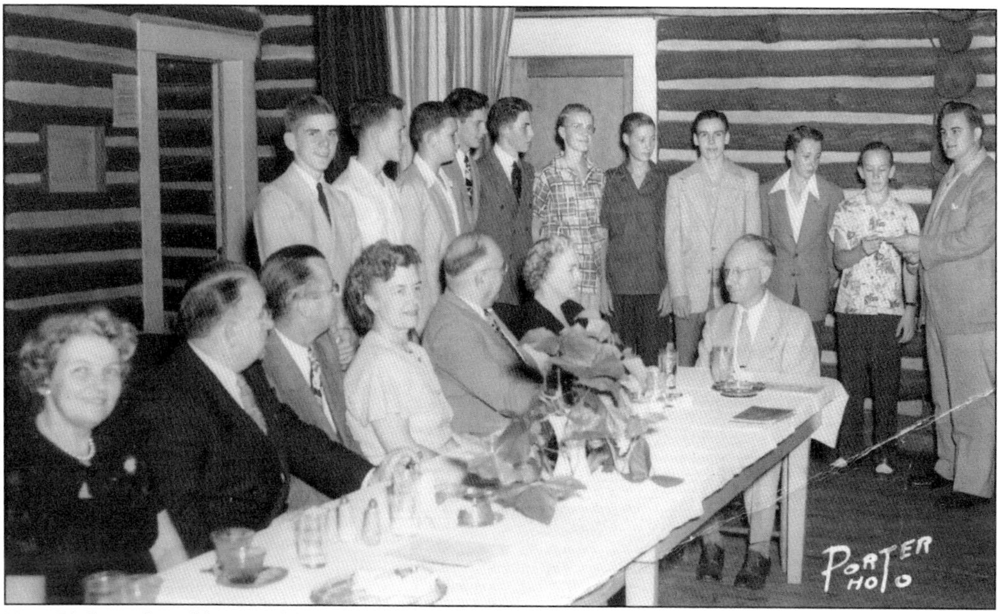

Key Club is the oldest and largest service program for high school students. It is a student-led organization that teaches leadership through service to others. Members of the Kiwanis International family, Key Club members build themselves as they build their schools and communities. Pictured standing from left to right at the officers' installation in 1947 are the following members: Bob Baker, Dick Sparling, Russell Bryan, Jerome Parker, Dixie Royal, Philip Owens, Clyde Mullins, Schalah Stephens, Jack Parker, Steve Johnson, and Martin Kirkland. Seated, from left to right, are Kiwanis sponsors Lucille and Harold Hippler and Jack and Bena Allen, Mr. and Mrs. Joe Brown, and Harry Myers. Members of the Key Club in 1948, pictured below with Principal Ellis Moore are (seated) Clyde Mullins and, standing from left to right, Dixie Royal, Russell Bryan, Jack Parker, Philip Owens, Steve Johnson, Johnny Sanwald, Jerome Parker, Schalah Stephens, unidentified, Bob Baker, and Dick Sparling. (Both photographs UHS.)

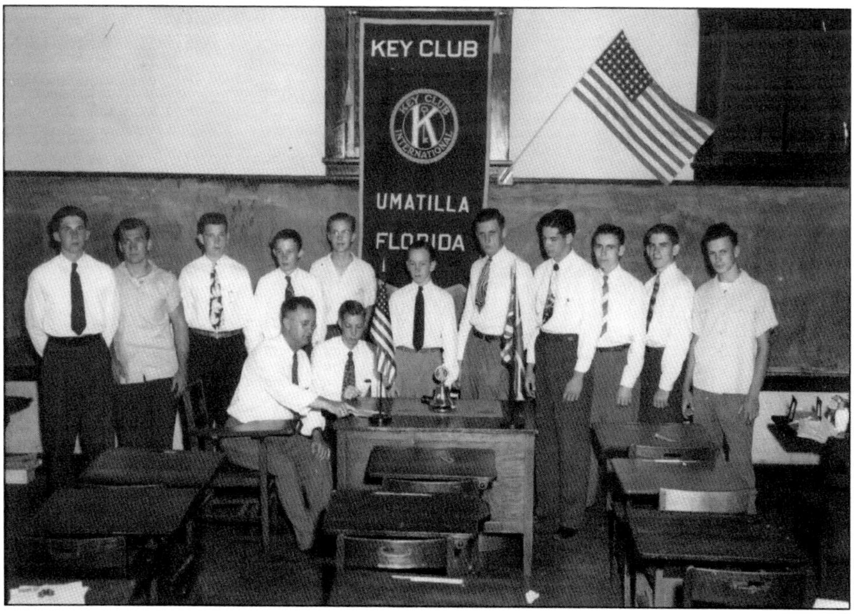

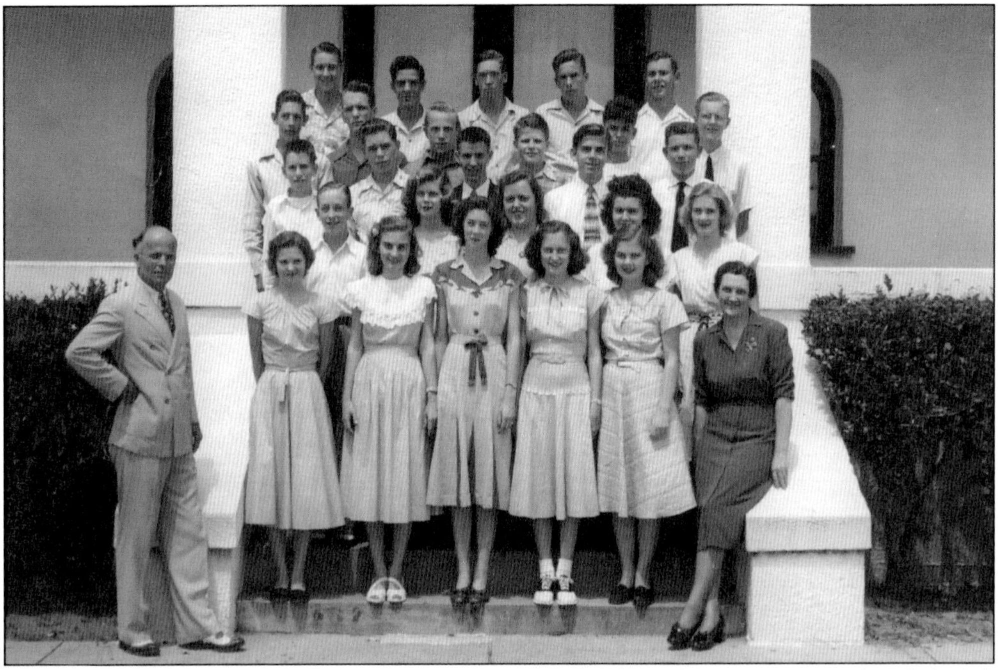

Umatilla High School principal Joe Brown (left) is shown with teacher Marguerite Edwards (right) and members of the sophomore class of 1948, including (in alphabetical order) Bob Baker, John Bates, Barbara Ann Bledsoe, Russell Bryan, Duane Caldwell, Henry Cross, Med Curry, Clifford Halford, Franklin Hall, Glenn Jividen, Steve Johnson, Herman Kenny, Billy Latner, Roberta Latner, Lillian McAvoy, Virginia Murt, Evelyn Newman, Gertrude O'Neal, Philip Owens, and Jo Earle Wolfe. Below, the classes of 1949–1950 pose on Florida's capitol steps in Tallahassee. Pictured are the following, from left to right: (first row) Rep. Hartley Hethcox, his daughter Mary Ann Hethcox, Gov. Fuller Warren, Bob Baker, his father, Sen. J. Ed Baker, and Rep. Tim Sellar; (second row) Elsie Zellman, Drucilla Allen, Ida Mae Carlton, Principal C. A. Vaughn Jr., and Marguerite Edwards. The remaining class members are unidentified. (Both photographs UHS.)

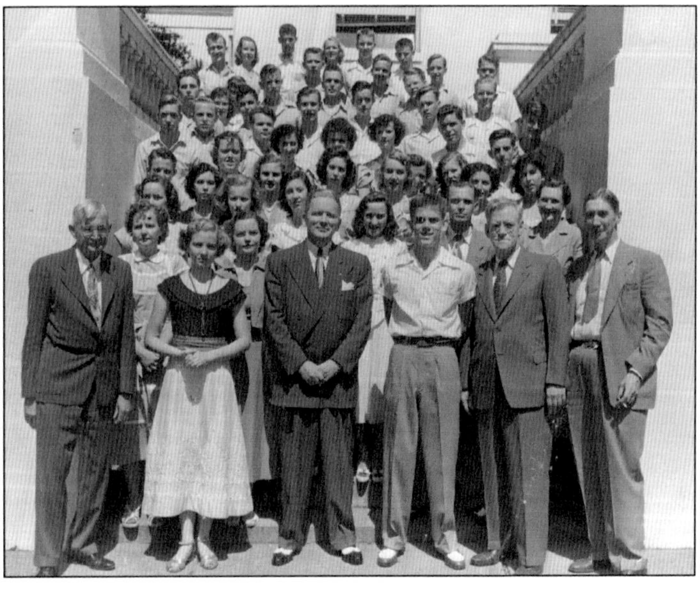

Three

Church Life

Before 1875, there were no established religious services in the small Florida village of Umatilla. Whenever available, circuit riding preachers held services in the log schoolhouse. William Whitcomb's mother taught a Sunday school class to adults and children. For protection from possible attacks by Native Americans, local men and even children carried shotguns to church, which were placed in the corner during services.

The Baptists met at the Live Oak Baptist Church near Eustis as early as 1862. In 1875, they moved their services to Umatilla and formed the First Baptist Church of Umatilla. The members first met in the Bay Springs schoolhouse, just south of the cemetery. In April 1889, Nathan Trowell donated land at the corner of Orange Lane and Trowell Avenue to build a church, which was dedicated in September 1892. In 1904, the Church of Christ built their sanctuary next door, and in 1914, an addition was made to the original church.

The Methodist Episcopal Church was first organized at Glendale but built its sanctuary in Umatilla in 1886 on land donated by Benjamin Yancey. It is Umatilla's only designated National Historic Landmark. The final service of the First United Methodist Church of Umatilla was held June 28, 2009, and the building's future is unknown.

On January 3, 1886, Rev. Asahel Enloe organized a Presbyterian church with nine members in Umatilla. The first service in the Kentucky Avenue church was held June 12, 1927, and in 1987, its centennial was celebrated with the dedication of the Enloe Bell Tower.

Gertrude Smith recalled that during the horse and buggy years, the churches often rotated evening services and in the morning would sometimes share services, especially when some outstanding person came to town. According to those whose memories go back to the late 1800s and the early 1900s, much congeniality existed between the Baptist, Methodist, and Presbyterian churches, with much visiting back and forth between them. "In those days," reminisced Lou Trowell Crow, "it was as if we were all together."

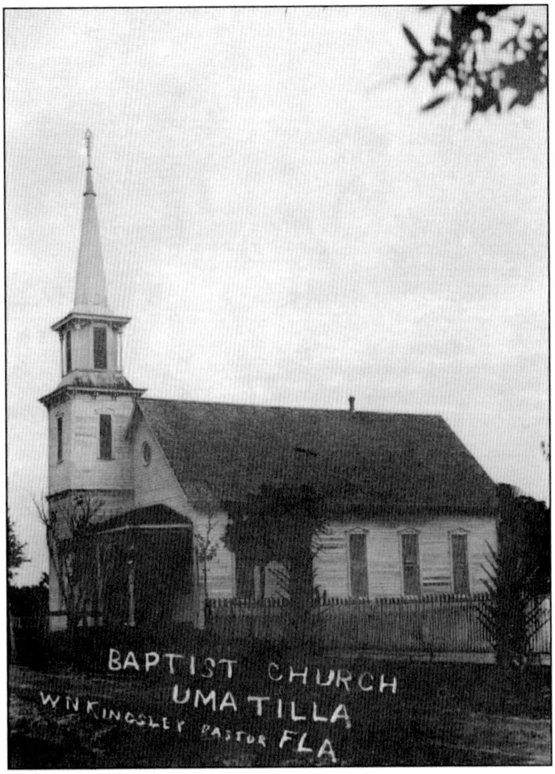

The original Baptist church is pictured at left in 1903. Members of the Live Oak Baptist Church first met as early as 1862, in a location closer to Eustis. Around 1875, they began meeting in the Bay Springs schoolhouse and then in the Osceola Park schoolhouse in Umatilla. Nathan Trowell donated the land on which this building was built in 1889. The name of the church was changed from Live Oak Baptist Church to the First Baptist Church of Umatilla, Florida. This was the first house dedicated since the church began. As the church grew, so did the building. Pictured below is an addition of new rooms built for Sunday school, completed in 1914. (Left CB, below LCHS.)

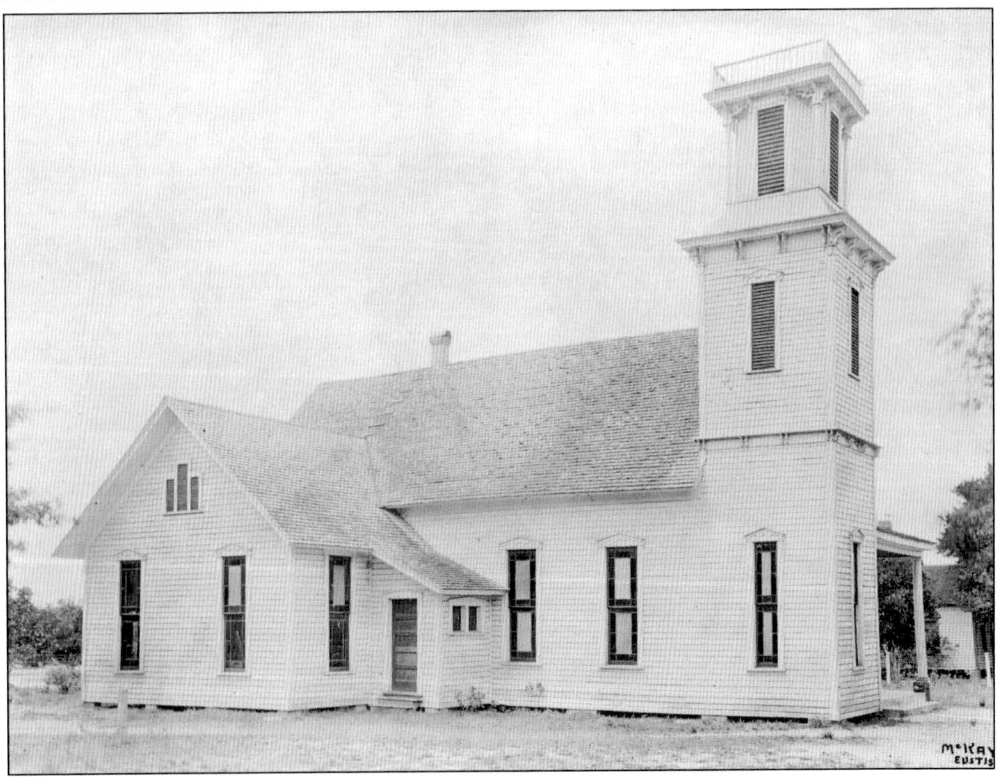

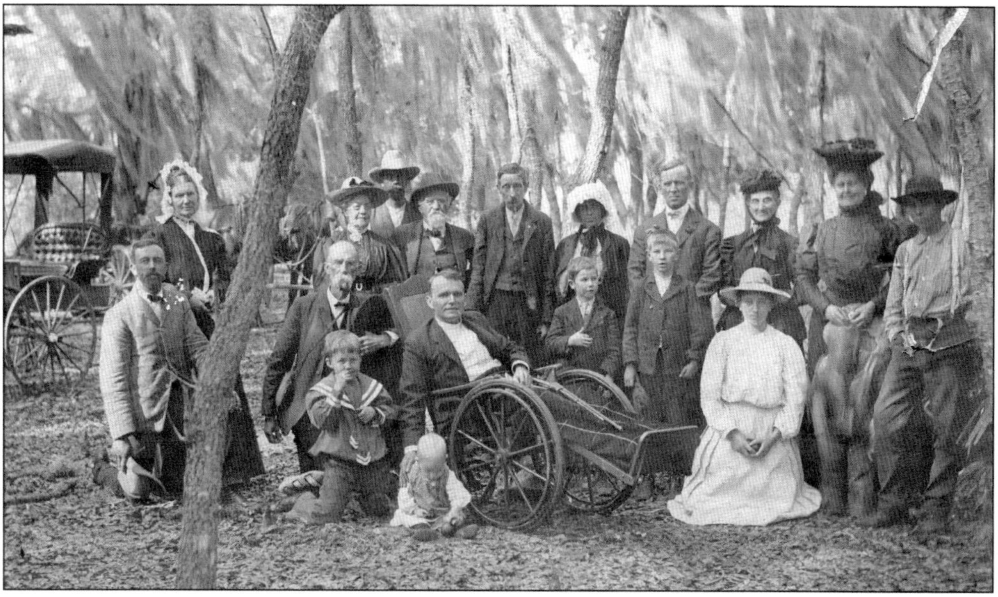

Umatilla's early social life centered around its churches, and picnics were a popular way of spending time together in fellowship in the surrounding beautiful outdoors. This photograph was taken at such a church picnic in the 1890s. The ancient oaks draped in Spanish moss make a dramatic background, and provide shade for the horses and carriages. Charles Giles, a veteran of the Spanish-American War, is seen in a wheelchair. Robert Lee Collins is on far left. Below, possibly taken on the same day, this group proudly holds oranges in their hands. (Both photographs EAS.)

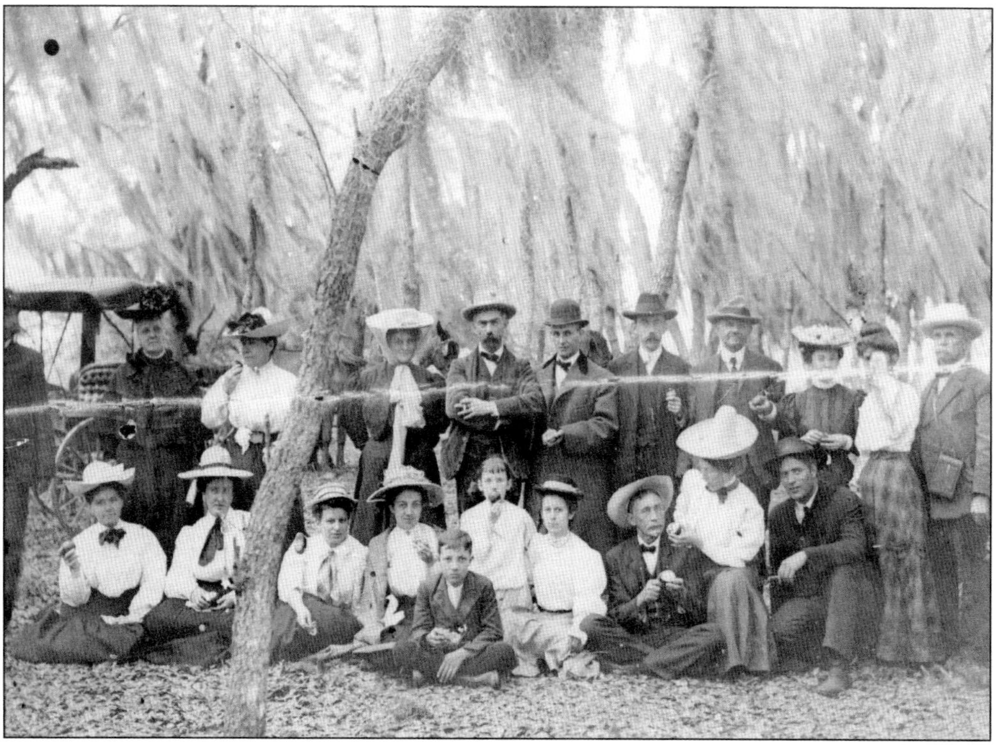

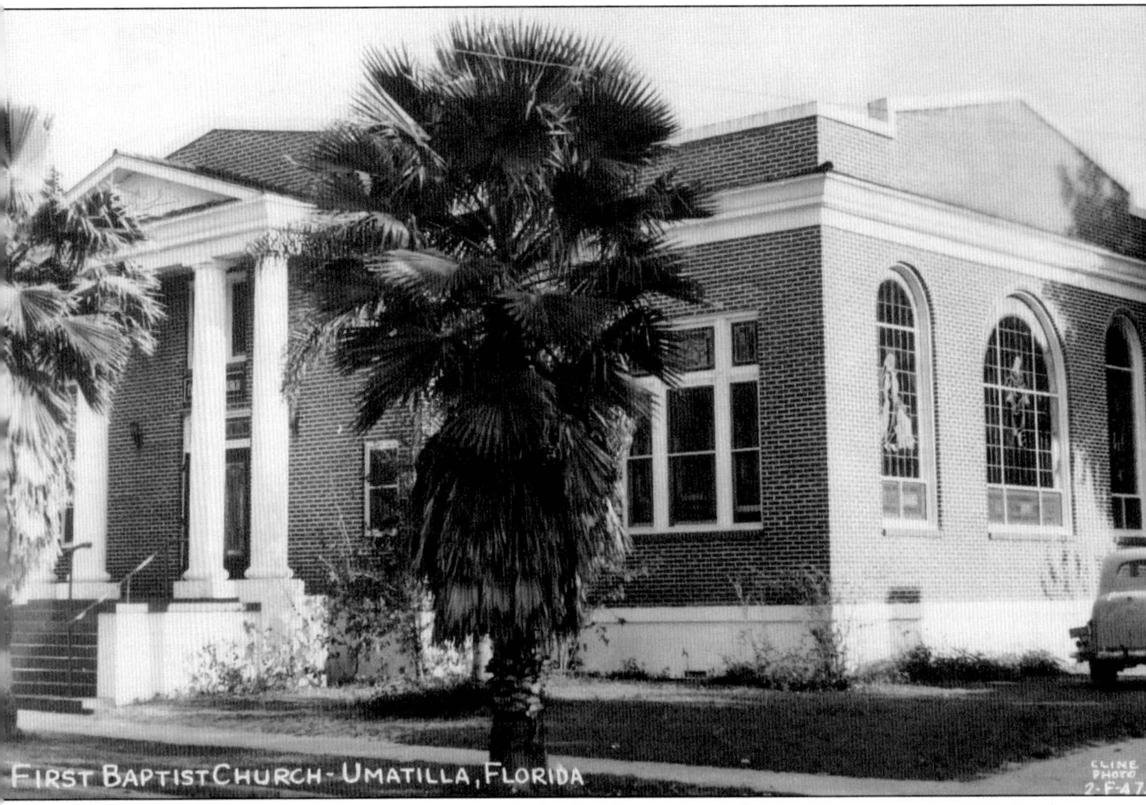

The First Baptist Church of Umatilla built this brick pastorium during the pastorate of J. L. Jenkins in 1926. In 1949, the congregation had 500 members, equal to almost half the population of Umatilla. The church established missions in Lindale, Mount Dora, Crows Bluff, Astor Park, Higley, and Grand Island. In 2001, the church moved to its present location on Hatfield Drive. (MG.)

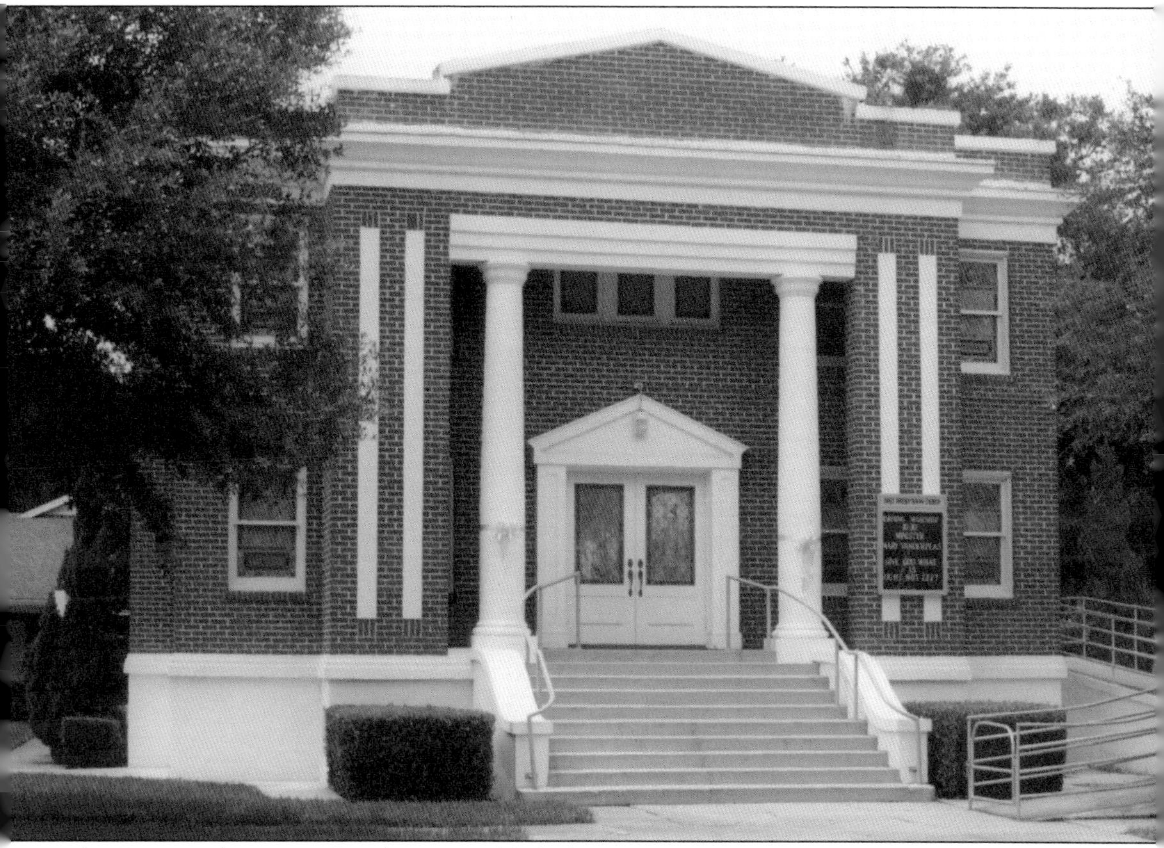

The First Presbyterian Church was established in 1886 with nine members under the Rev. Asahel Enloe. The church merged with neighboring Glendale Presbyterian church in 1887. Rev. Enloe, also a cabinetmaker, constructed the pulpit, which is still used to this day. Charter members were William H. Freeman, Frank P. Gillespie, E. C. Grayson, Gertrude Mitchener, Ella Freeman, L. F. Gillespie, Fanny Fortson, Jane Grayson, and Benjamin C. Yancey. Yancey deeded a lot in March 1888 for the site of the church. Its bell dates it as being built in 1891. This church building, constructed in 1927 on Kentucky Avenue, is where the membership continues to worship. (LCHS.)

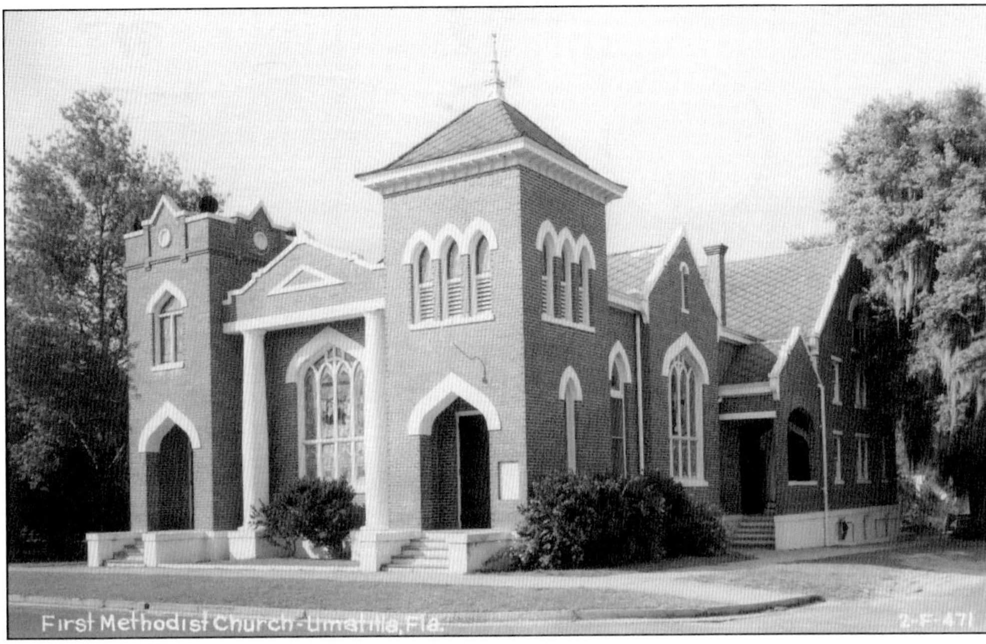

The Umatilla Methodist Episcopal Church was established in 1881 and originally worshipped in Glendale. In 1886, Benjamin Yancey, a member of the Presbyterian Church and friend of the Methodist Church, donated the lot for a new church building in Umatilla. Seen here is the sanctuary of the Umatilla Methodist Church, built in 1922. This is Umatilla's only structure listed on the National Register of Historic Places. The church's final service was held June 28, 2009. Pictured below, the membership gathers for a photograph taken in 1930, beside the sanctuary. (Above CB, below RBD.)

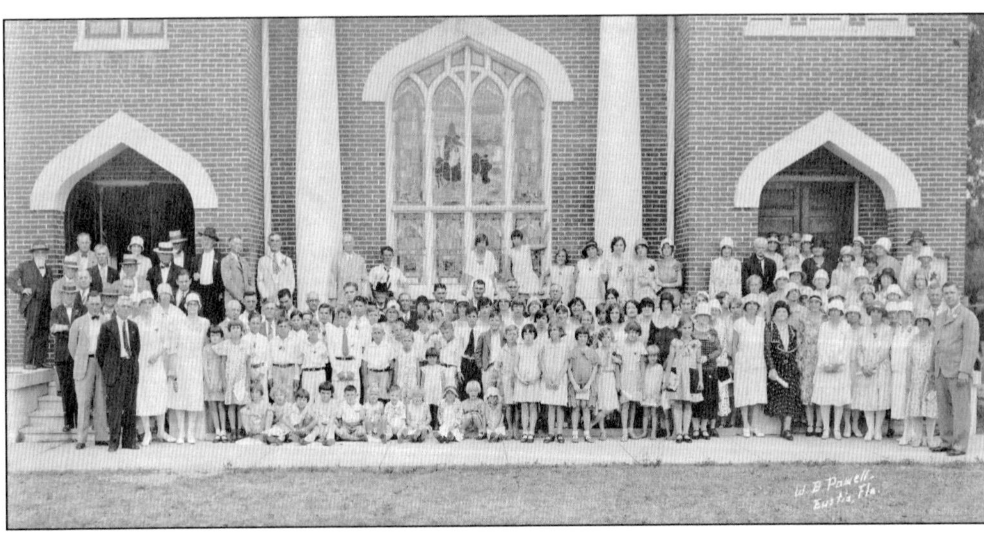

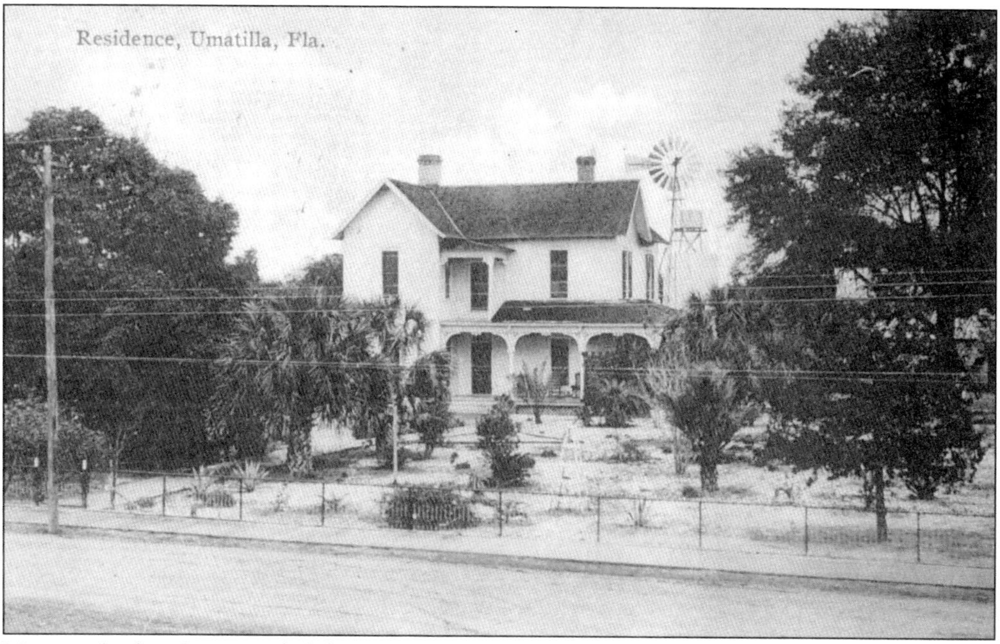

Many early churches provided their ministers a parsonage, manse, or rectory in which they could live while serving their congregation. In 1913, George DeVault donated a lot at Rose Street and Trowell Avenue on which the Methodist parsonage was built. The parsonage is pictured here in the 1920s; it no longer belongs to the church and is now a private residence. (CB.)

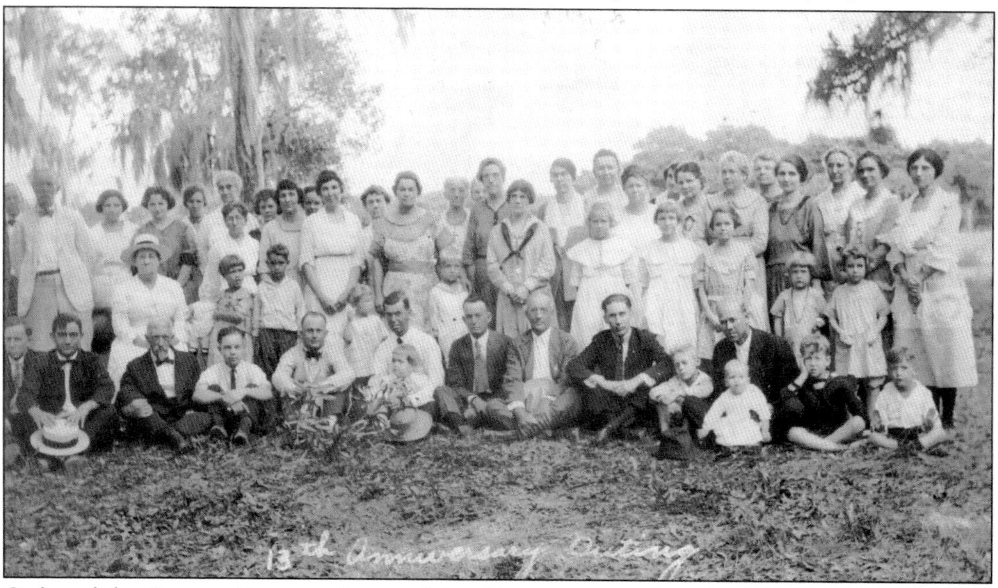

Order of the Eastern Star members and families are pictured at their 13th reunion in 1922. Umatilla's Order of the Eastern Star, chapter no. 32, was chartered April 22, 1909, with Retta L. Kennedy as the first Worthy Matron and Walter E. Stoops the Worthy Patron. The Order of the Eastern Star is a social order comprised of persons with spiritual values, but it is not a religion, and membership is open to followers of monotheistic faiths. Its appeal rests in the true beauty of the refreshing and character-building lessons that are so sincerely portrayed in its ritualistic work. A deep fraternal bond exists between its members. (RBD.)

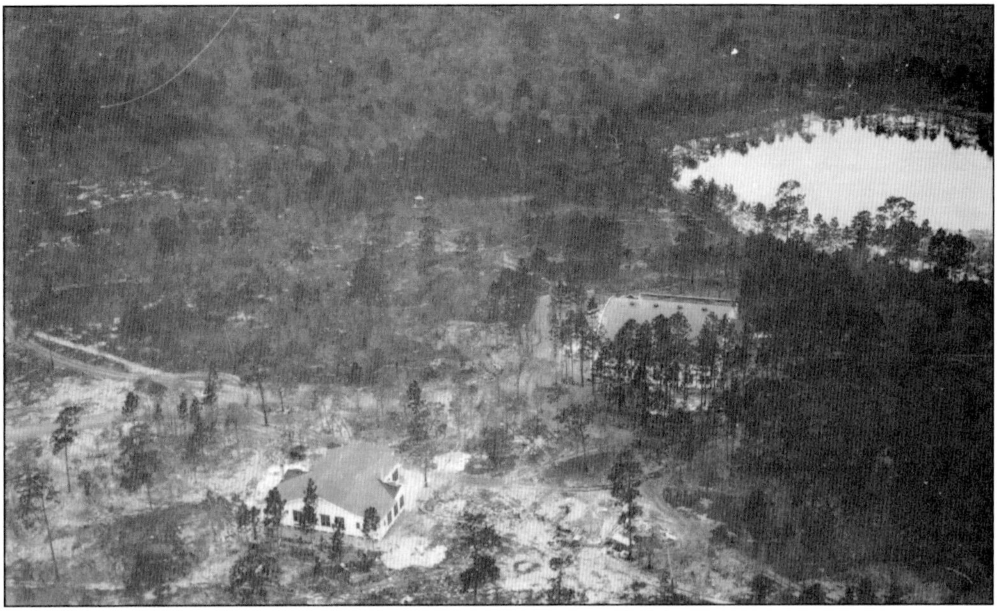

An aerial photograph taken in 1926 shows the grounds of the Baptist winter assembly in Umatilla. Hugh Rowe donated 130 acres of land to the educational board of the Southern Baptist Convention for the location of a winter assembly in Umatilla. Rowe's offer was supplemented later by another donation of 20 acres by Messrs. Kendall and Shouse of Eustis. Named Assembly Hill, a massive auditorium was built and opened February 23, 1926, rivalling the historic Chatauqua Institution of New York. The cafeteria is visible in the foreground and the auditorium in background. In the hand-retouched newspaper photograph below, a crowd is leaving an assembly in 1928. The assembly closed in February 1932 when the trustees could not raise the money to pay the mortgage. (Above BJM, below LCHS.)

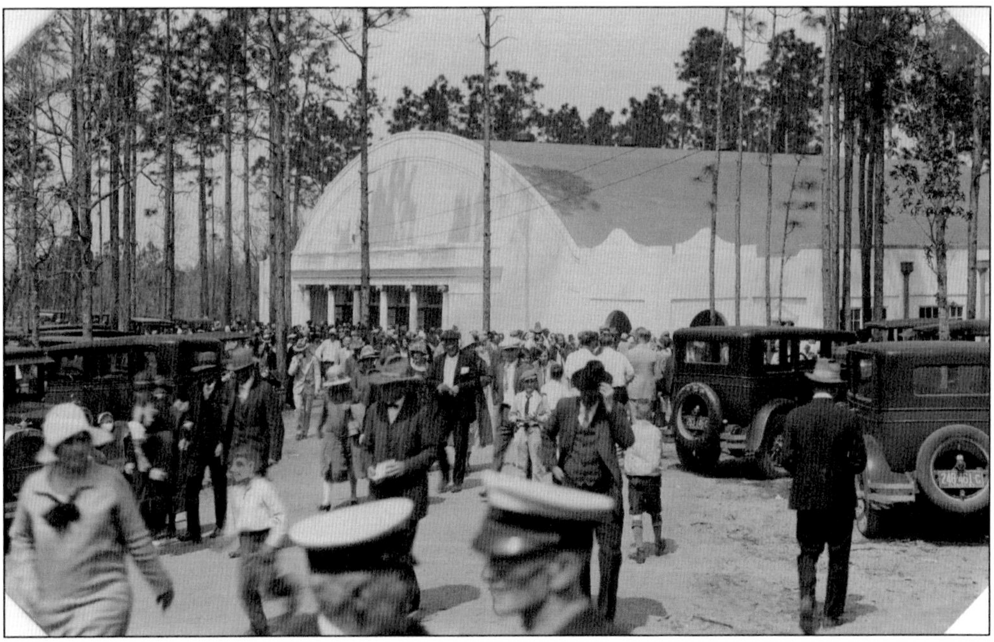

Four

SETTLER SOCIAL NETWORKING

Umatilla's community spirit was shared by families who were devoted to religious and school activities. The beauty of the countryside and the climate offered rare advantages for gathering together in the attractive lake region of the state. Towns grew along the St. Johns riverbank, but few penetrated the interior of Florida. Settlers living in central Florida depended on each other and created generational bonds of friendship.

In early days, one yearly event often participated in together was the community Christmas tree, a tall tree that was decorated with popcorn strings and cranberries. Sometimes the tree was in the town park, sometimes in one of the churches. Christmas trees in homes were not yet in vogue; stockings filled with candy, nuts, and fruit were used instead. The custom of having a joint community Christmas tree continued into the 1920s.

George Washington's birthday celebration in Eustis was looked forward to in the old days. Bena Collins Allen Gamble recalled in 1987, "Every February 22nd, the trip was a day-long event. People stayed until dark to watch the fireworks, then plodded home in the buggy. In rainy weather, the wheels sometimes were mired in the mud."

Summertime introduced many activities, and a few families planned a beach vacation. *The Umatilla Progress* wrote, "In summer fish-fries on some of the many lakes were not infrequent, at which the whole community would collect, being provided with frying pans and fishing tackle, bringing with them also baskets well filled with bread and other extras, such as fowls prepared in various forms, pies, custards, coffee, milk, syrup with which to sweeten the coffee and the universal potato pone . . . Large quantities of fish were caught and carried through all the necessary manipulation for the table and in short such a feast was prepared as would tempt the appetite of the most fastidious epicure that ever lived. Ye Gods! How it makes one's mouth fairly water to recall these scenes, coupled with the good cheer and heartiness of the occasion."

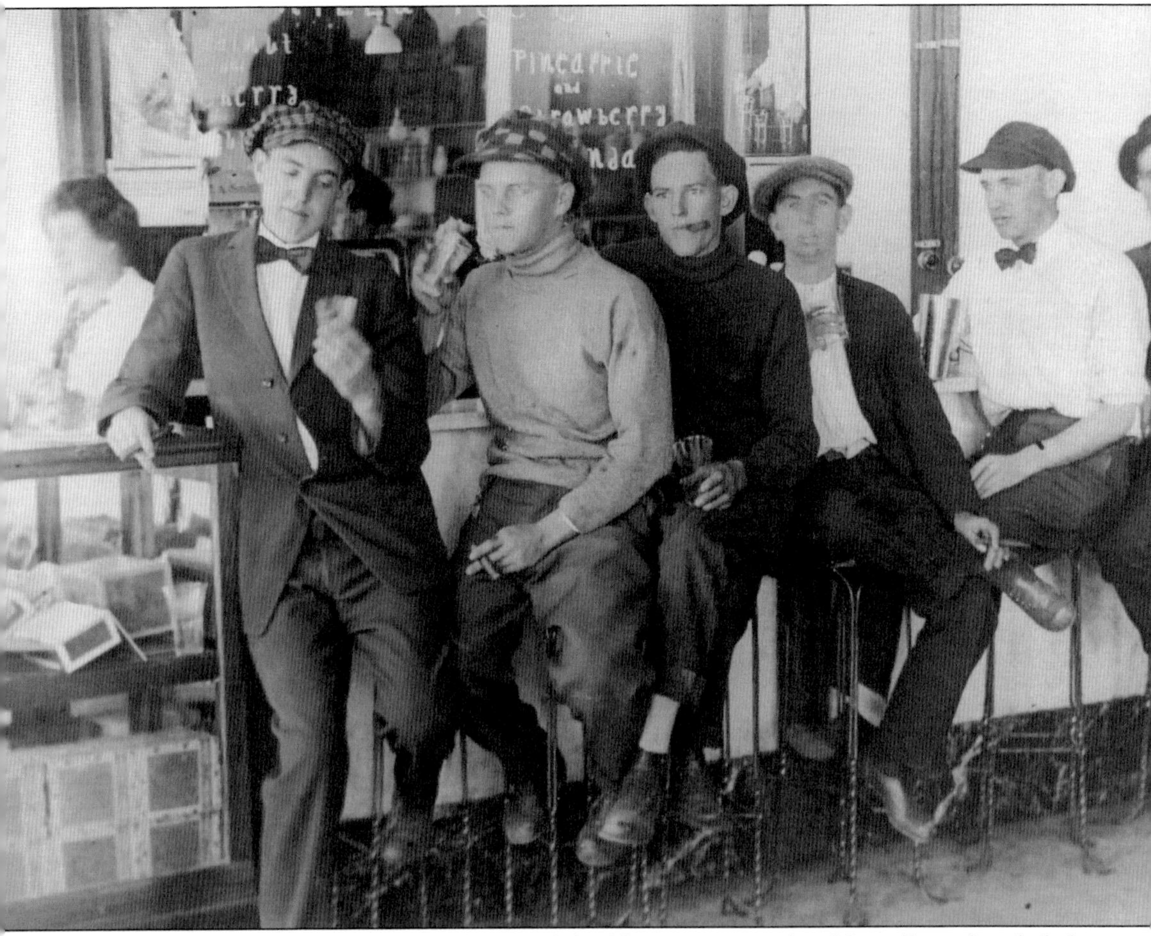

T. A. Smith's Mercantile was the first brick building constructed in Umatilla and included a barber and a confectionary shoppe. The mirror behind the soda fountain advertises pineapple and strawberry lemonade. In this photograph from the early 1900s, an unidentified group of dapper young men are enjoying cigars (probably from the display case on the left) with their milk shakes. (MG.)

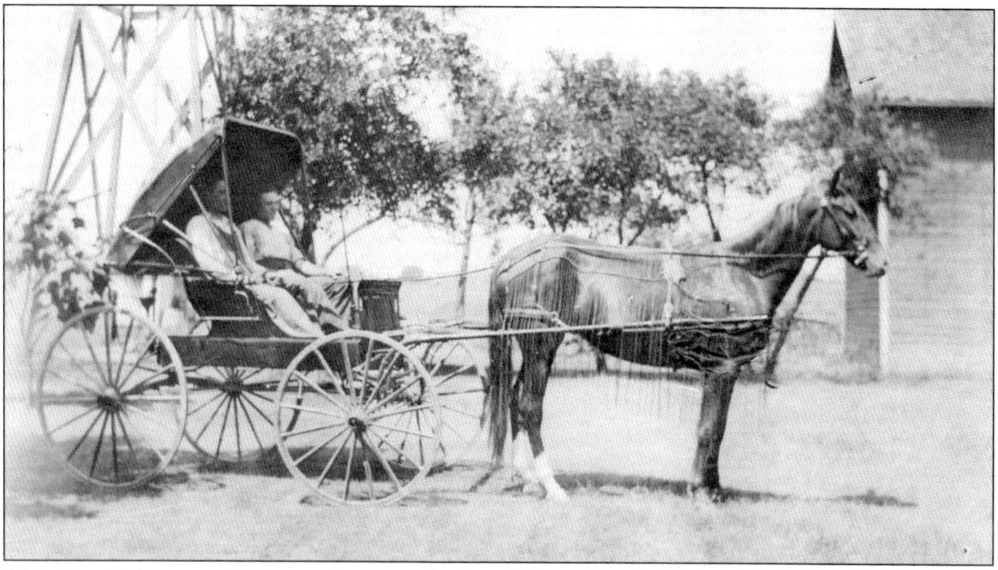

This Florida horse and surrey, photographed in 1914, is dressed in its finest. Mules, horses, and oxen were the preferred means of transportation on Umatilla's roads, where wheels were often mired in the deep sand and the animals were able to pull them free. (EAS.)

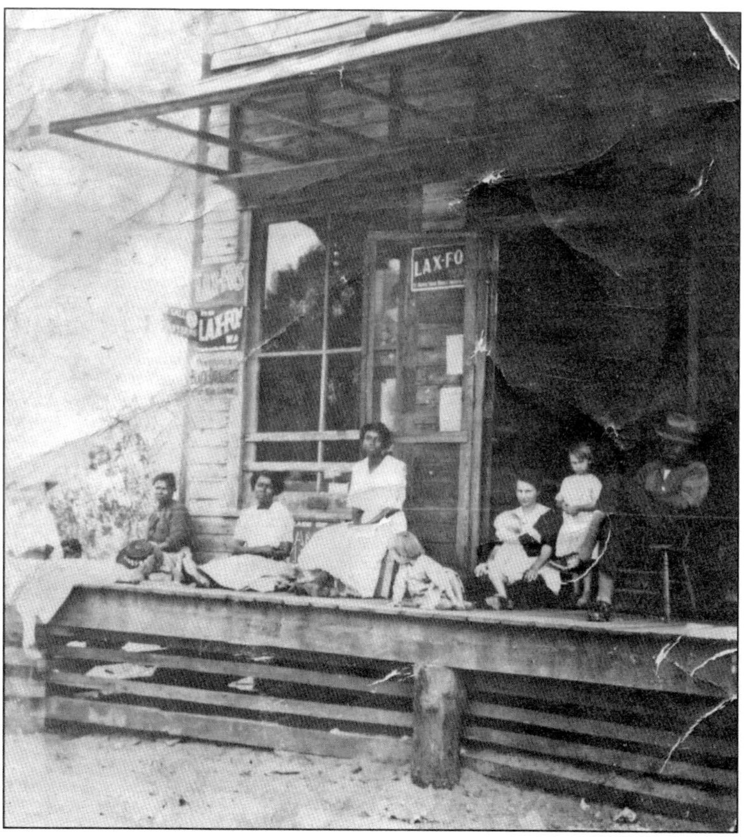

Higley was a little settlement located a few miles west of Umatilla on Lake Yale. The little town was one of many that simply faded away in the years following the big freeze of 1895. Pictured on the porch of the old store in Higley, in 1912, are the Nunn family (African American), with, from left, Ella Vaughn, Halye (Vaughn) Barber, Lou (Vaughn) Livingston, and baby Clyde Vaughn. (IV.)

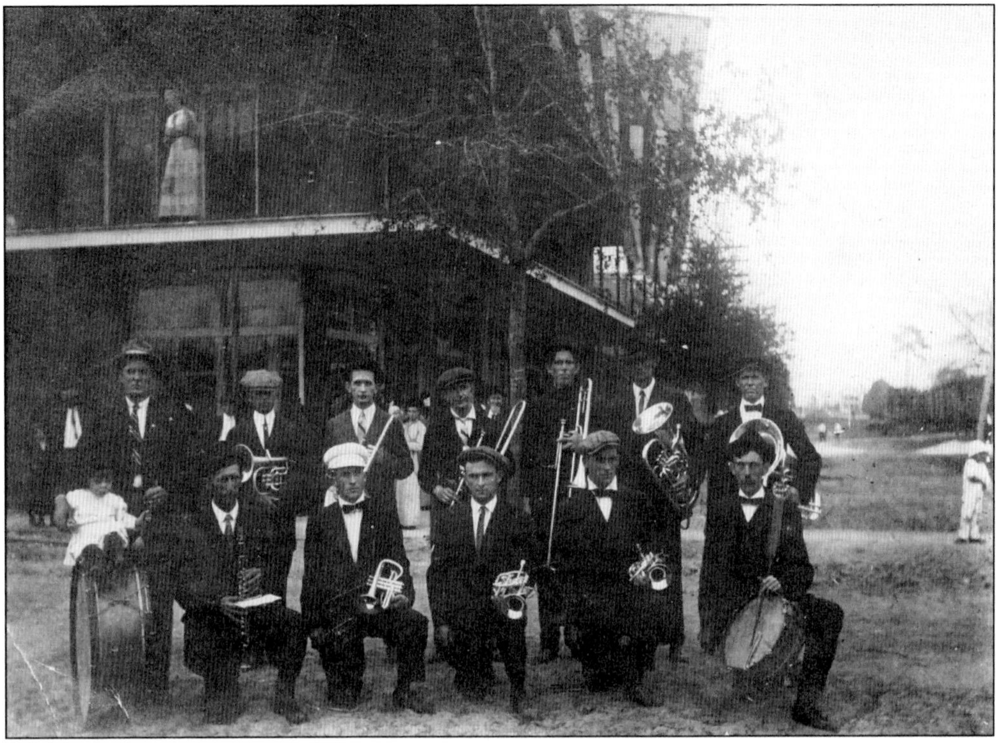

The Umatilla marching band poses in downtown Umatilla in 1909, with a baby sitting on the bass drum. Umatilla's band performed weekly concerts in the park during the 1920s. The band included the customary instruments as well as a banjo, which was unusual for a marching band. Identified members include Mitt Stroebel (back row, center) and Radford Collins and Ted Epps (back row, far right). The band represented Umatilla by performing for parades, celebrations, holidays, and civic gatherings. In the 1914 photograph below, the Umatilla band leads a parade down one of Umatilla's sand roads. (Above BJM, below MG.)

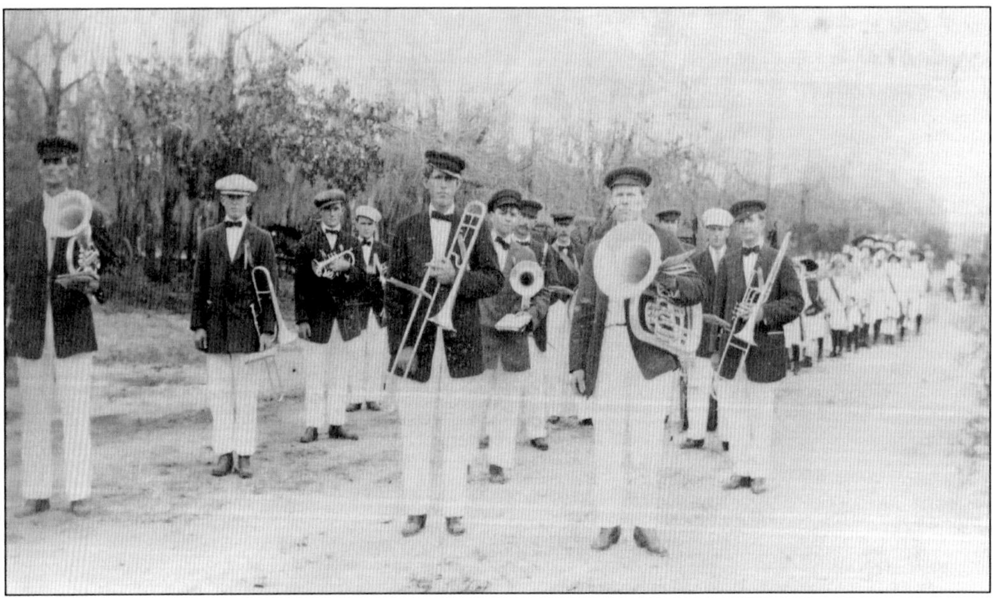

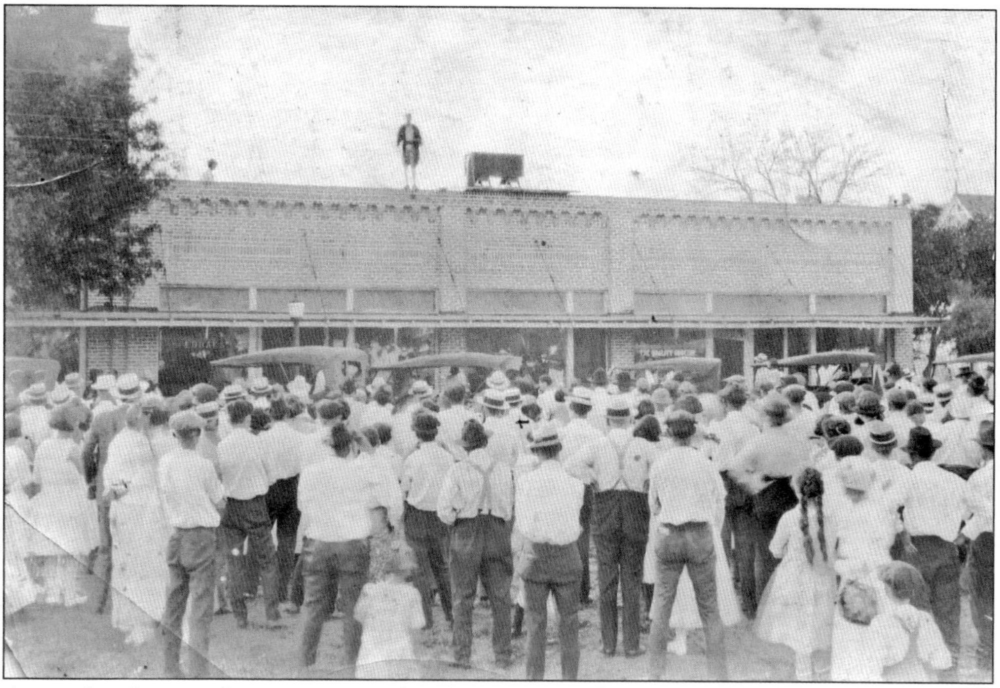

A crowd gathers in the street to watch a magician's performance in 1921. Since there was no theater or arena in Umatilla, the magician uses this one-story building downtown as a stage. The storefronts are, from left to right, Kodaks, The Quality Grocery, and Mary Told Millinery Shop. The new post office and Mason lodge on the left corner are not pictured. (BJM.)

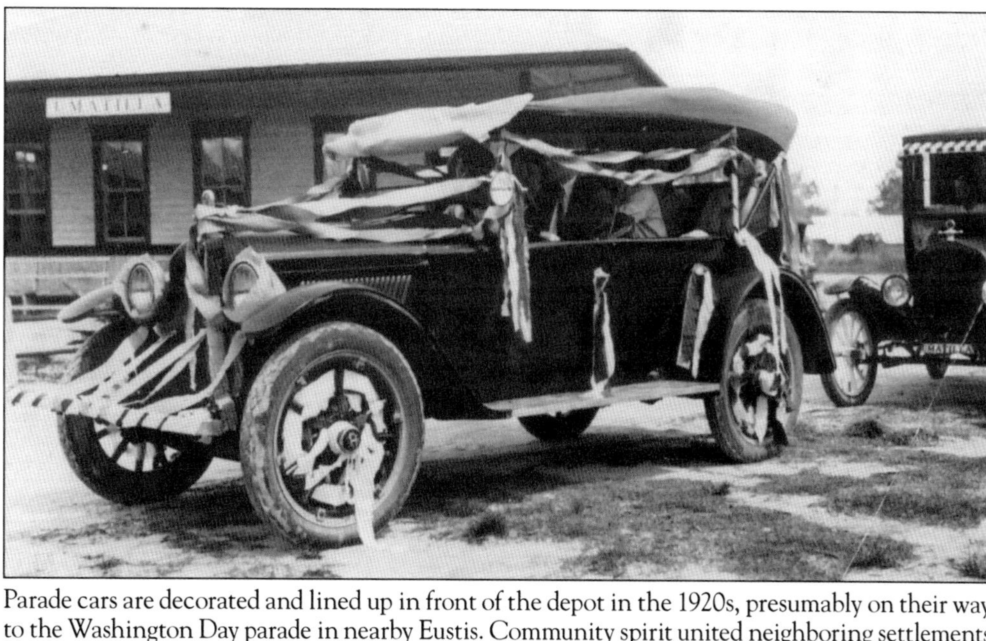

Parade cars are decorated and lined up in front of the depot in the 1920s, presumably on their way to the Washington Day parade in nearby Eustis. Community spirit united neighboring settlements and brought them together several times a year for such celebrations as the Washington Day parade and decorating the community Christmas tree. (BJM.)

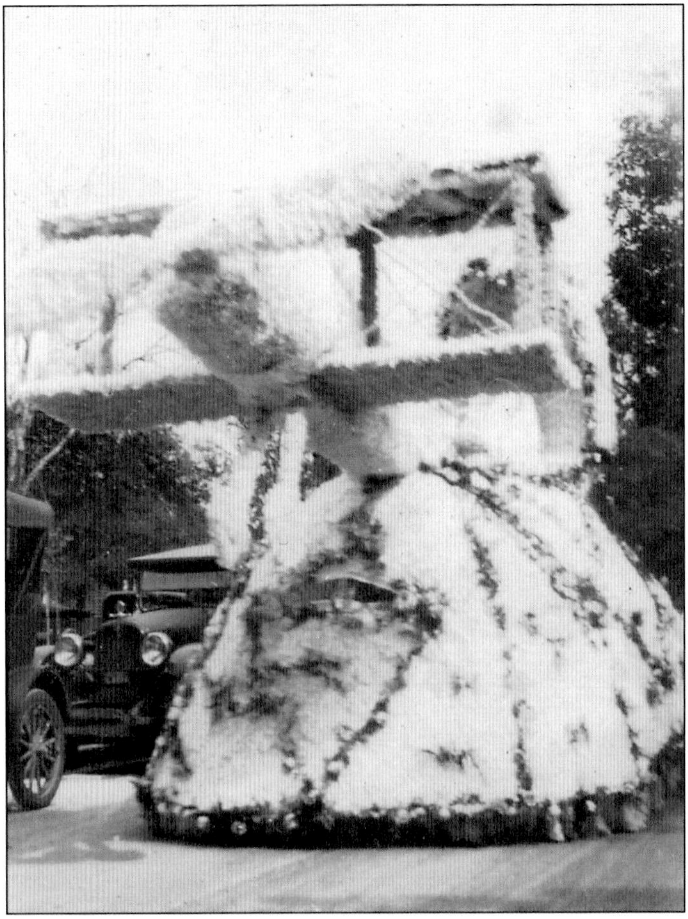

Elaborately decorated with flowers depicting a "new" flying machine, this float was part of the 1921 Washington Day parade in Eustis. Not many citizens had ever seen a bi-wing plane, and this float was all the rage. The annual parade in Eustis is the oldest continuously running celebration in the state of Florida, sometimes celebrating George Washington's birthday with as much as a two-week-long celebration. Pictured below, representing Native Americans familiar to the early settlers of Florida, the children on this float are clothed in native wear, including headdresses, and traditional weapons. The float is complete with palm branch teepees, and moss-draped ground cover. (Left IV, below RBD.)

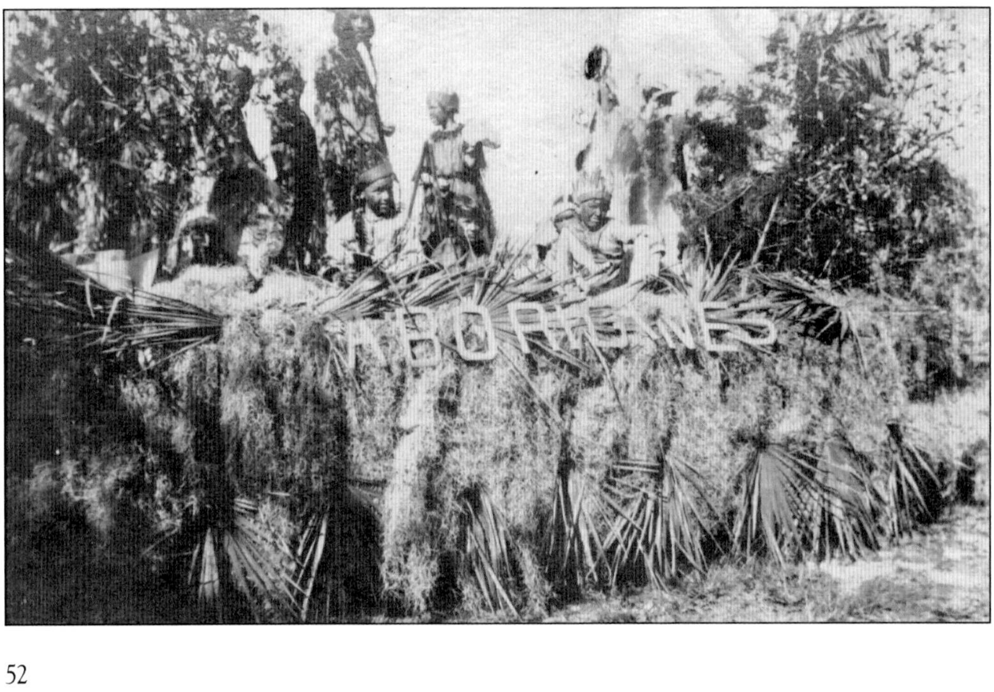

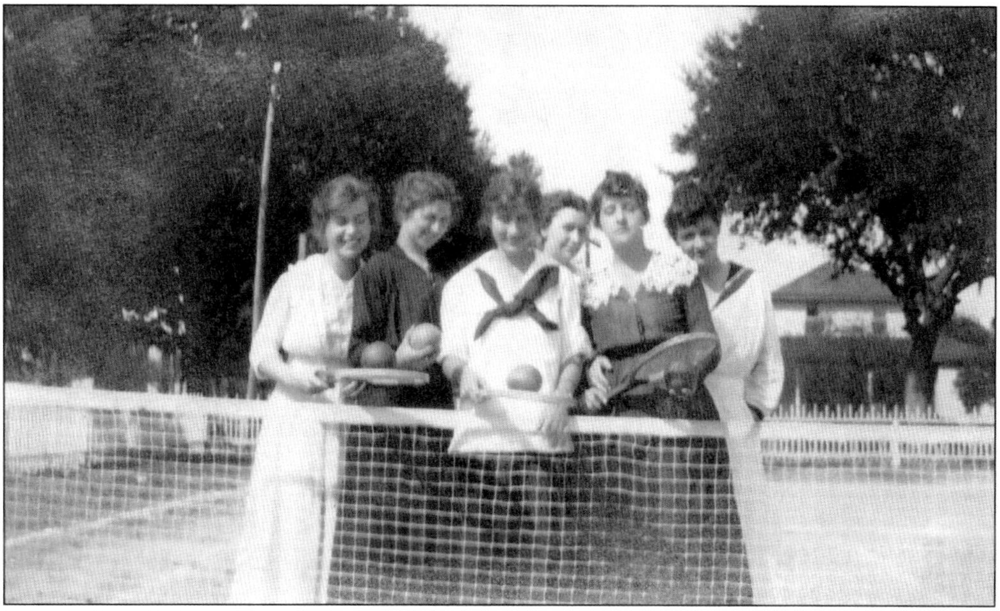

Bena Collins (left) poses with five unidentified friends in the 1920s on the tennis courts of her parents' (Drucilla and Robert Collins) estate. When examined closely, it is evident that their tennis balls are actually grapefruit. (EAS.)

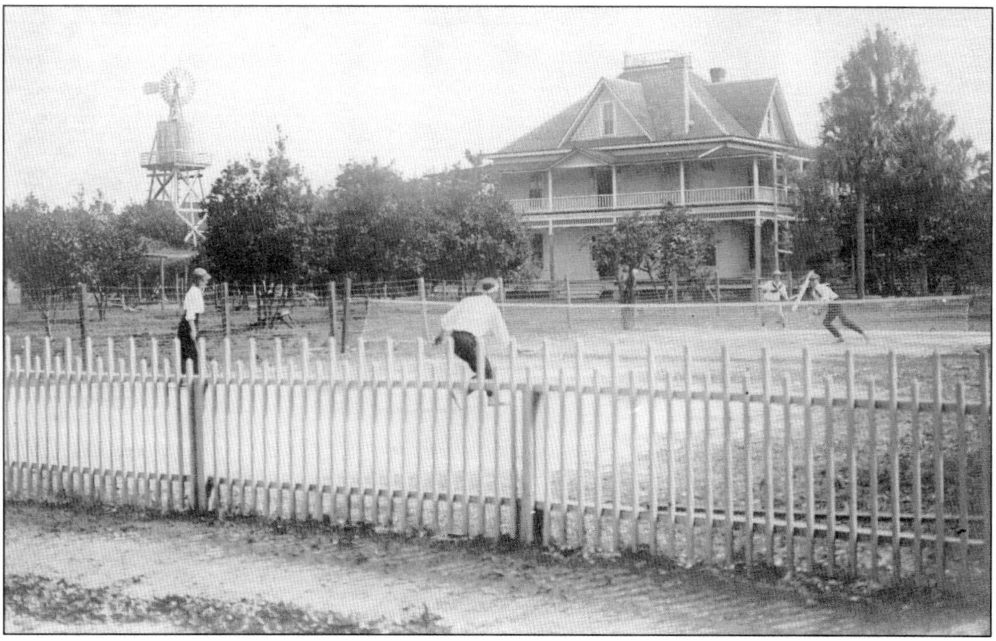

The Collins estate was built in 1904 and included every modern amenity for homes of the day. Clearly visible in the background are the Collins' water tower and windmill-driven water pump for the house. Near the windmill, the family barn housed a cow that provided milk and butter. In this 1911 photograph, a game of tennis is played on the sand court. All players are unidentified. (EAS.)

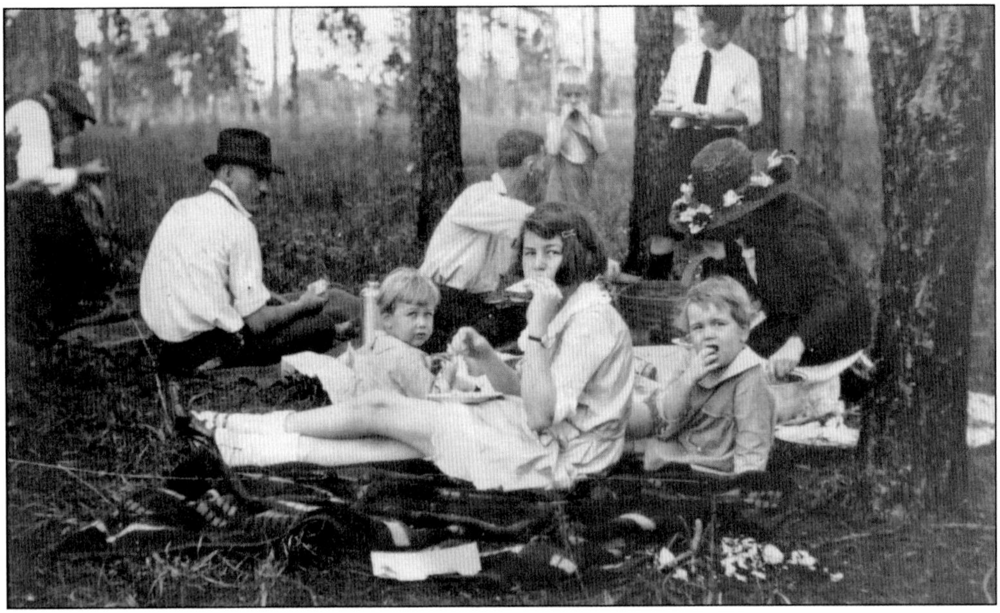

Pictured in April 1921, from left to right, are Don Dickinson, Jack Allen, members of the Collins family (Mary, Harry, Evelyn, Bobby, Bill, and Carolyn) and Bena Allen (wearing hat). The extended family often enjoyed a picnic in the scrub, combined with an afternoon of swimming and relaxing in one of the nearby springs. Pictured below in Collins's orange grove on Lake Pearl with two unidentified friends are Jack Allen, Robert Lee Collins, and Harry Collins. Fish fries were messy work, often staged outdoors. Sometimes fish fries were impromptu events, but just as often they were planned social events for the entire community to enjoy. (Both photographs RBD.)

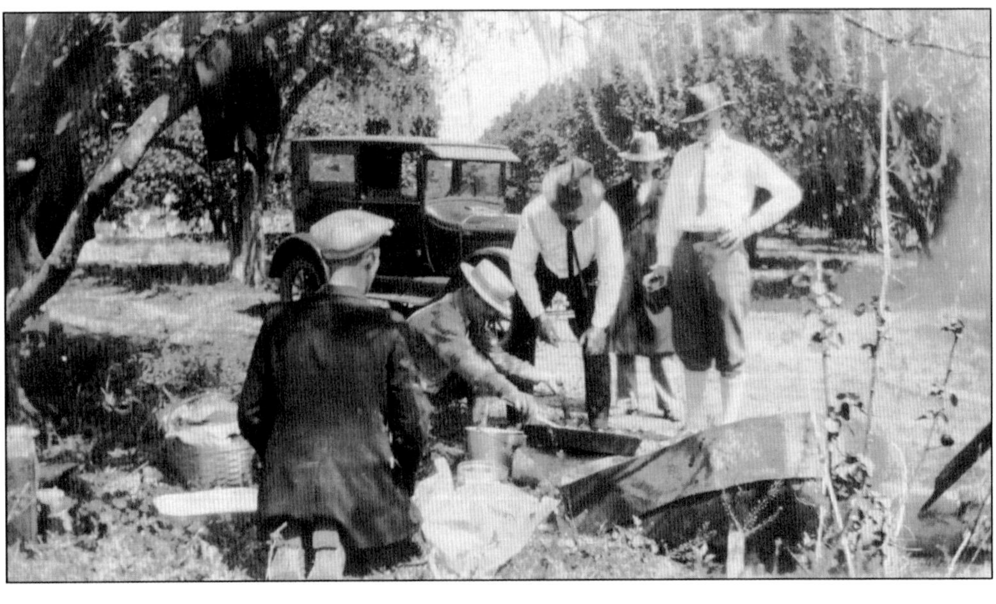

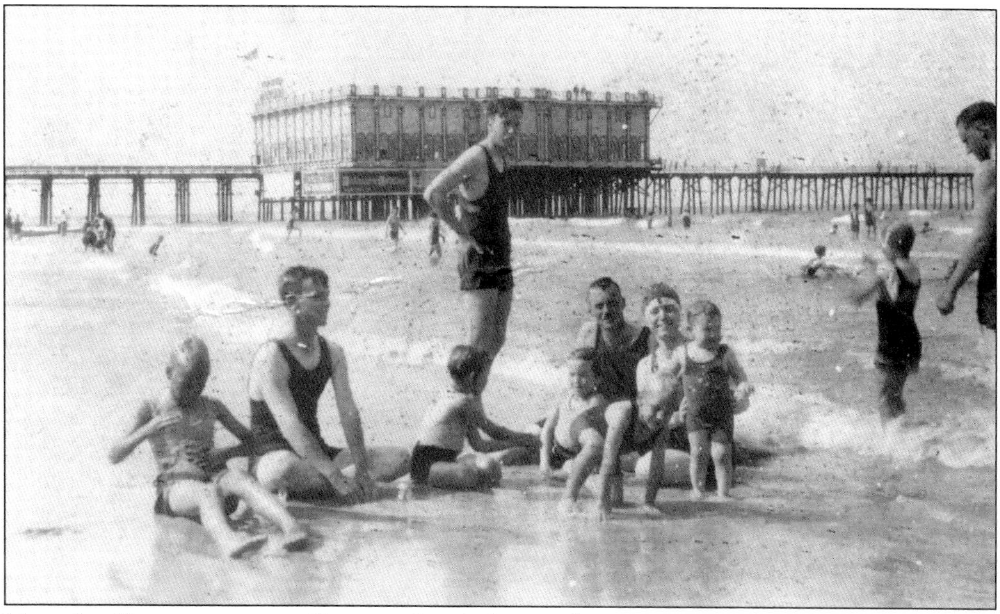

Many families spent time at Daytona Beach during the summer months, often to escape the malaria outbreaks that tended not to affect the coast. Enjoying the surf at Daytona Beach in this 1926 photograph (with the historical pier in the background), are, from left to right, Bobby, Harry, Mary, and Carolyn Collins, Jack Allen, unidentified, Bena Allen, Harry Collins Jr., and Virginia Collins. Homeowners along the beach built little shade huts where bathers were able to enjoy the beach without getting too much sun. Seen below taking a break from the water are, from left to right, Bena Allen, Harry Collins, and an unidentified woman photographed in 1924 at Daytona Beach. (Both photographs RBD.)

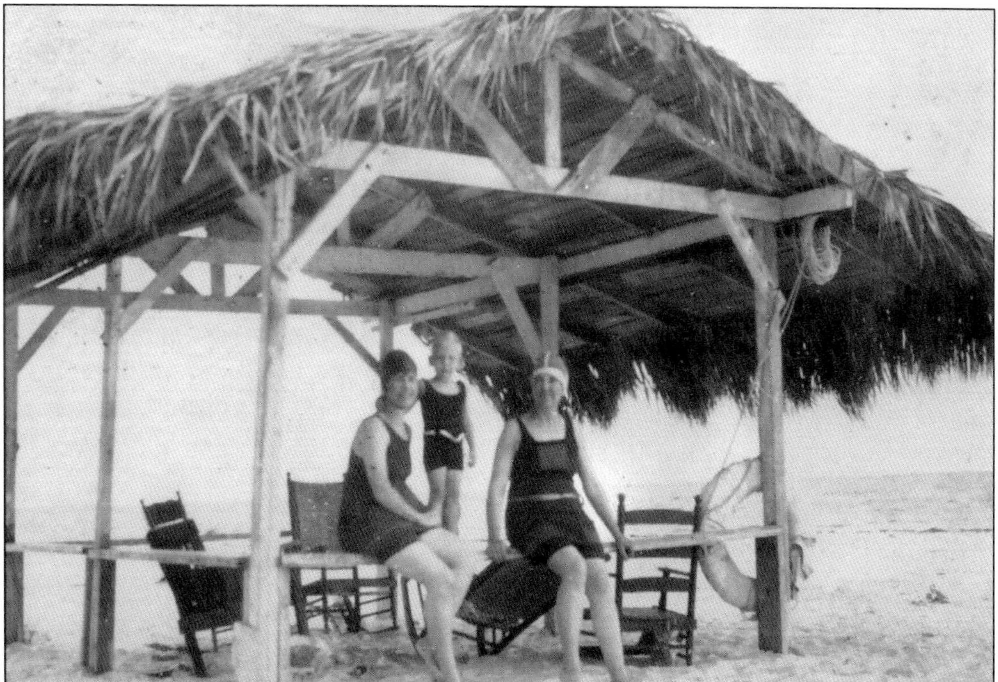

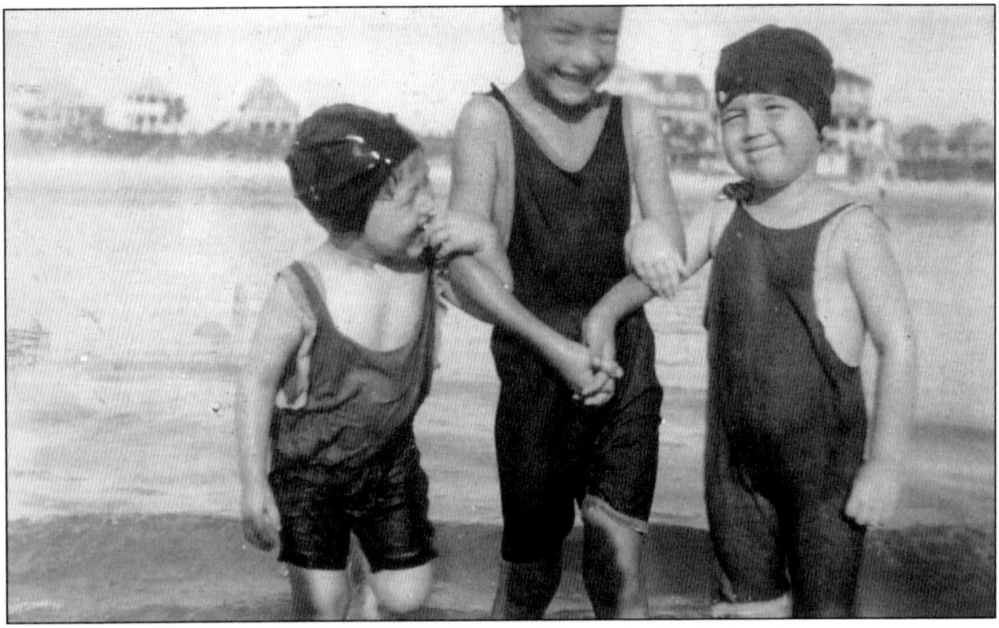

Mary, Bobby, and Carolyn Collins stand in the waves on Daytona's famous white sand beach in 1920. Below, modeling the swimwear of the era, the group includes (in no particular order) Bill, Evelyn, Lucy, and Bobby Collins. Bena Allen Gamble remembered every summer starting for the coast with her parents and two younger children in a surrey and the older children in a cart pulled by an Indian pony. The two vehicles went east to Crow's Bluff, where they spent the night with relatives. That day-and-a-half trip can be driven today in about an hour. (Both photographs RBD.)

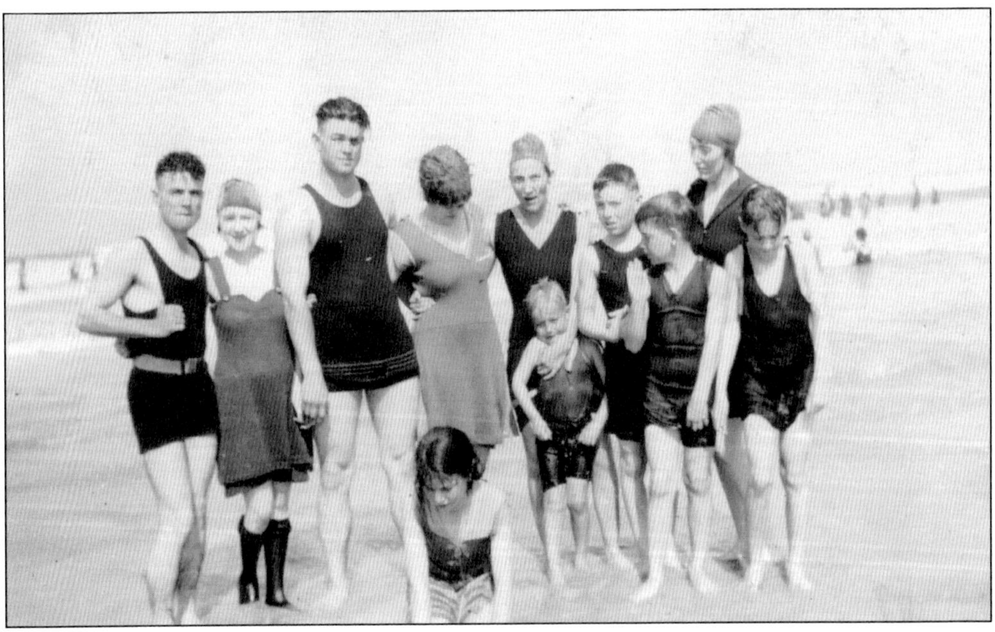

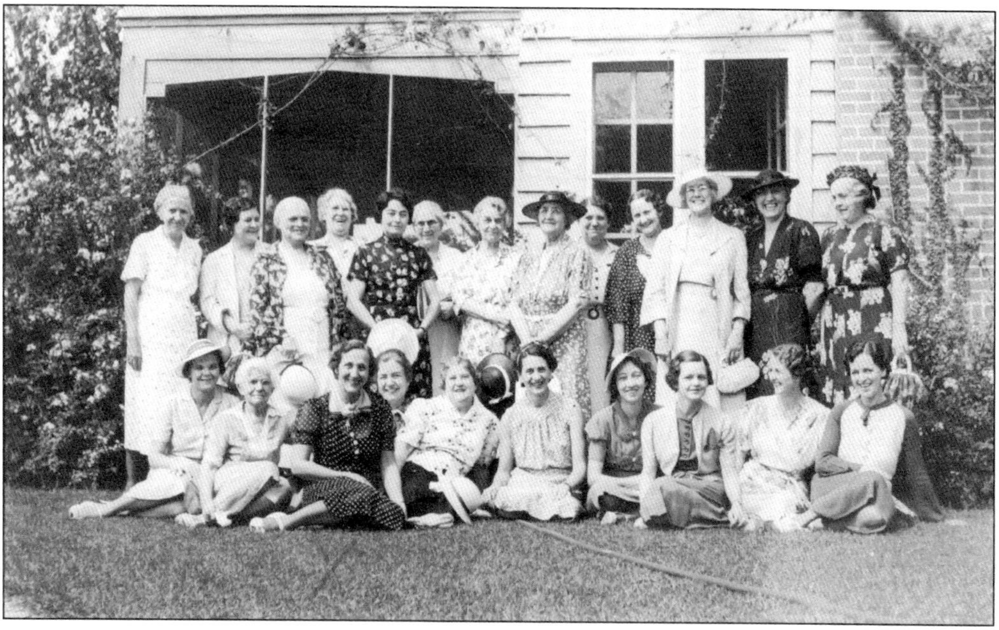

In 1917, the women of Umatilla began a library in an upstairs room over a store on the corner of Central Avenue and Orange Lane. This was the beginning of the Umatilla Women's Club, still active today in its service to the community. Pictured in 1934 are the following members, from left to right: (first row) Dorothy St. John, Beth Needham, Lucy Collins, Bena Allen, May Webster, Betty Taylor, Jean Arnold, Cleo Calhoun, Fanny Kassulker, Betty Rush; (second row) Mrs. Harry Williams, unidentified, Lorraine Smith, Grace Davis, Loretta Shouse, unidentified, Drucilla Collins, two unidentified women, Lister Barger, Elsie Replinger, Patty Hoover, Mrs. Club, and Kathryn Baker. The women's club began meeting in the new community building in 1940. In the photograph below, the members are gathered in the front of the log building. (Above RBD, below EAS.)

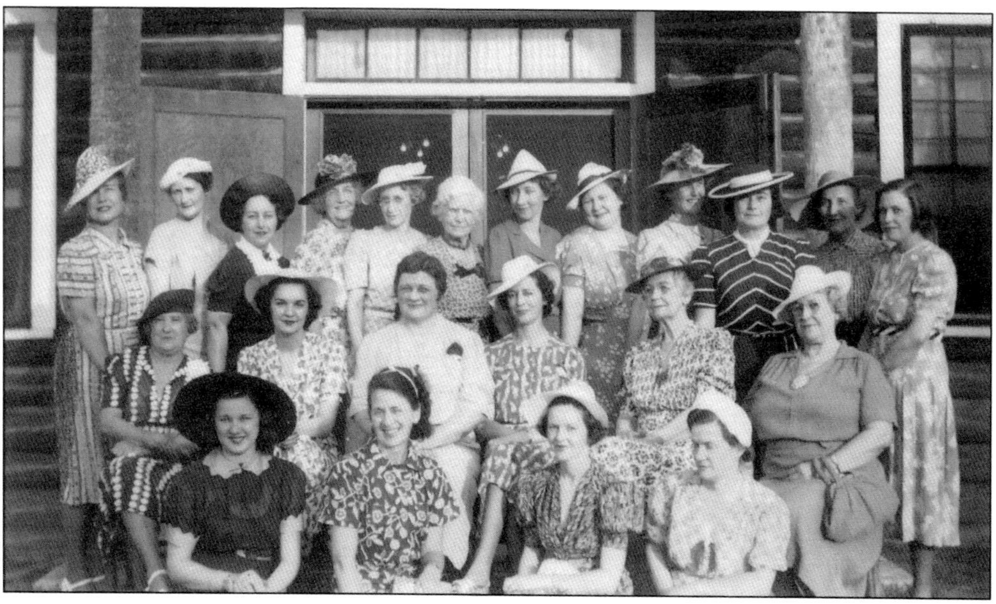

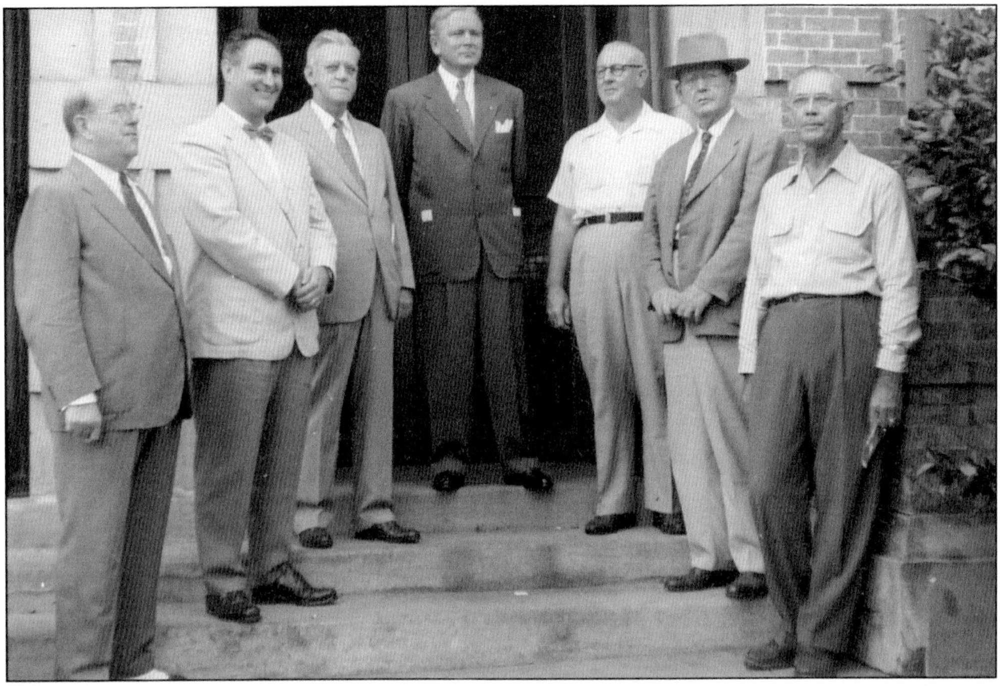

Pictured at a political gathering are, from left to right, George J. White (president of the First National Bank of Mt. Dora and a member of Florida's state board of control), Troy Hall (judge), J. Ed Baker (senator from Umatilla), Fuller Warren (governor), Carl Duncan (state representative), Truman Futch (judge), and Sanford C. Colley (doctor from Mount Dora). While governor of Florida from 1949 to 1953, Fuller Warren laid the foundations for the state's turnpike system and instituted the Florida reforestation program. During his tenure, quality control programs were established for Florida's citrus crops and new laws were established that forbade cattle to wander freely. (UHS.)

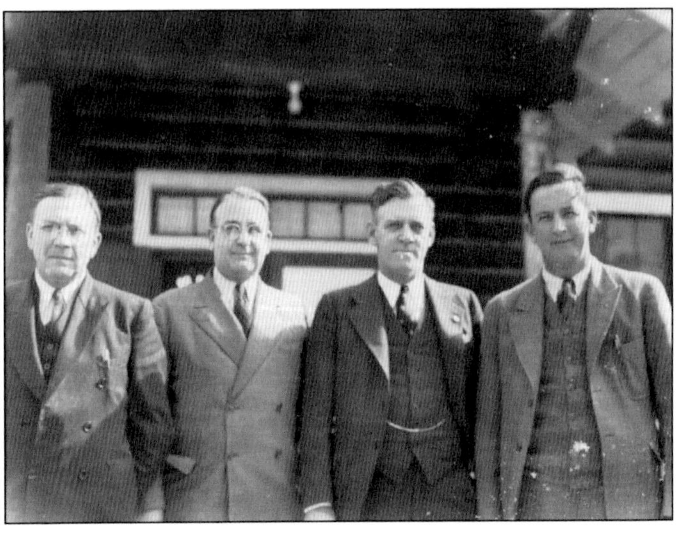

Kiwanians pictured outside the community building in the 1940s are, from left to right, Dr. Lee Ashton (Umatilla), Harold Hippler (Eustis), J. Ed Baker (Umatilla), and W. A. "Lex" Skinner (Umatilla). Kiwanis International is a global organization of volunteers that promotes service to youth using two approaches—directly improving quality of life and encouraging youth leadership. (UHS.)

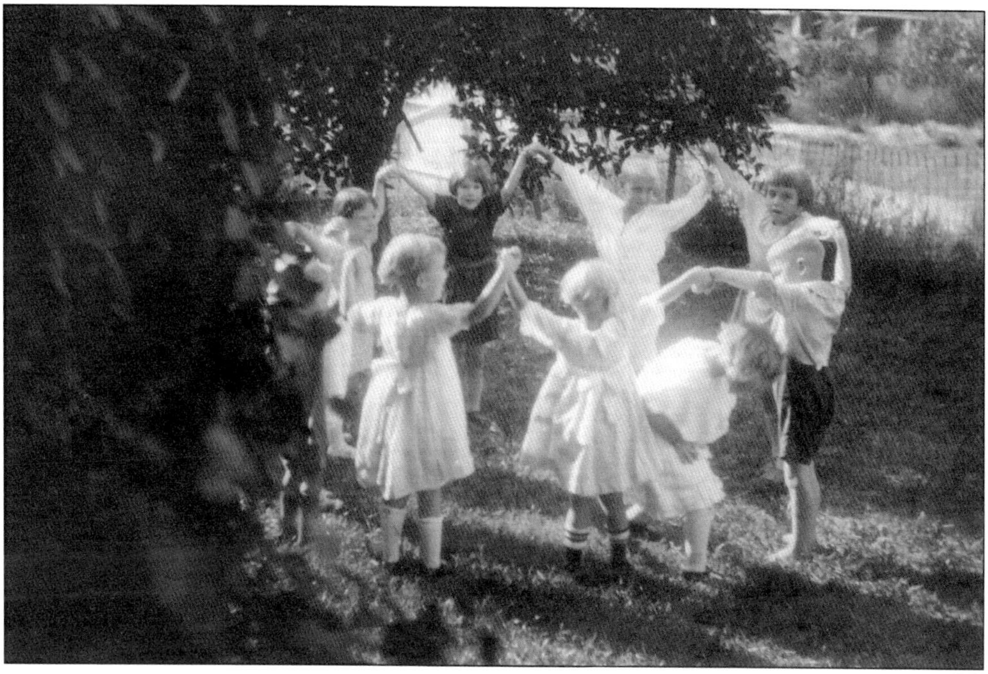

Birthday parties were a special time for friends and family to gather in celebration. Pictured in 1924, the Collins children and their friends play among the orange trees, where the sunlight reflects the magic of the moment. Below, Bobby Collins appears ready to catch his fish with either the cane pole in one hand or the hammer in the other. Five unidentified friends join Carolyn (second from right) and Mary (in a wicker pull-along stroller) Collins. (RBD.)

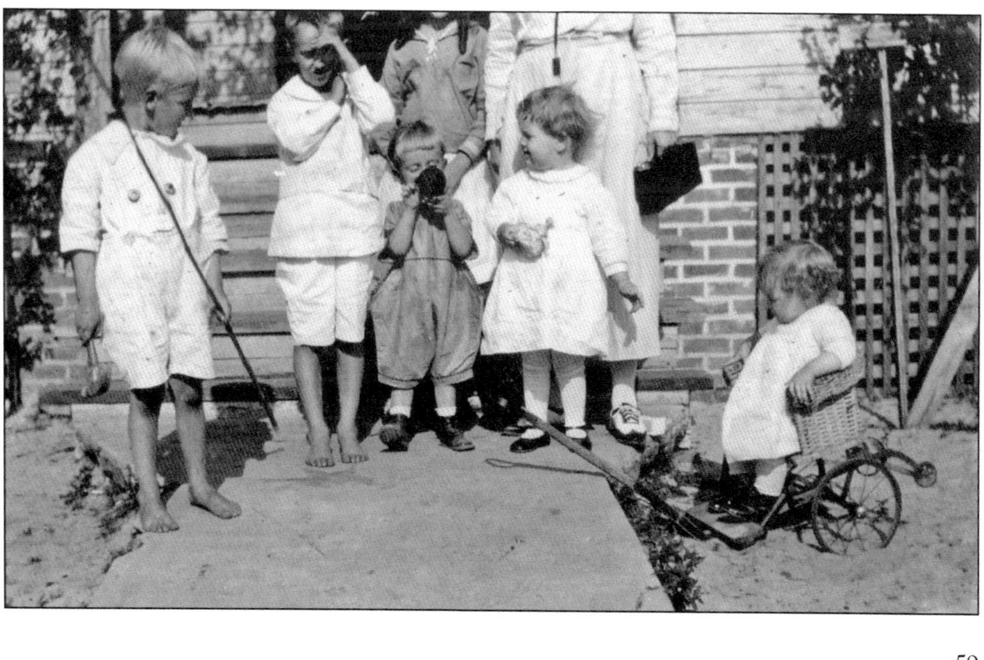

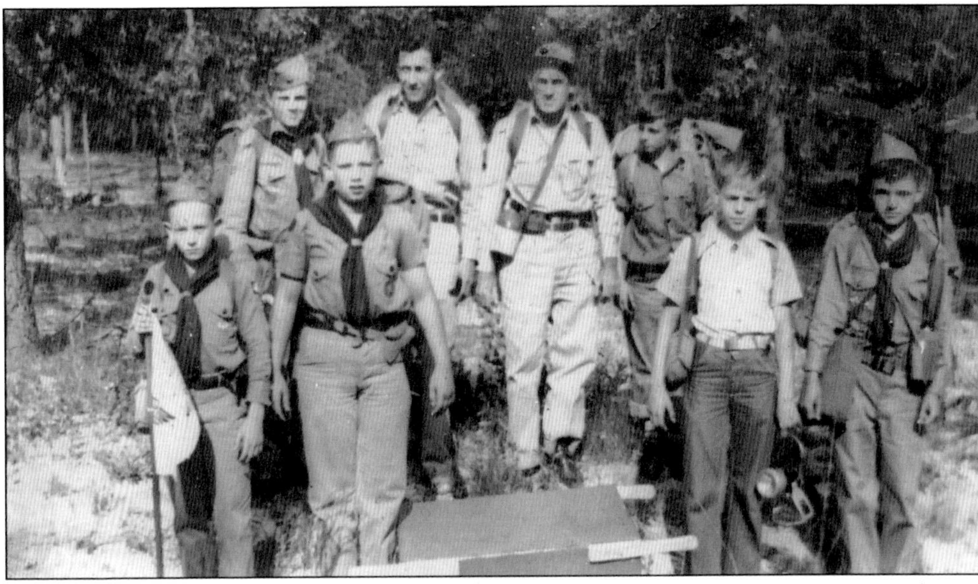

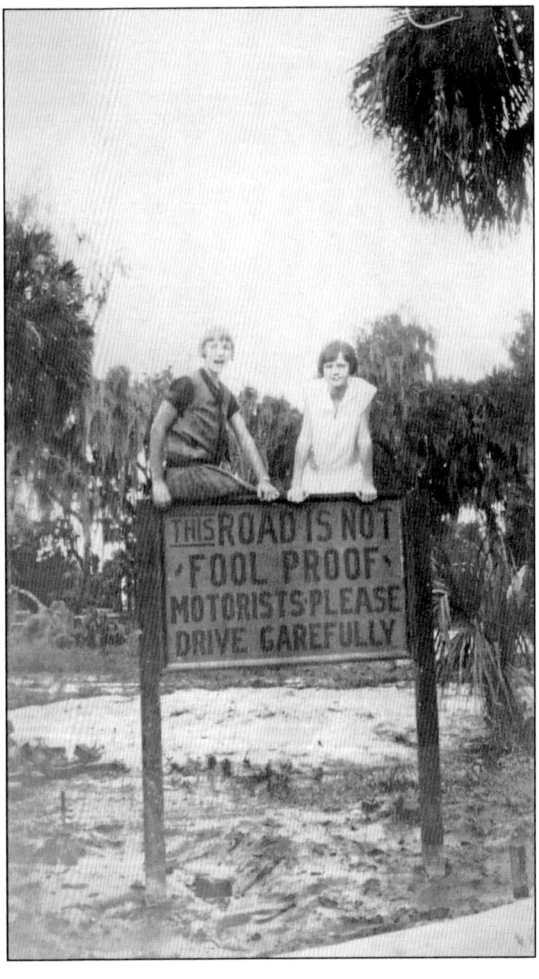

Boy Scout Troop 45 was sponsored by the Kiwanis Club of Umatilla. Jack Allen served on the board of the Central Florida BSA Council; J. D. Wingfield, Clyde Marteeny, and others were on the local committee. Pictured on a hike in 1944 are "Doc" Hatfield, scoutmaster (second row, left); and Glen Bolles, assistant; with (from left) Steve Johnson, Russell Bryan, Phillip ?, Bruce Crow, unidentified, and Charlie Allison.

Early roads in Umatilla were deeply grooved sandy paths—hardly foolproof. Before the national numbered highway system was established in 1926, traffic followed paths blazed and promoted by various trails associations, a system collectively known as auto trails. Umatilla's main roads were part of the Dixie Highway system. Halye Vaughn (right) and friend pose on a sign warning of the dangers of driving in the 1920s. (IV.)

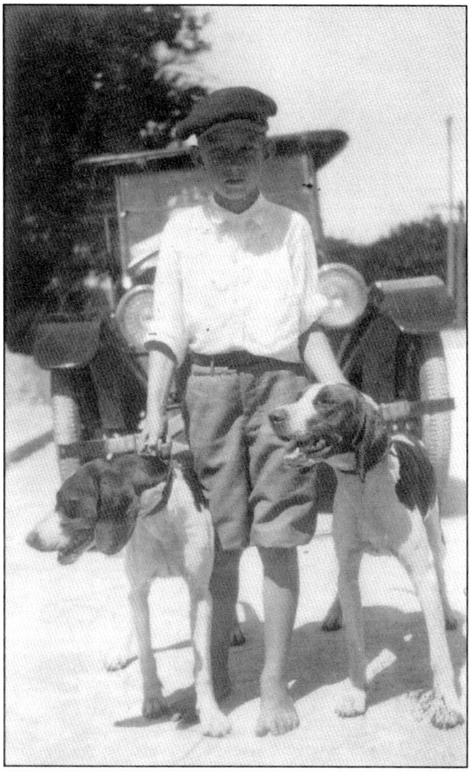

Bob Vaughn poses in front of a Model T Ford with two of his family's hunting dogs. "Gone Hunting" signs were common on closed shops in hunting season. Fine hunting dogs were known to receive care and affection equal to that given children, as hunting was more than sport for families, which often depended on game for food. Seen below in the 1920s, with his piney woods rooter wild hog, Bob Vaughn stands proudly dressed, posing in his Sunday best. Most households kept livestock for food, and animal care was a part of everyday life. (Both photographs IV.)

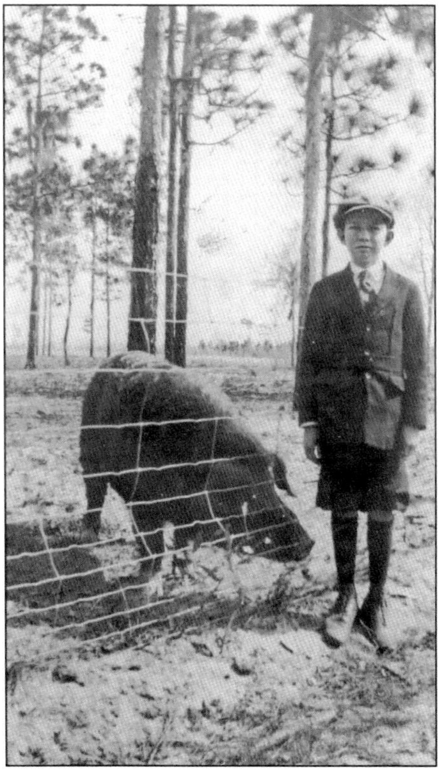

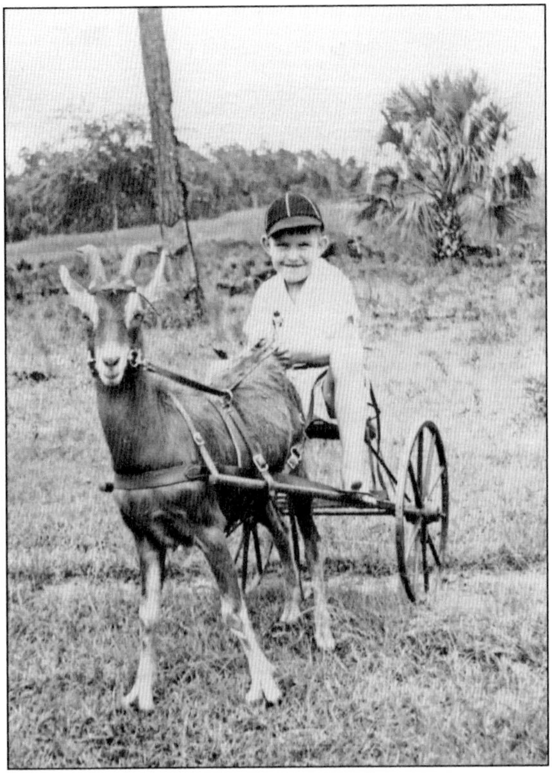

Perry Mark Turner is photographed in his goat cart in 1938, heading out for an afternoon ride. Goat carts were popular with children to drive, but goats also hauled light loads and have long been used for weed control in yards and pastures. (SA.)

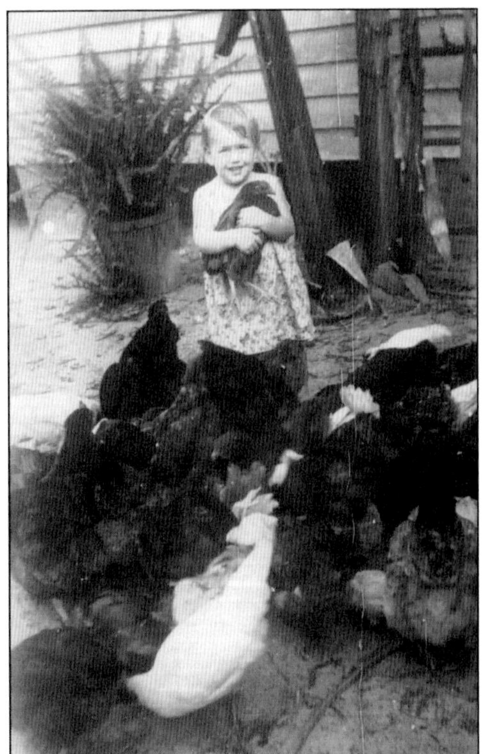

In 1928, most households kept their own chickens and livestock for eggs, milk, and meat as supplies for home consumption. Little Virginia Collins holds a favored chicken (possibly dinner?), while others rush in to get fed. Children learned responsibility by raising and caring for family animals and pets. (RBD.)

Five

A Change Has Taken Place

Remaining frontier country for over 300 years, Florida had been held for strategic purposes but only sparsely settled. Footpaths of Native Americans gradually became trails for explorers, then byways for wagons, and finally crude roads. Following the Civil War, small steamboats—uniquely tailored for the narrow, winding Oklawaha River—served growing communities near headwater lakes, including Umatilla. Larger steamers used the St. Johns, but only wagon trails connected Umatilla to their landings. An influx of settlers increased the need for improved transportation.

All things changed with the whistle of locomotives. The first train came through Umatilla on February 18, 1880. Nathan Trowell planned a big dinner and invited the entire countryside to celebrate. Free rides on the train's flatbed cars were offered by train officials.

The new rail line was called the St. Johns and Lake Eustis Railroad and covered 28 miles from Astor to Eustis. Henry Plant bought most of the rail lines through western and central Florida between 1882 and 1887. In 1902, the Atlantic Coast Line Railroad took over Plant's lines and served communities along its route until 1944, when trucking transportation began to replace rail lines.

The arrival of the railroad signaled an unfolding panorama in the development of the frontier settlement of Umatilla, "infusing of a new life, departure from the old paths, changing of once-existing conditions, until the country does not seem by any means to be what it once was. At this time, travel in any direction you may choose, you will see comfortable homes, families contented and happy, well tilled farms, thrifty orange groves, a far better grade of horses, mules and cattle, improved agriculture implements, neat and substantial churches, school houses."

Loren Stover expressed the drama of the railroad era: "Bands and ball teams, tourists, local excursionists, weekend traders, farmers, merchants, and businessmen—all of these and many others rode the first dinky, slow, midget trains that opened the land to be known as central Florida with Lake County at its heart."

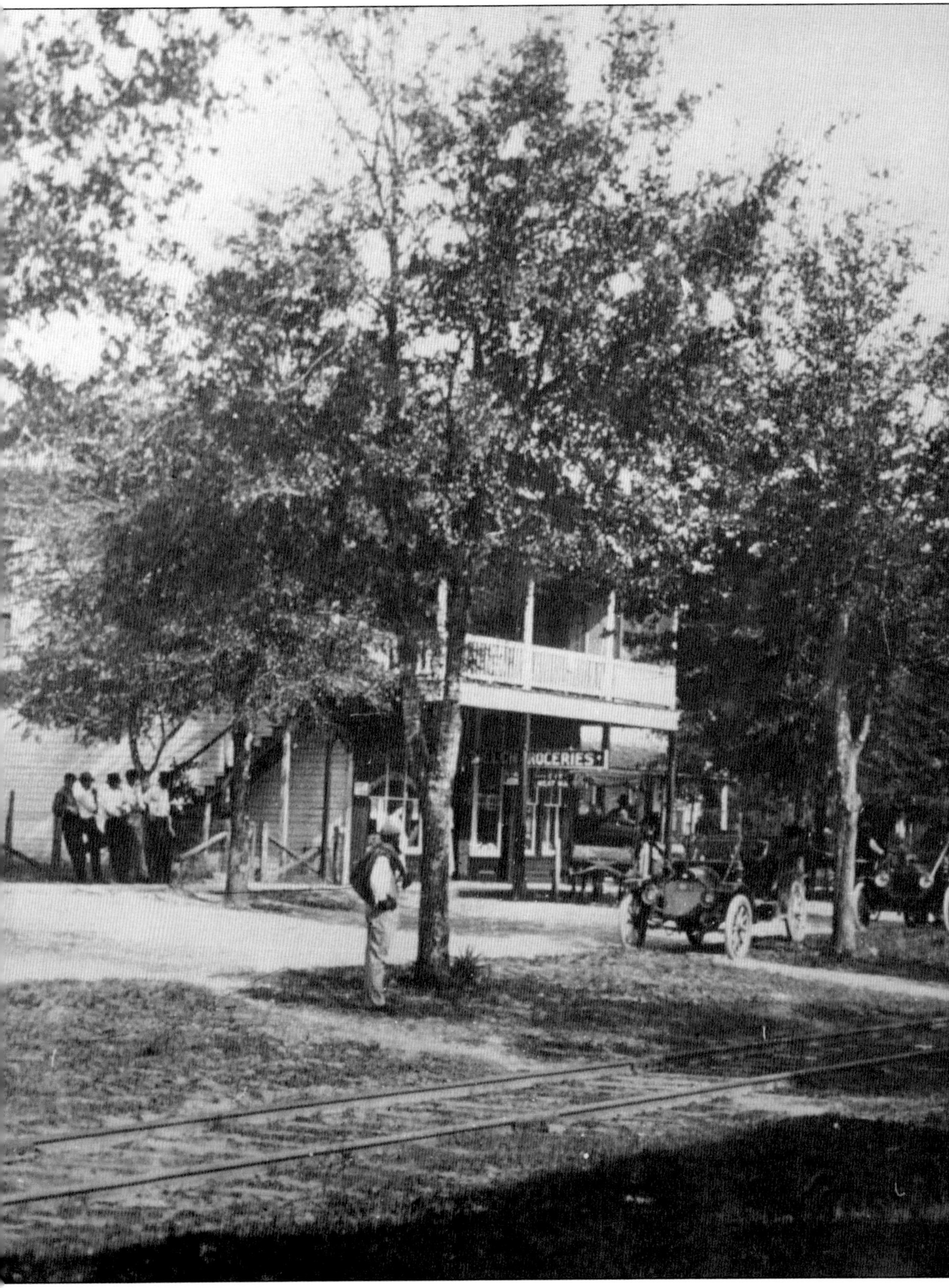

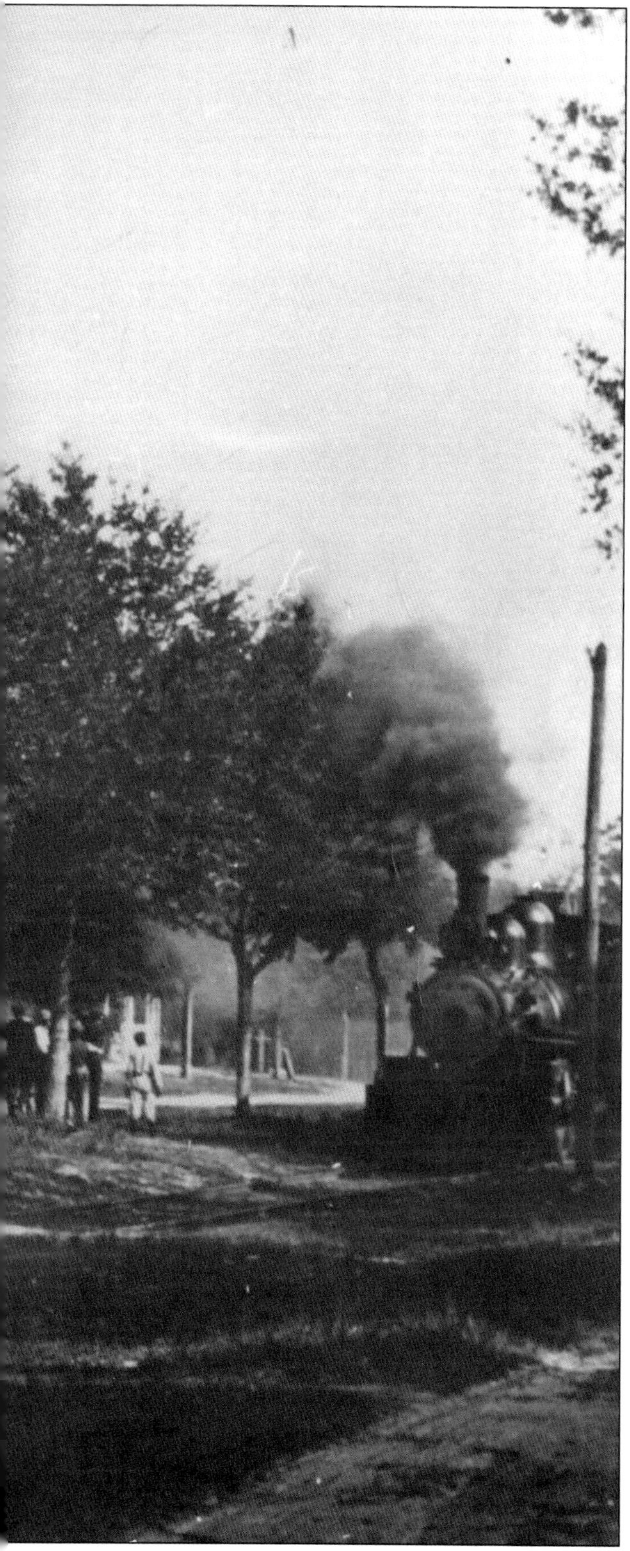

Folks gather to watch the St. Johns and Eustis "Old Smokey" arrive in Umatilla. The first railroad was narrow gauge—about 3 feet from one rail to the other. The trains that traveled these tracks were small. The tracks meandered among some of the 1,400 lakes that dotted and named the new county and provided a beautiful vista for passengers. Its arrival in 1880 created great economic opportunity by opening the interior section of Florida to new industries and settlers, and established Umatilla as a destination for winter and recreational visitors. In 1884, when Umatilla pioneer Anne Turner first sighted the train she exclaimed it looked like a "Thousand Leg," referring to the brown worm insect. The trains ran on unreliable schedules, but to the settlements and settlers along the route it was a marvelous improvement to their backwoods roads for travel. A train schedule from 1884 lists the following schedule for Train No. 1: Astor at 8:00 a.m., Summit at 8:50 a.m., Altoona at 9:24 a.m., Umatilla at 9:55 a.m., Fort Mason at 10:35 a.m., Eustis at 10:50 a.m., covering a trip of 28 miles in a mere hour and half. (MG.)

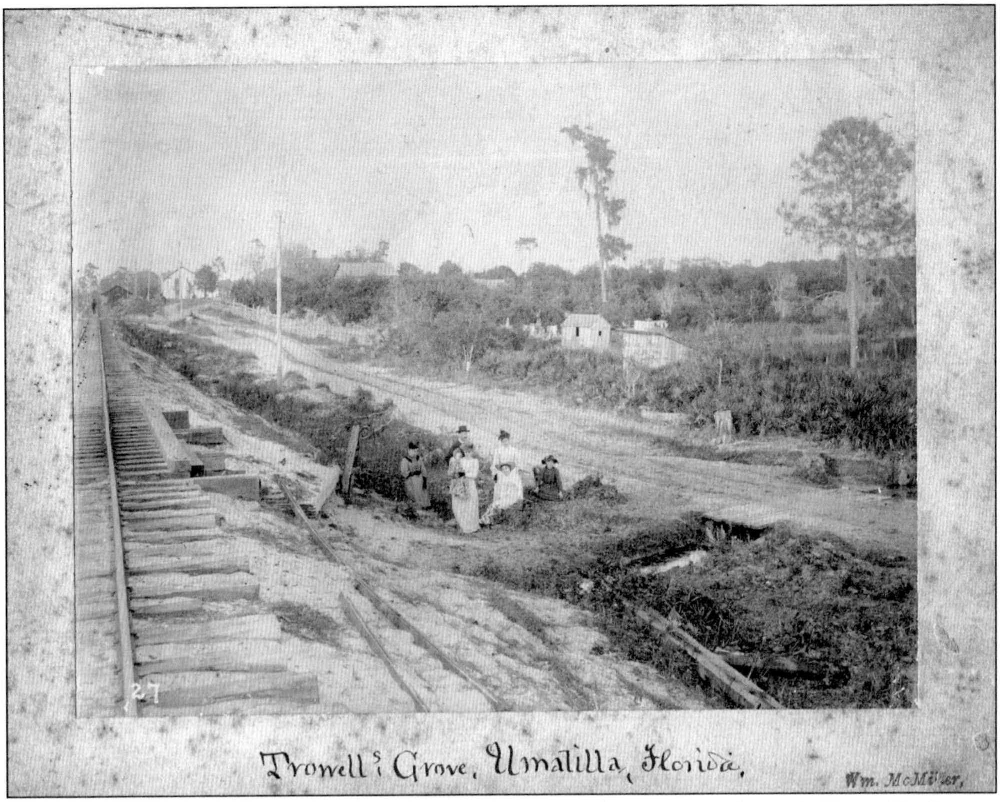

An unidentified family poses beside the new train tracks running through Trowell's Grove, now known as Umatilla in 1880. The deep sandy road beside the tracks clearly shows why the train would be a preferable means of transportation, as roads were unpredictable at best. In the background, an unidentified gentleman walks along the tracks toward the photographer. The very same vista is pictured on a postcard from the early 1900s, showing the improved landscaping along the tracks leading into downtown Umatilla. Both photographs were taken facing north into town where the tracks run beside Lake Umatilla on the right. (Above BJM, below CB.)

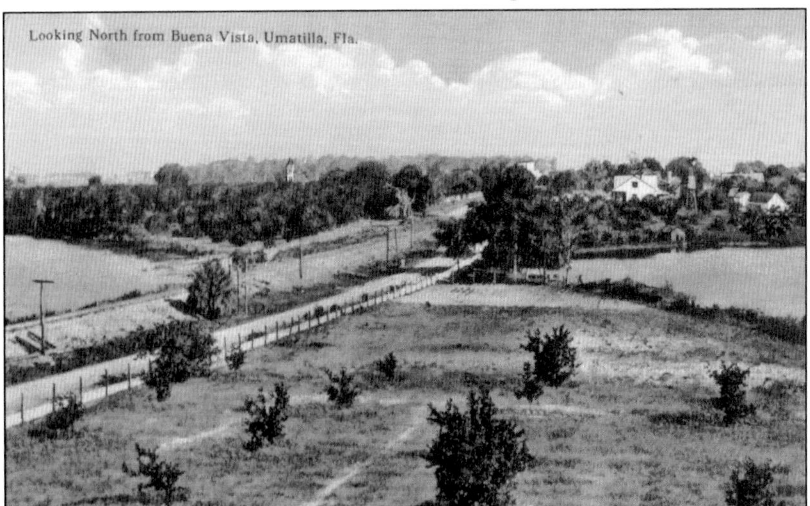

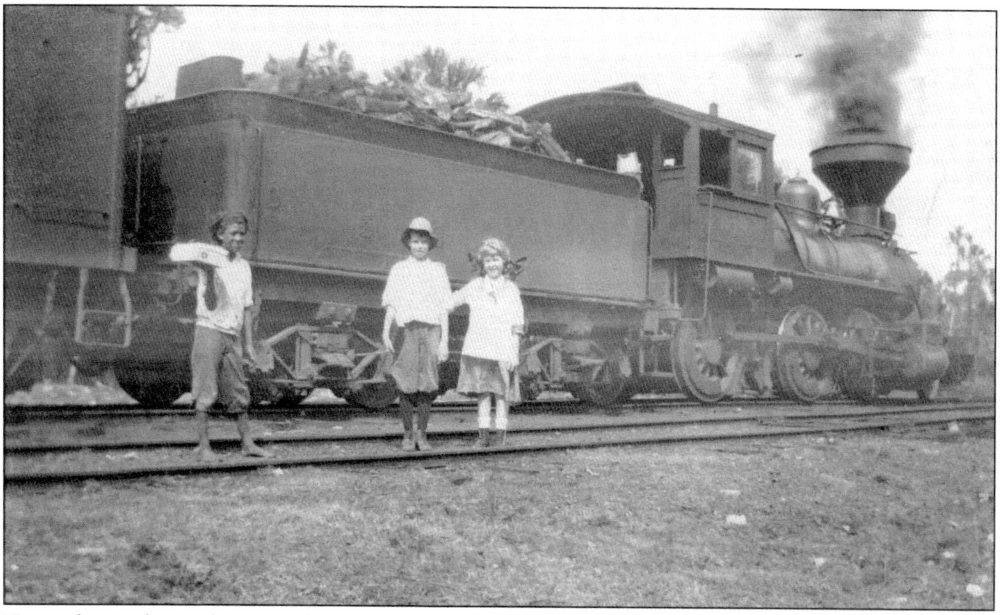

Trains have always fascinated children, and the sight of the first train coming through Umatilla was an event worthy of celebration by the entire community. Three unidentified children pose in front of "Old Smokey" in the 1880s. Seen below, at age 13, is Willis V. McCall posing beside the old depot in his Sunday best. McCall was elected Lake County sheriff in January 1945, and served until June 1972. He had outspoken beliefs, and controversy regarding his pursuit of the law is part of his legacy; however, many citizens retained their confidence in him. (Above EAS, Right SA.)

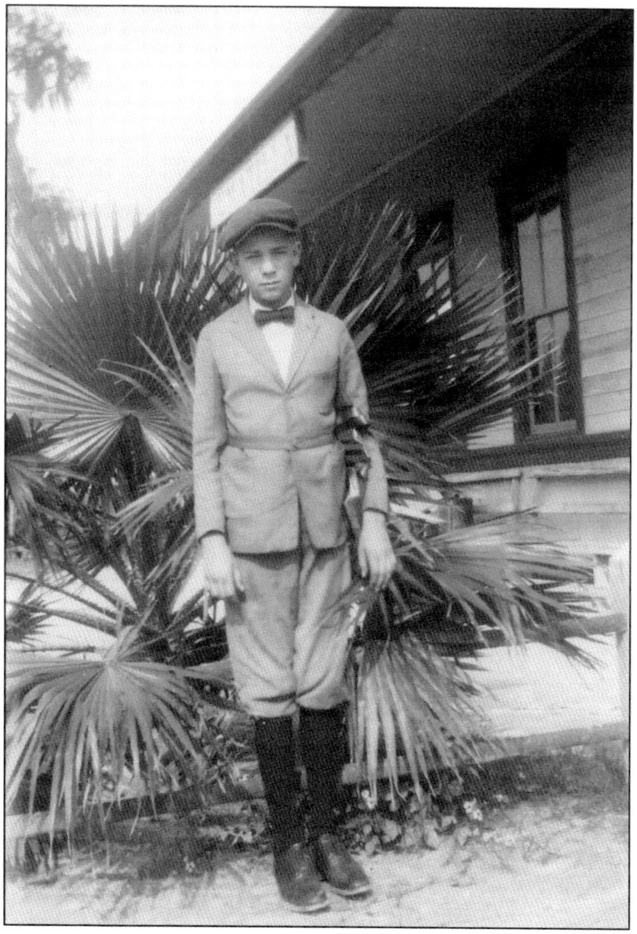

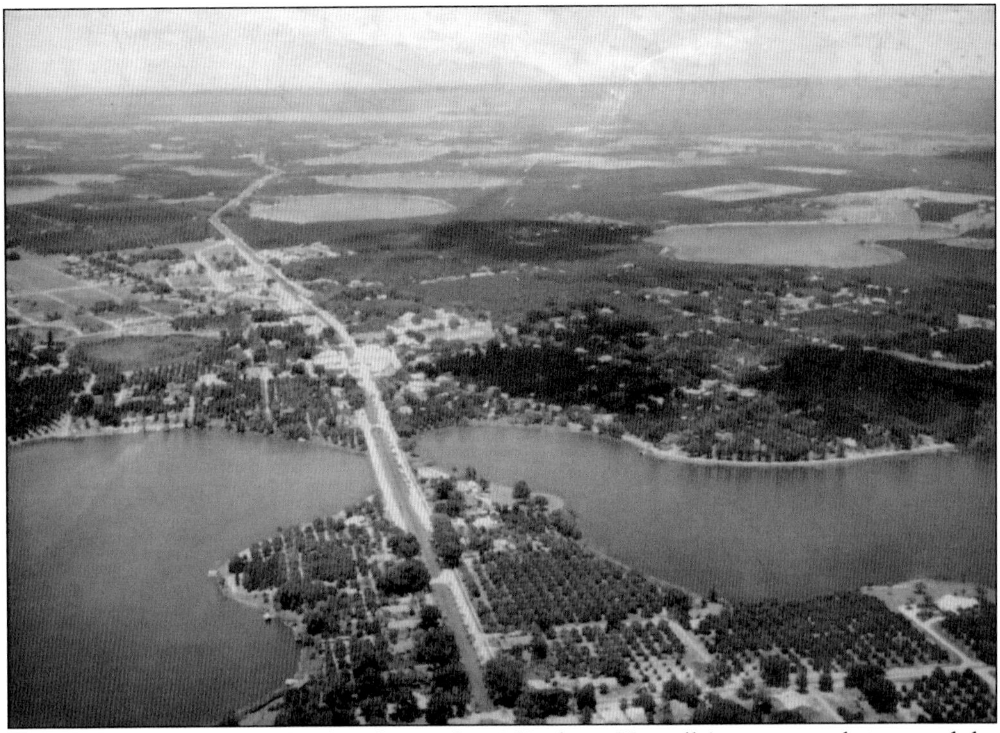

Above, an aerial photograph taken during the 1950s shows Umatilla's commercial citrus and the business growth along the Highway 19 corridor. Residential growth also is evident; most houses were tucked into groves, or groves were planted around them. The map shown below is drawn by Benjamin F. Adams and titled "Map of Part of West Orange County and the Great Lake Region of Florida." The map shows the route of the St. Johns and Eustis railroad line, which ran 28 miles from Astor to Eustis. The map was drawn before 1887, when Lake County was carved from portions of Sumter and Orange counties. (Above RBD, below DS.)

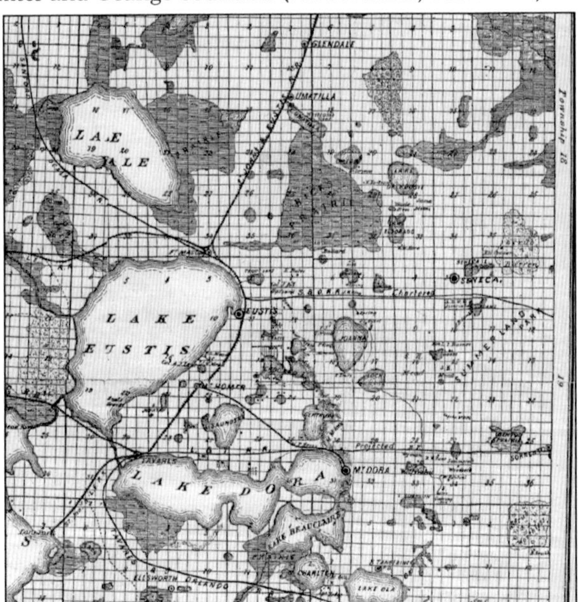

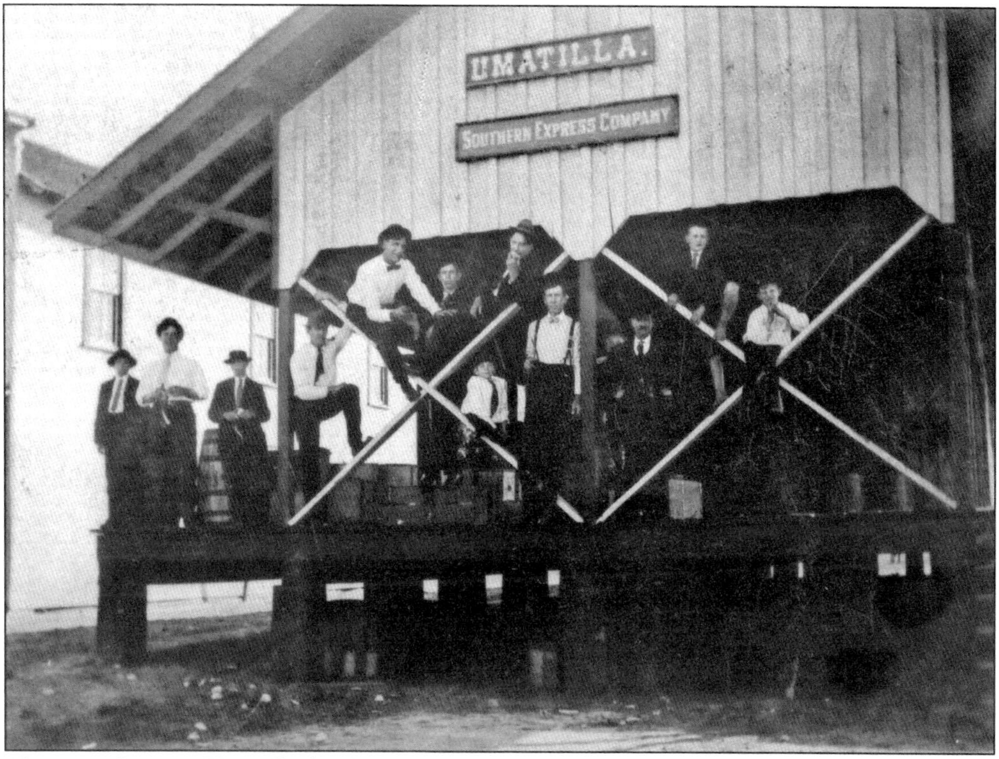

The train depot in Umatilla for the St. Johns and Eustis line is shown in this 1890 photograph. The original depot stood on the east side of the tracks, across the street from the Collins building. Above, men and boys pose on the old depot in 1912 with barrels ready for the train. This line ran from 1881 until 1928, when increasing highway traffic made passenger boats and trains obsolete. The final leg from Astor to Umatilla was abandoned in 1928 when paved roads from Astor to Umatilla, Eustis, Tavares, and Leesburg were completed. (Both photographs EAS.)

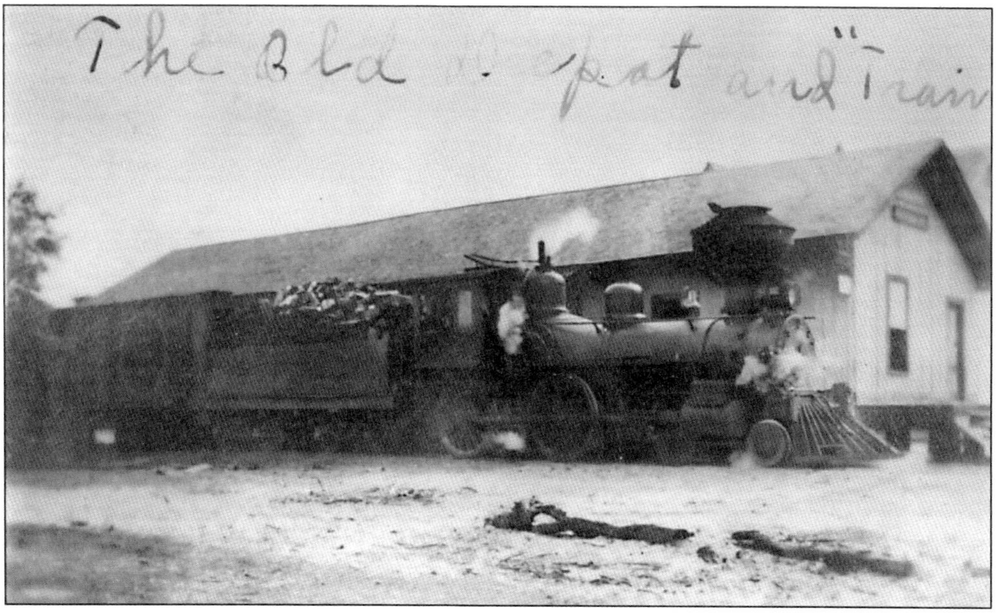

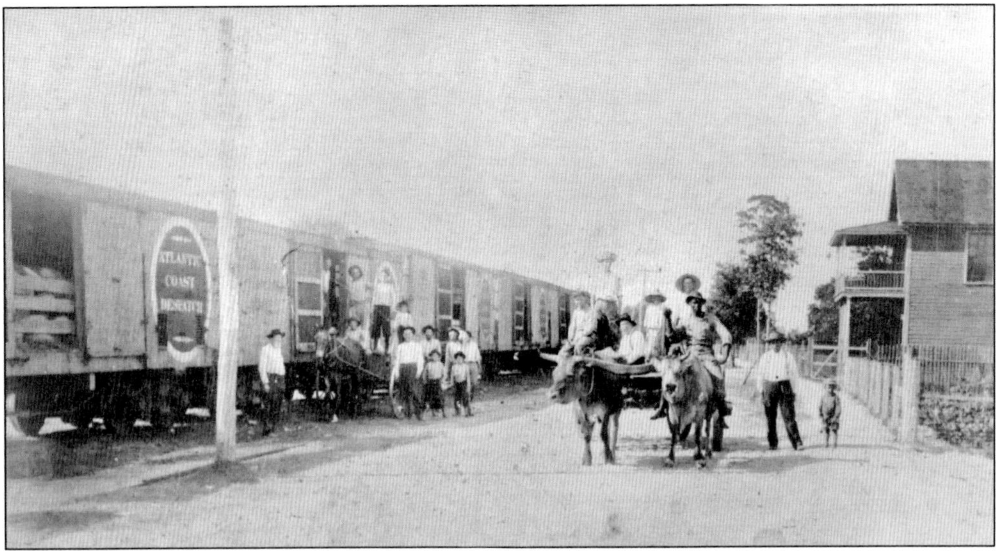

The train waits for melons to be loaded from both a mule cart and an ox cart with produce ready for shipping. The open train car reveals how produce train cars were lined with crates for shipping melons. C. B. Patrick is pictured standing beside the ox cart, with a small boy, Claude Patrick. In 1912, D. McCullough (mayor of Umatilla) recorded that 118,000 boxes of fruit were packed, netting growers $175,000. Pictured below, a row of 15 mule carts and one automobile wait with oranges ready to load the train in Umatilla in 1894. (Both photographs EAS.)

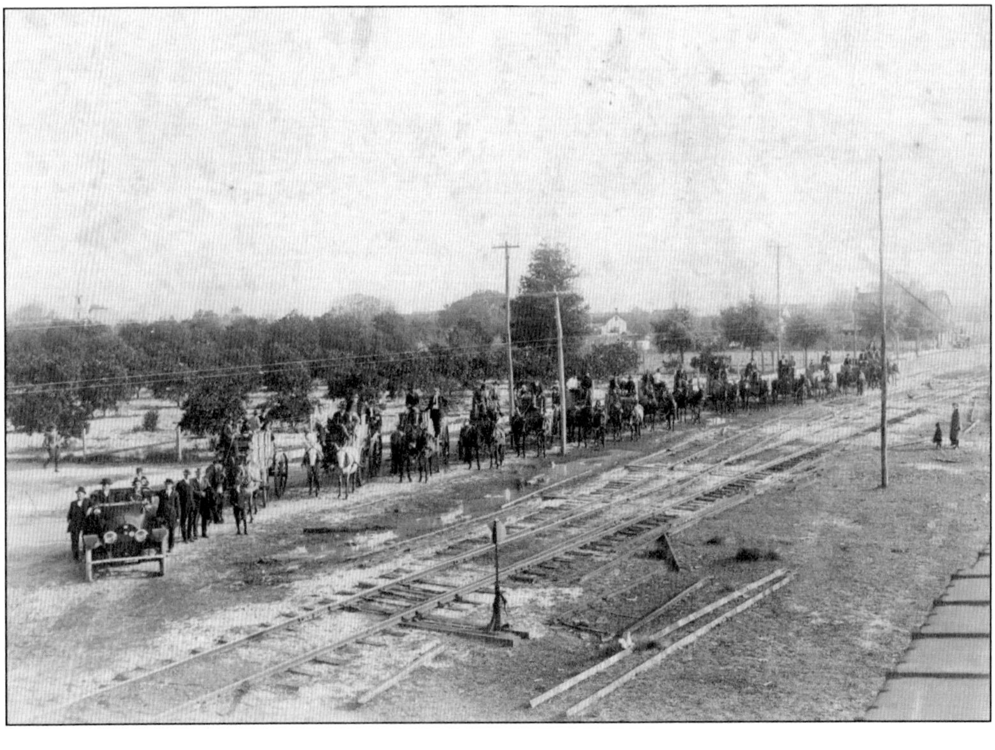

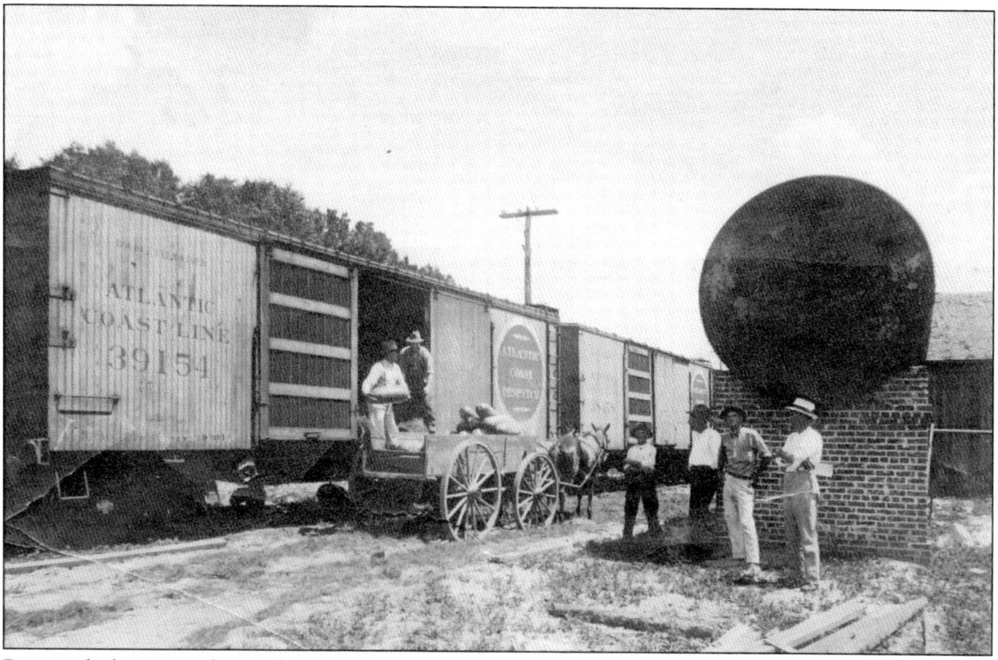

Pictured above in the early 1900s, a train is being loaded with melons. In 1914, Robert Lee Collins sold his watermelon over the water when he entered the Cuban market, shipping by train to Key West and then by boat to Havana. This lucrative market, where melons sold for a dollar each in the early days, closed with the advent of World War I. By mid-century, an average of 500 freight car loads of watermelon were shipped during the growing season and at least as much again went to market in trucks. Seen below, Rep. Hartley Hethcox, a successful melon and cotton grower, poses with a shipment of watermelon being loaded for markets in the north. (Above UHS, below JCG.)

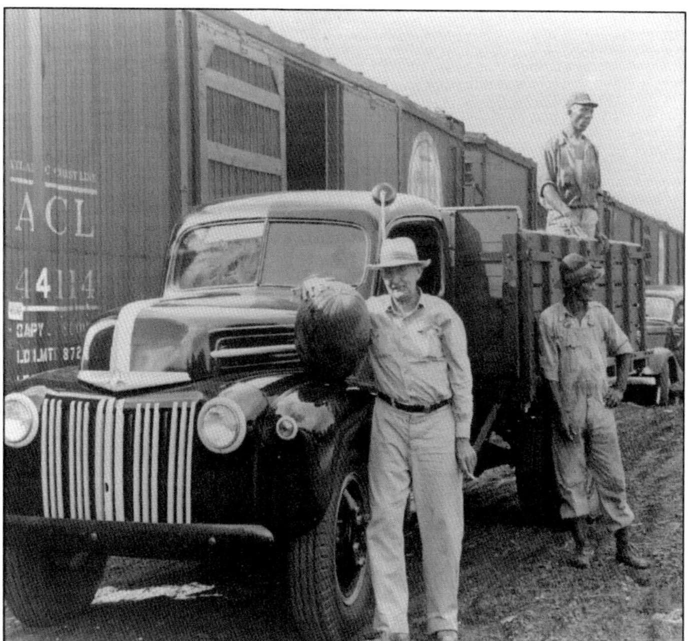

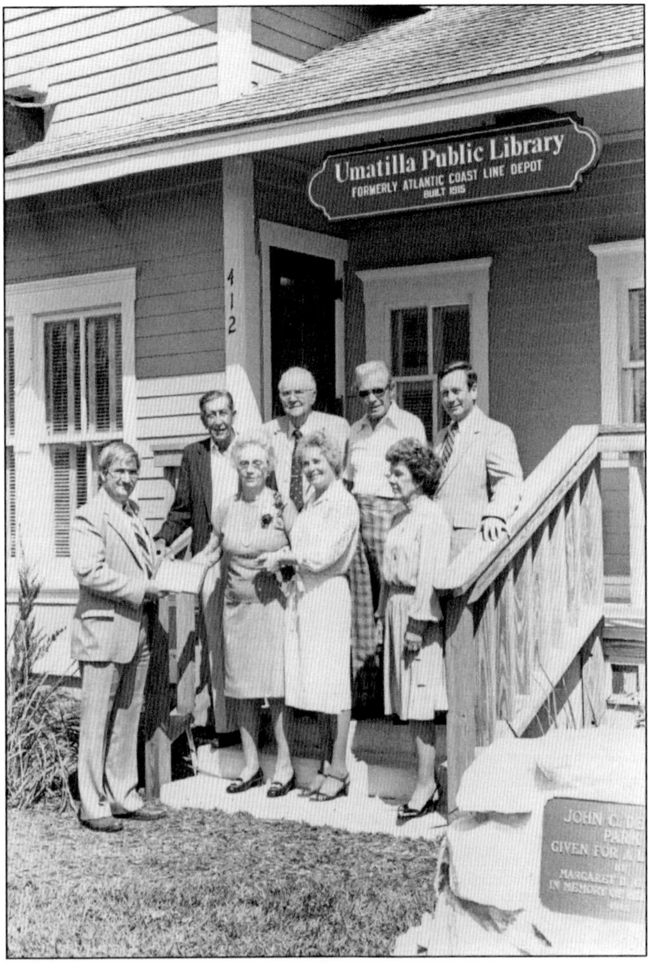

This photograph was taken in 1981, at the dedication of the John C. Deavor Park to be used for the site of the Umatilla public library. Pictured from left to right are the following: (first row) Doug Hasley, Margaret Atkinson, Mary Ellen Babb, Janet French; (second row) Dr. Franklin Hatfield, Lawrence Atkinson, Alton Epps, and Steve Johnson. The 1,600-square-foot Atlantic Coast Line train depot, built in 1915, was donated to the city to use for the library. Land was donated by Margaret Deavor Atkinson, and money was raised for its renovation. Seen below, the depot converted into the library with an eye-catching red caboose and antique mail cart. The railroad theme is carried throughout, making the building quite a conversation piece among the community. (Both photographs BJM.)

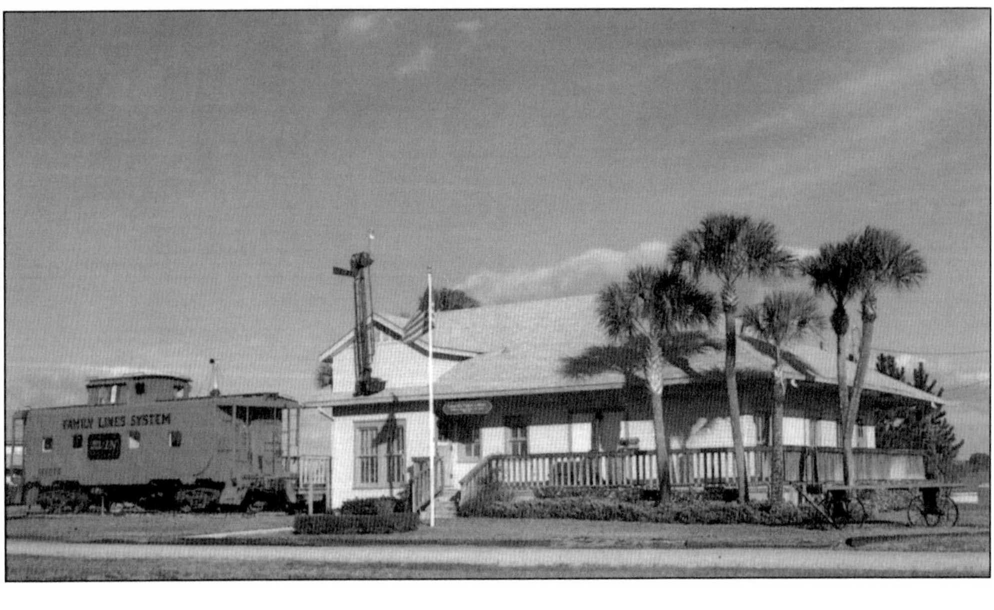

Six

Winter Visitors Find Paradise

When I leave Florida, it will be to go to the only better country—the Florida of the Soul—where we will be young and well and happy forever.

—Dr. Edward Guerrant
evangelist and Umatilla pioneer

Umatilla shares a long history of winter visitors with its neighboring central Florida towns. It was considered an earthly paradise to those returning year after year to spend winter in the sunshine. Umatilla did not claim any spectacular amusements, but offered a home-like atmosphere and the hospitality of friendly neighbors. When visitors came, they were welcomed, and people came to Umatilla because they liked the hunting, fishing, boating, or simply the people.

The winter resort of a great many people, Umatilla was especially favored by families from Kentucky and Tennessee. Much of the early social life was centered at the Kentucky House on Lake Umatilla, operated by Fletcher Smith, who hosted an annual gun shoot at which marksmen from all over the South competed for prizes. Rosedale Hunting Preserve was the home of Mr. and Mrs. Megargee, with 335 acres lying on a chain of 15 large freshwater lakes, 4.5 miles outside of Umatilla. It was considered one of the most romantic spots in Florida. The Umatilla House, owned by the Mitcheners, hosted operas and concerts in downtown Umatilla.

Along with being only a stone's throw from the Ocala National Forest and its bounty, Umatilla offered its visitors beautiful natural vistas, magnificent moss-draped great oaks, the heady fragrance of citrus groves in bloom and temperate winter weather. The town was nearly hidden among the trees, groves, and lakes that set the path of its roads. Many winter visitors contributed to and enjoyed Umatilla's church and social life, and quite a few built homes where they retired and established permanent residency.

These words from the Eustis Lake Region newspaper's first edition, dated October 23, 1884, are still true today, "Umatilla offers a homey town, 'by the side of the road'—each citizen of which is a 'friend to Man.' . . . This town welcomes all newcomers who desire a healthful location with wholesome surroundings. There's hospitality in the air / Of our charming little town, / Umatilla claims no great / Or wonder renown."

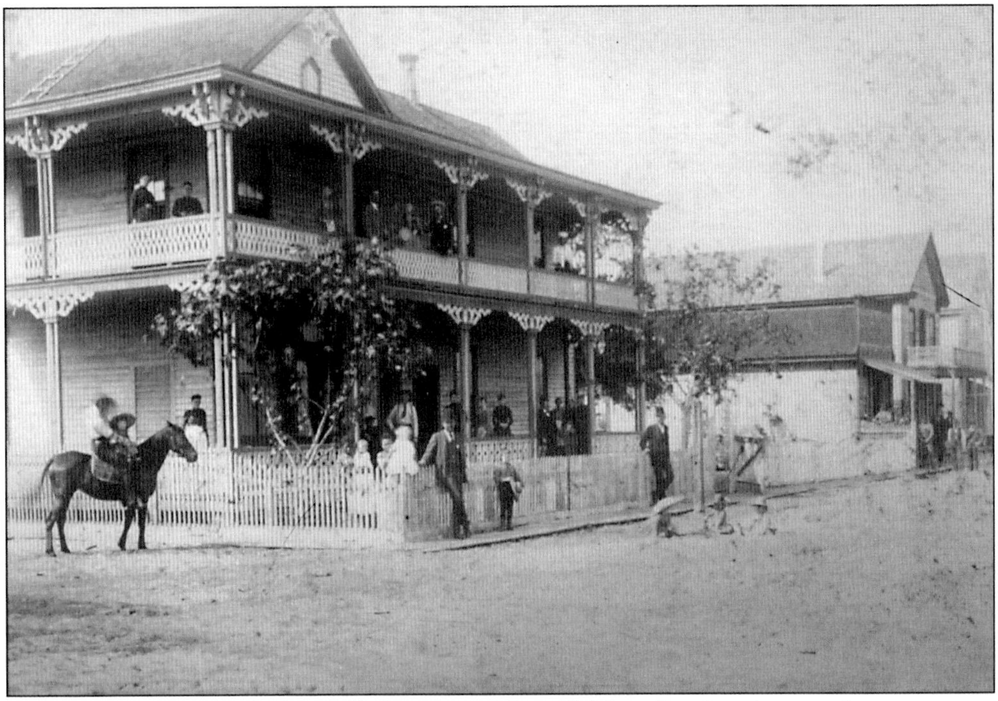

Photographed in 1886, the Umatilla House was Umatilla's lone hotel at the time this picture was taken. The hotel later became known as the Mitchener's Hotel and was an attraction not only to guests from out of town, but also for locals who enjoyed the operas and concerts performed in the hotel. The new St. Johns and Eustis train made travel to Umatilla easier for its winter residents and year-round visitors. Perhaps the turn-of-the-century postcard below romanticizes the experience of train travel through Florida's orange groves, but anyone who has breathed the heady orange blossom will enjoy the romantic notion of the picture postcard. (Above BJM, below DS.)

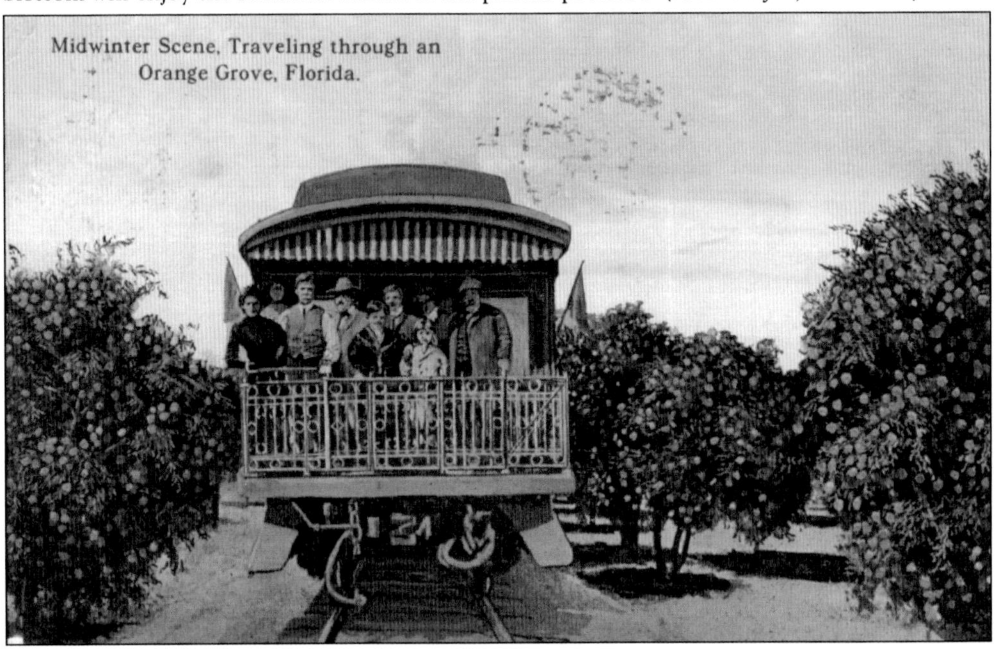

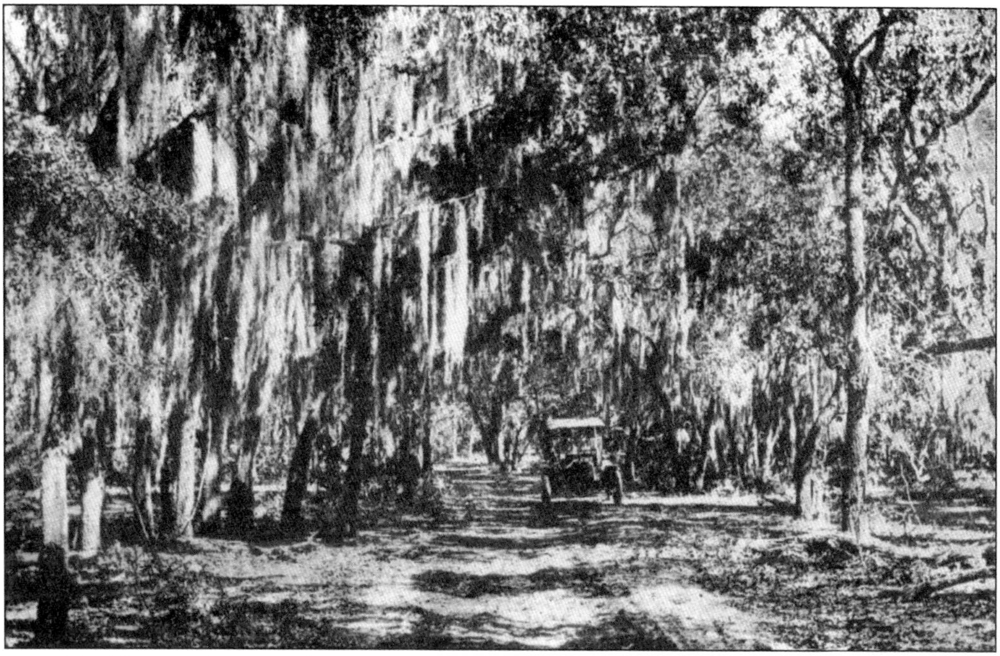

Rosedale Hunting Preserve, known as one of the most romantic spots in Florida, was tucked into the landscape 4.5 miles outside of Umatilla. The preserve included 335 acres, skirted Lake Yale, and was on a chain of 15 large freshwater lakes. Rosedale abounded with numerous small game (including quail, duck, wild hogs, and turkeys), and the lakes afforded unlimited fishing, boating, and bathing for its visitors and winter residents. Also on the property were 12 acres of groves bearing orange, satsuma, and grapefruit. Pictured below, Rosedale was the home of its owners, Mr. and Mrs. C. G. Megargee (formerly of Philadelphia), beginning in 1886. (Both photographs EAS.)

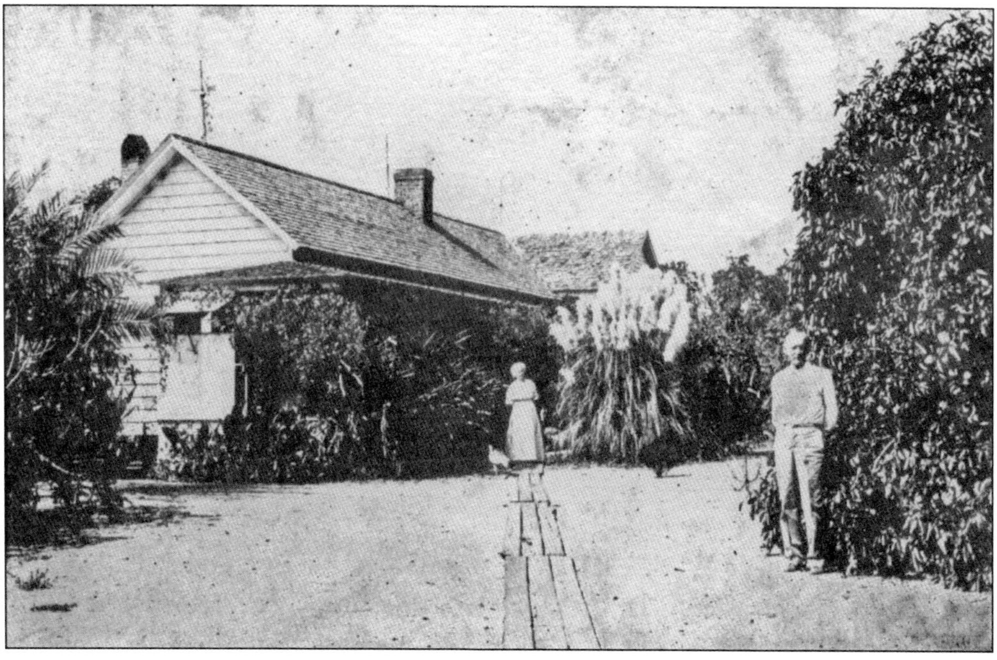

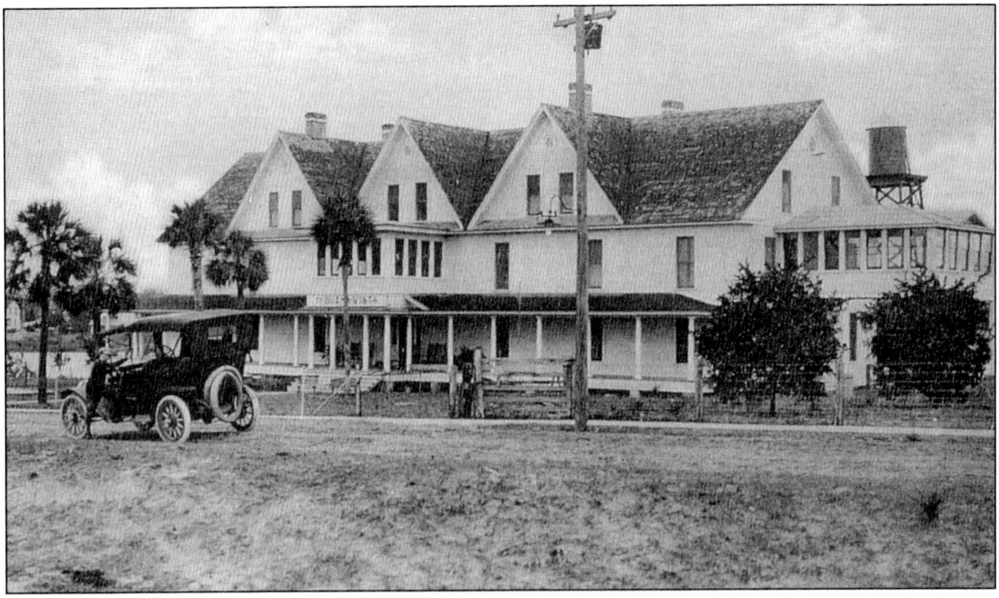

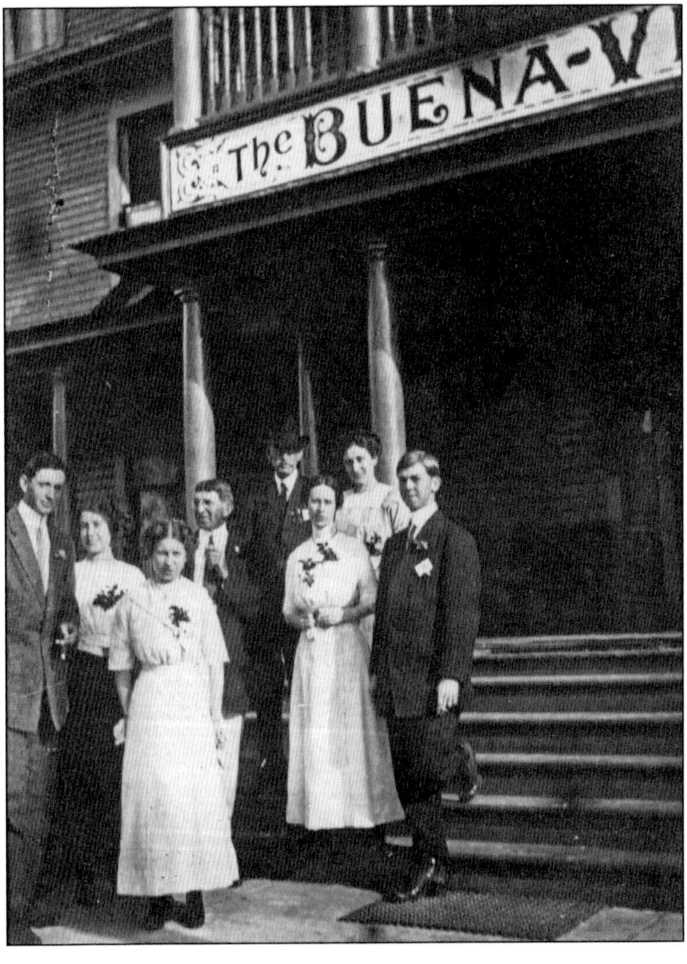

The oft-photographed Kentucky House, which later became the renowned Buena Vista Hotel, was operated by F. C. Smith and family. Smith hosted an annual gun shoot at which marksmen from all over the south competed for prizes, and he was also the town barber. A 1920s hotel brochure listed room rates between $3.00 and $7.50 a day. Meals were 50¢ each—breakfast, lunch, or dinner. Umatilla became the resort home for many winter visitors following the arrival of the railroad in 1880. Pictured at left in 1915, a group of young people, including Bena Collins (second from left) and Harry Collins (at far right) pose in front of the Buena Vista dressed for a social gathering. (Above CB, left BJM.)

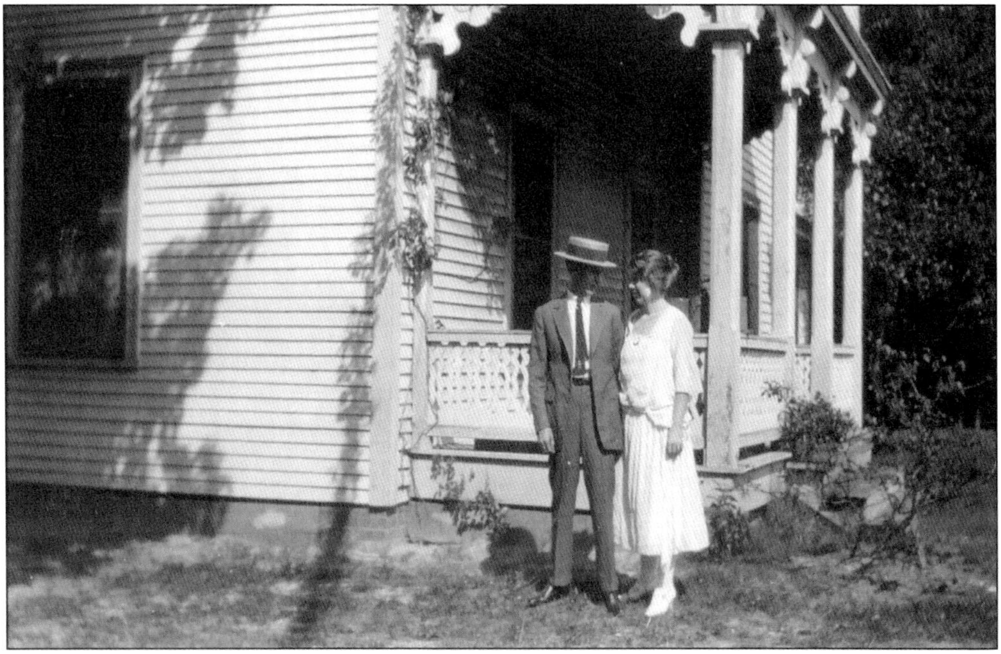

Two of Umatilla's smaller inns, the Maple Shade and Whitley Inn, were favorites for their traditional family-style noon dinners. Seen here in the 1920s are Lucille and Alex Morrell, owners of the Maple Shade Inn, which was located at the corner of Central Avenue and Bulldog Lane. The Maple Shade was famous for its Sunday dinners, especially the homemade pecan pie. An unidentified group of people is pictured below at the grand opening of the Whitley Inn, which was located on the corner of Central Avenue and Guerrant Street. The Whitley Inn preceded the Umatilla Hotel, which continued the tradition of serving fine family dinners. (Both photographs JCG.)

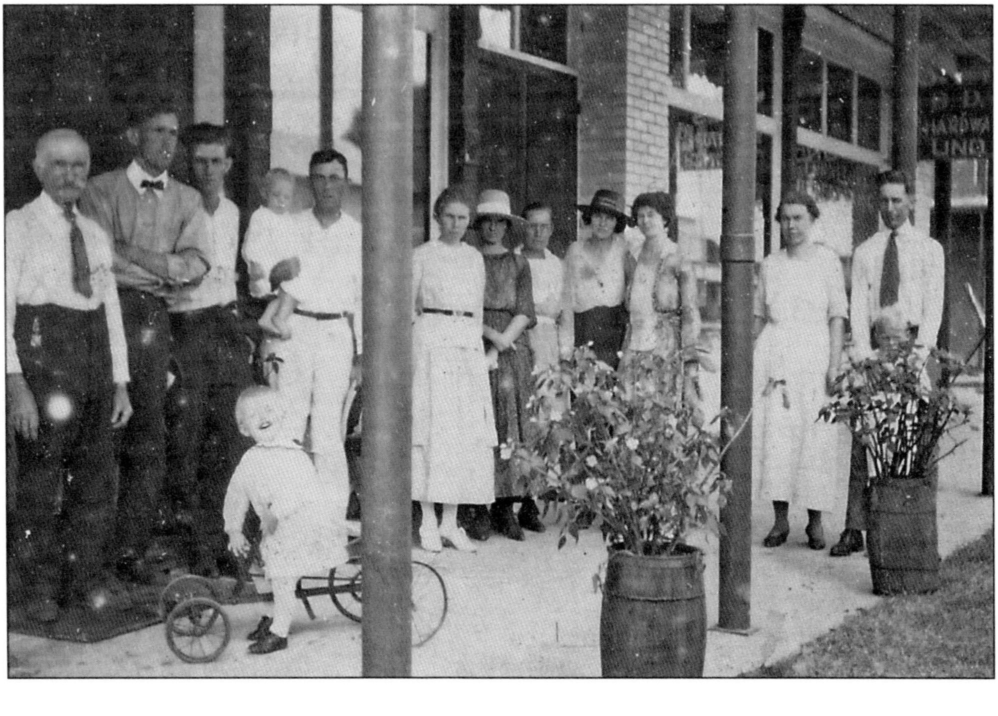

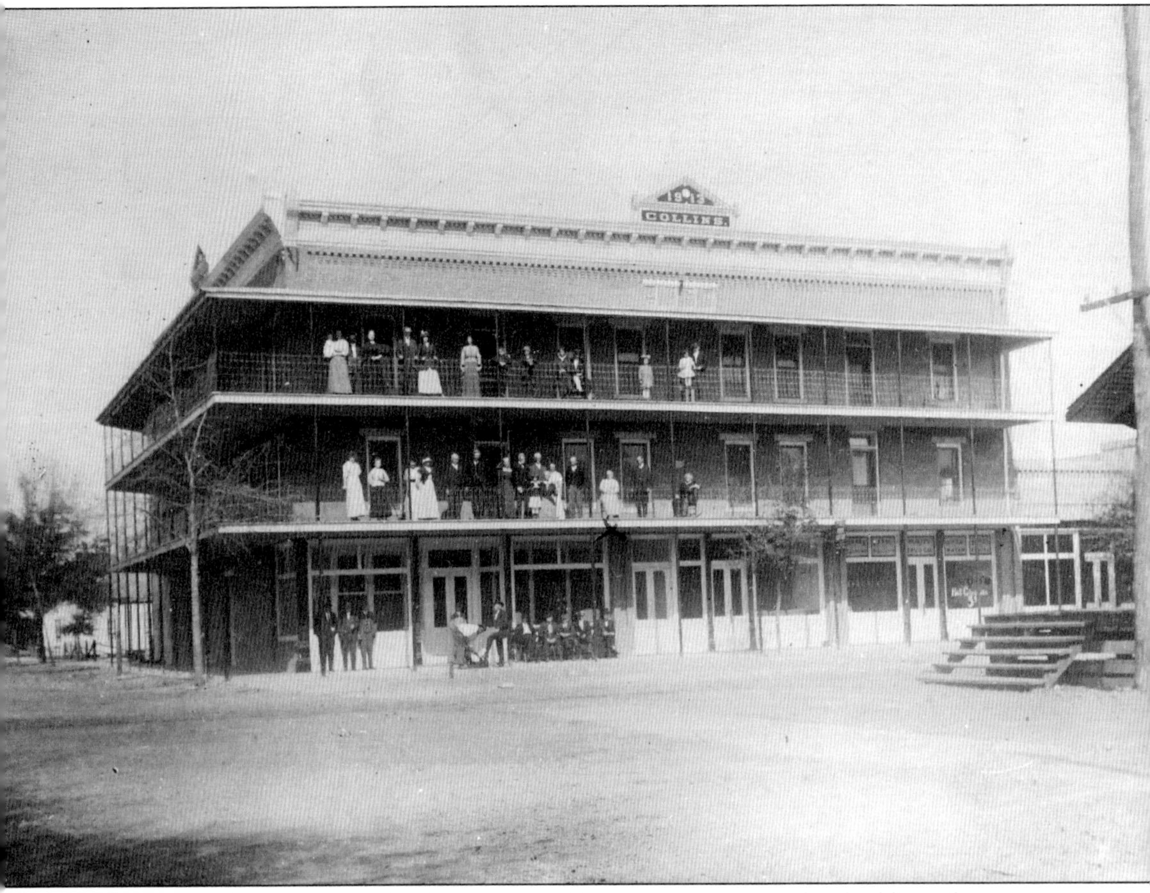

Umatilla's tallest structure, the three-story Collins Building, was the first building of consequence in Umatilla. The property on which it was built stood vacant for more than 10 years following the Alliance fire in 1899, which destroyed the entire business section on the west side of downtown. Robert Lee Collins was responsible for much of Umatilla's early redevelopment that signaled an end to the hard times following the disastrous 1895 freeze and 1899 fire. Hotel guests pose on the balcony of the second and third floors of the Colonial Hotel. The hotel opened in 1913 directly across the street from the first site of the train depot in downtown Umatilla. The Collins Building storefront included the Purity Drug Company, which advertised 5¢ hot chocolate, candy, stationery, cigars, and soda water. (RBD.)

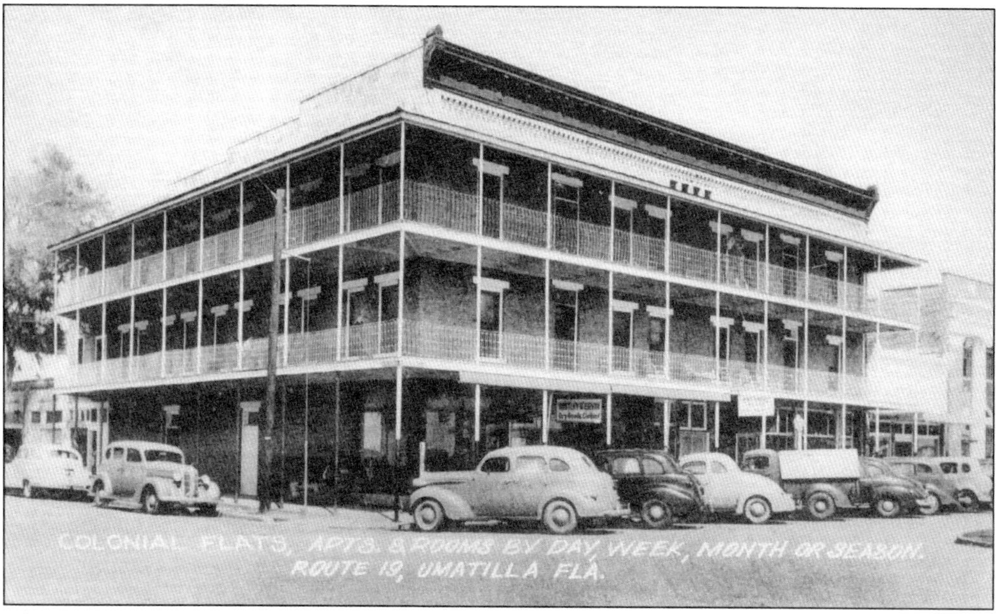

The transformation of the exterior of the Collins Building has always been a reflection of the decade in which the changes were made. Following the stock market crash of 1929 and the Great Depression of the 1930s, the Colonial Hotel added apartments in the 1940s. Guests could rent by the day, week, or season. Pictured below, another transformation reflects the style of the 1950s, when the awnings and siding were pink and turquoise—a trendy combination of the time. Umatilla and most of Florida enjoyed a number of decades of successful agricultural pursuits, and that prominence brought respect throughout the state of Florida. Umatilla citizens became influential in state politics and were a dominant part of Florida's booming citrus industry in the history-making years. (Both photographs CB.)

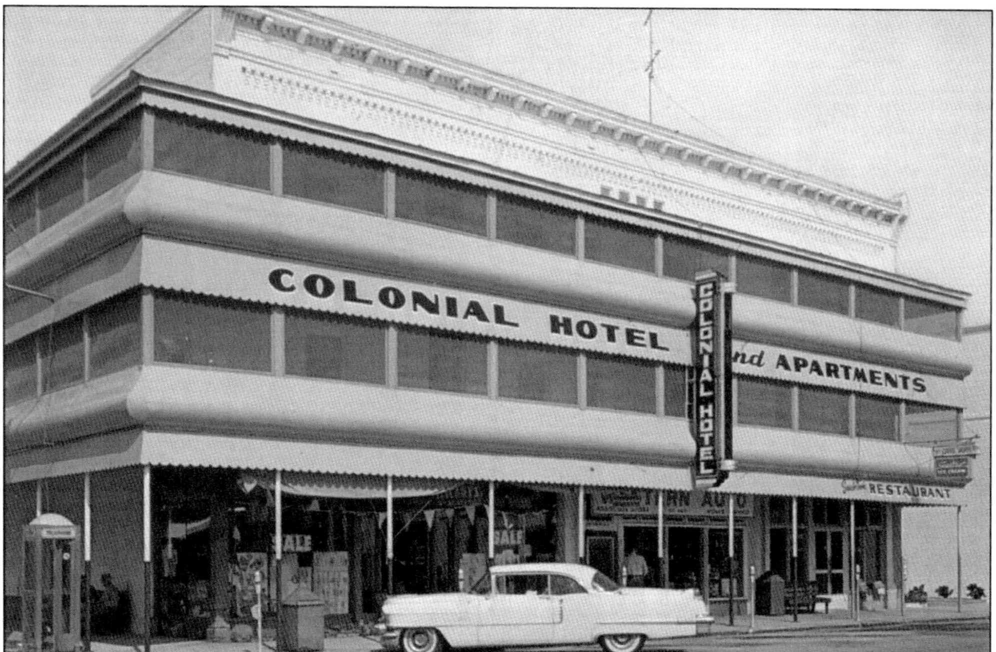

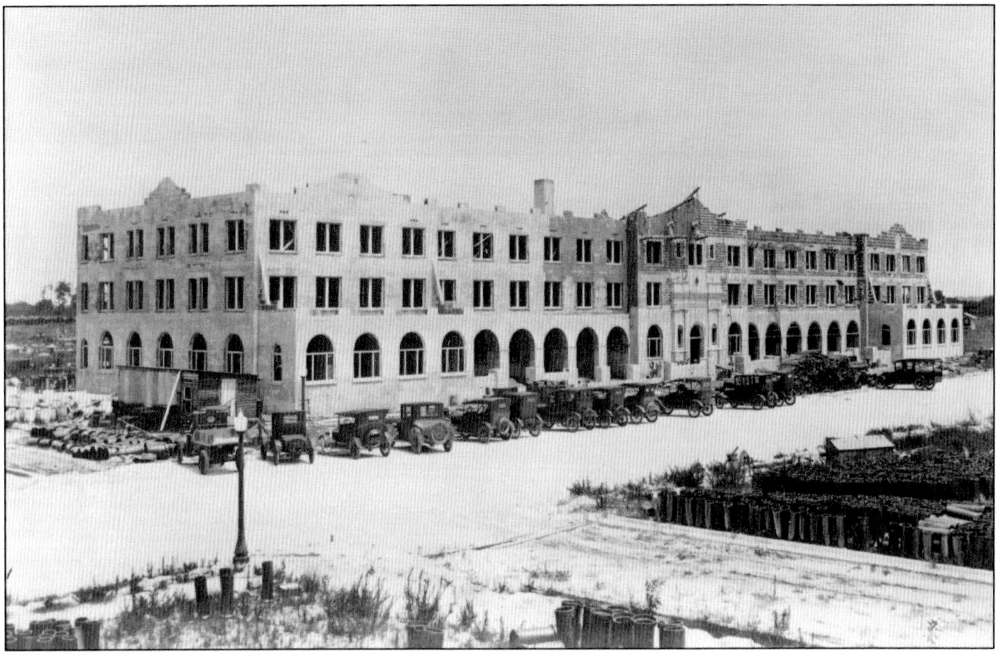

Umatilla became part of the Florida land boom of the 1920s when W. Hugh Rowe began an ambitious attempt to make the little town of Umatilla a resort town. Rowe bought 80 acres and built a theater, a business block, 10 or 12 houses, a garage, and a 100-room resort. This photograph of the Rowebuilt Hotel (the largest in Umatilla) was taken in 1925, while under construction. Rowe had also donated land for the Baptist winter assembly. When Florida's boom bubble burst after the stock market crash, the Rowebuilt was closed along with many boom-time dreams. The photograph below shows an aerial view of the hotel and its surroundings. (Both photographs BJM.)

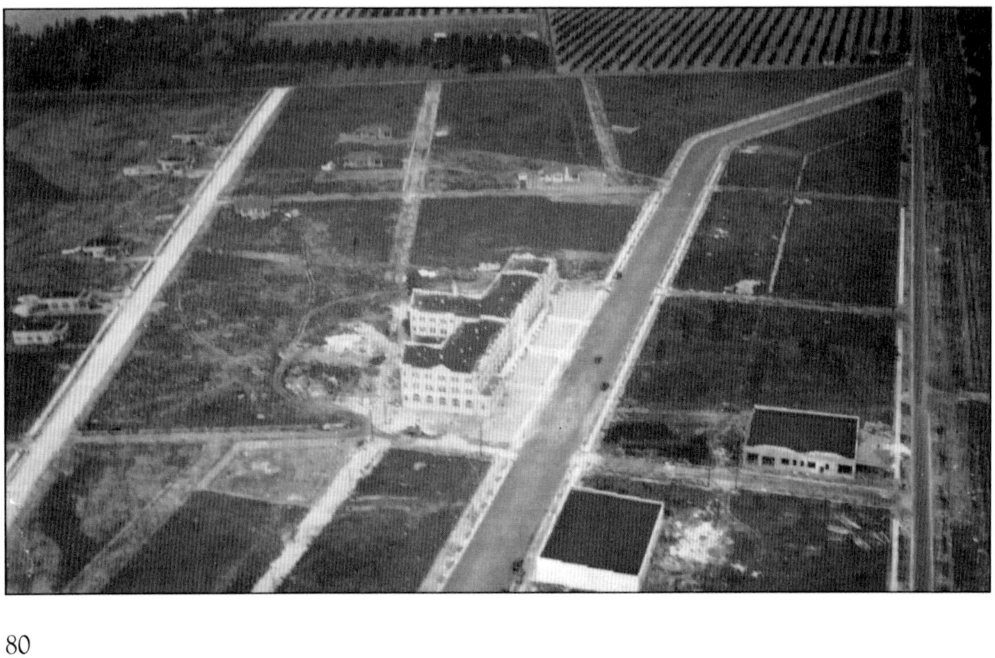

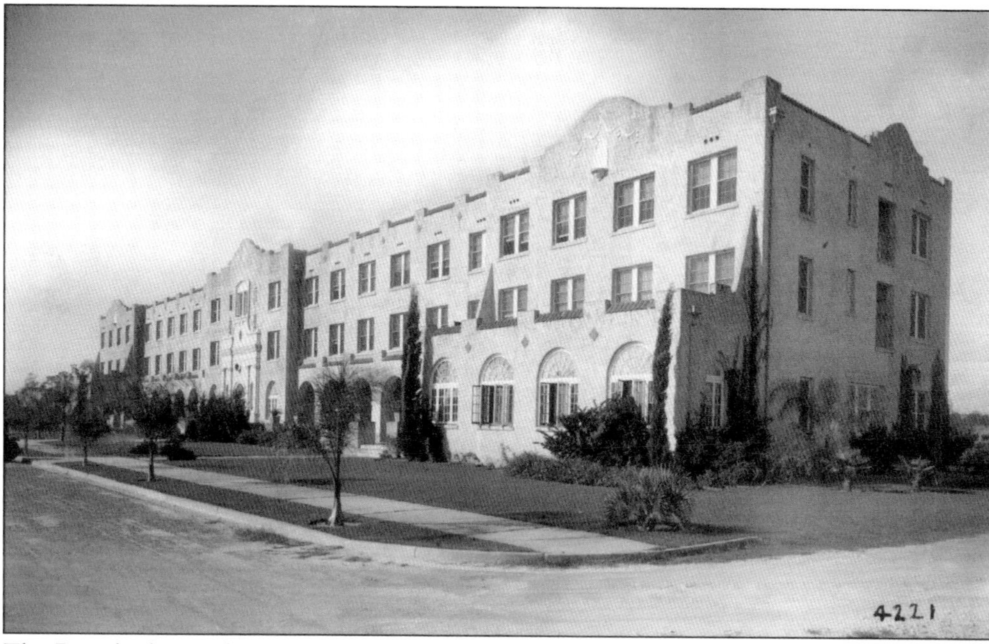

The Rowebuilt Hotel, seen completed, was open for only 15 days before it closed due to the economic aftermath of the stock market crash of 1929. Its most famous visitor was evangelist Billy Sunday, who preached at the Baptist assembly. Photographed after the hotel became the Harry-Anna Crippled Children's Home, the lobby gives evidence to the grandeur planned for the hotel. When ownership of the hotel passed to the mortgagor, Harry R. P. Miller of Eustis, he and his wife, Anna, donated it to the Florida Elks for the establishment of a children's hospital. Miller and Dave Scholtz (president of the Florida Elks who later became governor of Florida) stumped the state for contributions to support the conversion of the hotel into a hospital for crippled children. (CB.)

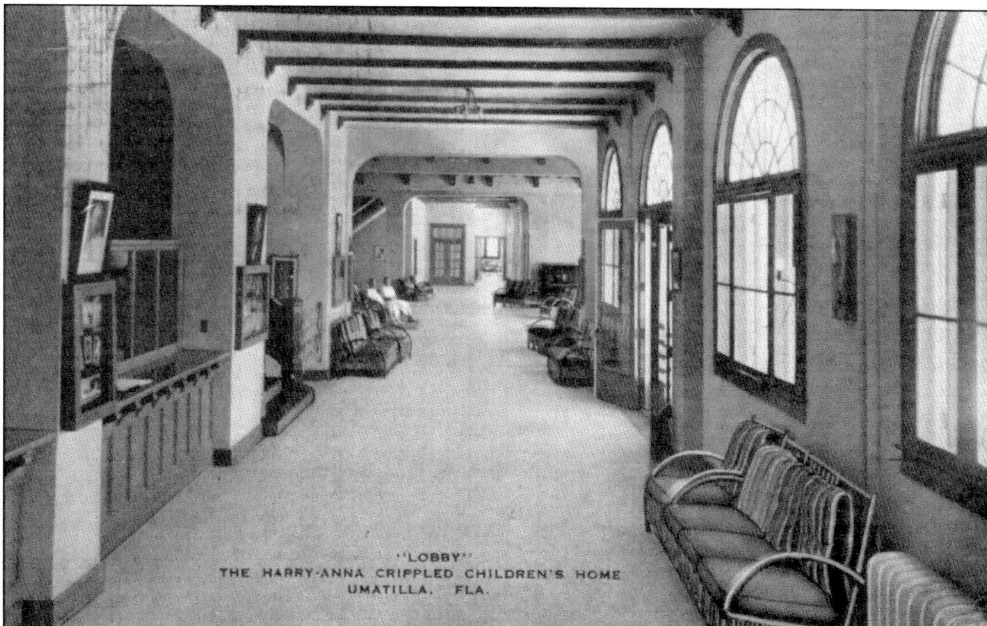

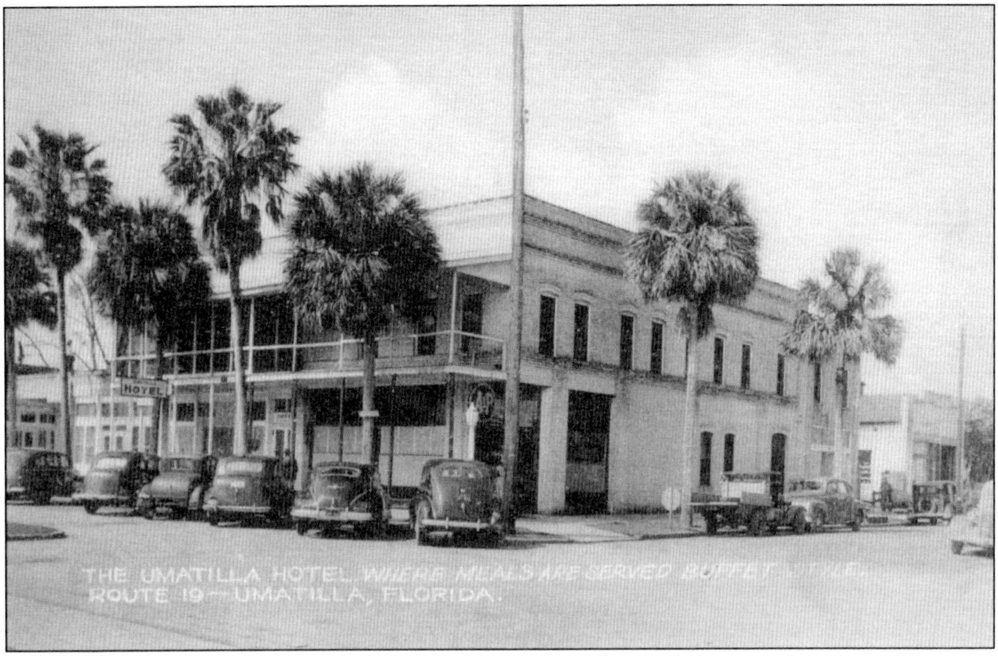

The Umatilla Hotel—"where meals are served buffet style"—was owned and operated by Jesse Lee Bryan Ramsey from 1956 until 1980. The upstairs apartments housed winter residents so happy with their accommodations that some paid a full year's rent to ensure they had a room at the hotel for the winter. Mrs. Ramsey's home-style cooking brought Umatilla and neighboring towns together for Sunday dinner after church. (CB.)

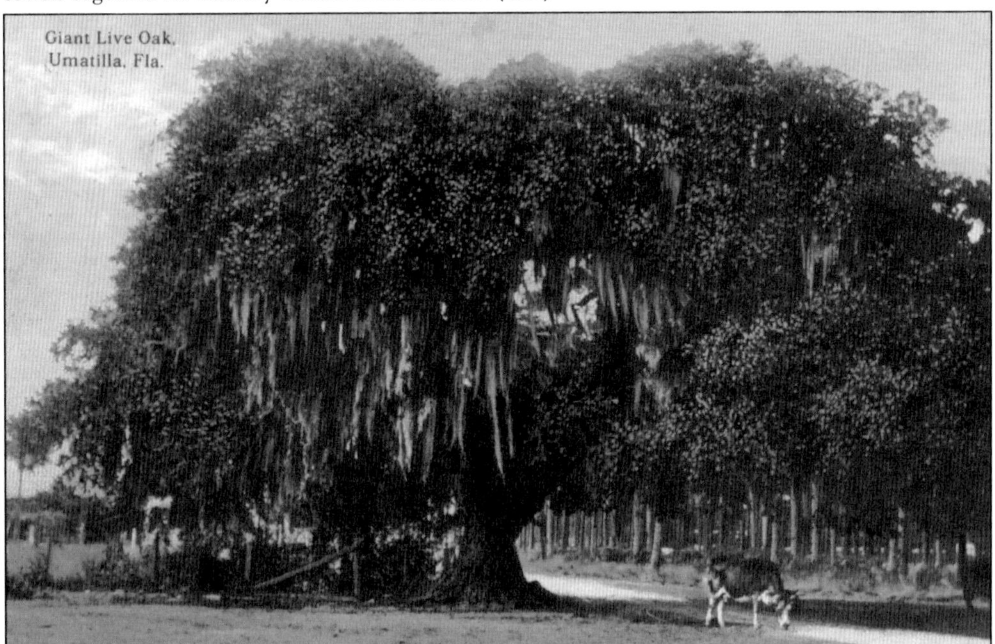

Umatilla boasted this natural landmark, an ancient moss-draped oak tree, seen here as it was in 1919. The old tree grew on the north end of Central Avenue and was a popular subject for picture postcards. The tree is most often remembered as Umatilla's "Lovers Oak." (UHS.)

Seven

A Town Grows in the Wilderness

In 1881, Benjamin Cunningham Yancey and his wife, Lucy Hall, moved to Umatilla. Yancey and Nathan Trowell agreed subdividing lots on the east and west sides of the railroad would encourage settling. Yancey bought property from Nathan Trowell and David McCredie, and it was subdivided along with property owned by Mitchener to create Umatilla's boundaries.

By 1886, Umatilla had a population of 200 people and the business section of town included seven stores, a gristmill, three churches, and a schoolhouse. Citrus, farming, lumber, and turpentine were standard business industries. In 1887, Lake County was carved from sections of Orange and Sumter Counties and Umatilla was a thriving, close-knit community.

The Big Freeze of 1894–1895 brought an abrupt end to growth. Disaster visited Umatilla again when fire broke out in the Alliance store shortly after midnight on July 2, 1899. The flames spread unchecked, and the entire business section on the west side was destroyed. Time seemed to stand still, and it was nearly 15 years before another building was constructed. Groves were replanted, and sawmills, logging and turpentine facilities continued operating in the expansive virgin timber forests nearby.

Umatilla slowly began recovery and was incorporated on November 8, 1904, with the city slogan "Best of All." It promoted itself as a friendly city, good for people's health. The first contracts for hard roads were drawn up in 1915, and the year 1926 brought the first bridge across the St. Johns River, as well as the paving of the road between Ocala and Astor. By 1926, Umatilla had a bank, ice plant, and electric generation plant.

Following the crash of 1929, citrus, cattle, farming, and lumber sustained Umatilla until World War II. During World War II, a prisoner of war camp was built in nearby Leesburg on the site of present-day Lake-Sumter Community College, and the Ocala National Forest contained a bombing site for training soldiers.

Umatilla became the heart of Florida's citrus industry and home of Golden Gem Growers, one of the largest citrus juice concentrate plants in the nation, until the devastating "Hundred Year" freezes of 1983 and 1985 changed forever the economic and natural landscape of Umatilla.

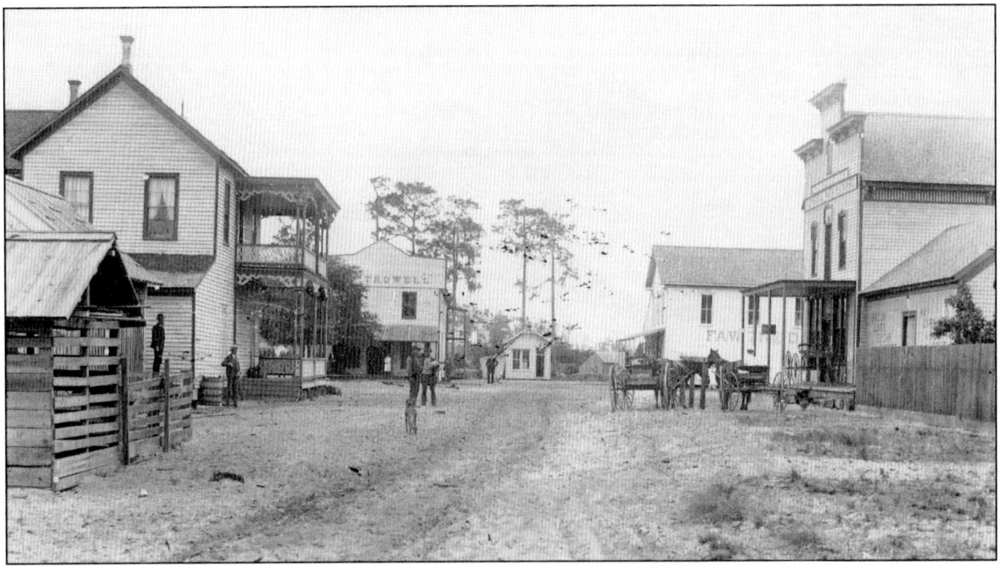

Downtown Umatilla, photographed in the 1880s, is now a little town thriving in the wilderness and developing a personality. Pictured above from left to right are the livery, Mitchener Hotel, Trowell's store, the offices of Dr. Hannah and Dr. Owens, Faw and Devault, and W. T. Whitley and Company. Pictured below, Theodore Augustus Smith's building housed his mercantile, including confectionary, hardware, building supply, and grocery stores. Upstairs was the meeting hall for the Woodmen of the World, the largest fraternal benefit society with open membership in the United States. After the fire of 1899, Smith kept his store open until the mail came in, and Mr. Fink, the postmaster, would take his lantern to the store and stay until the train came. (Both photographs MG.)

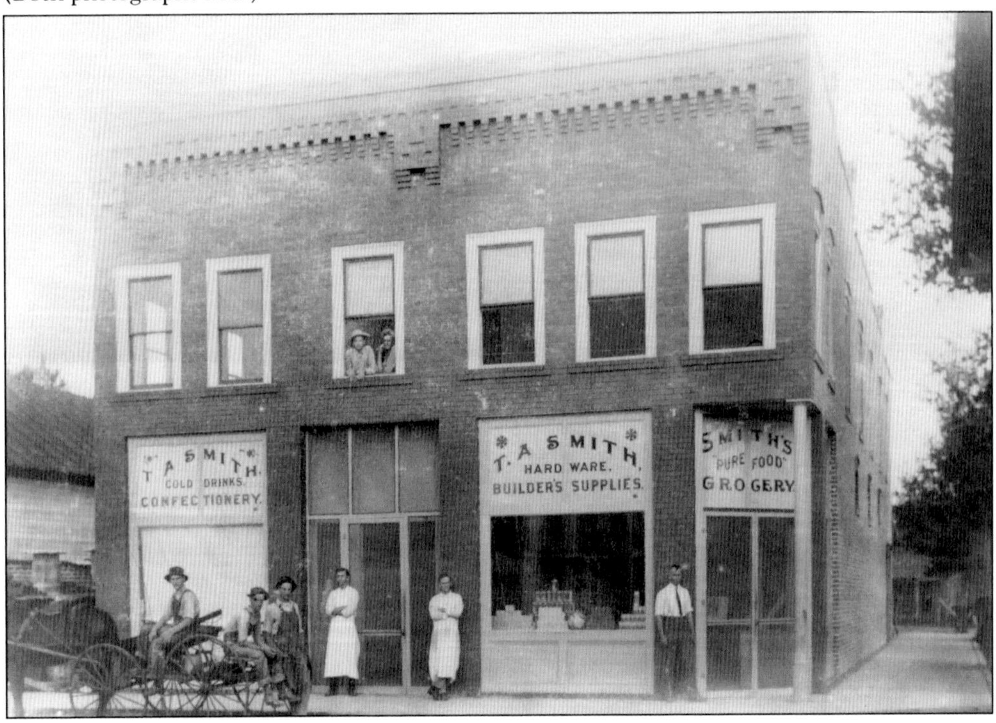

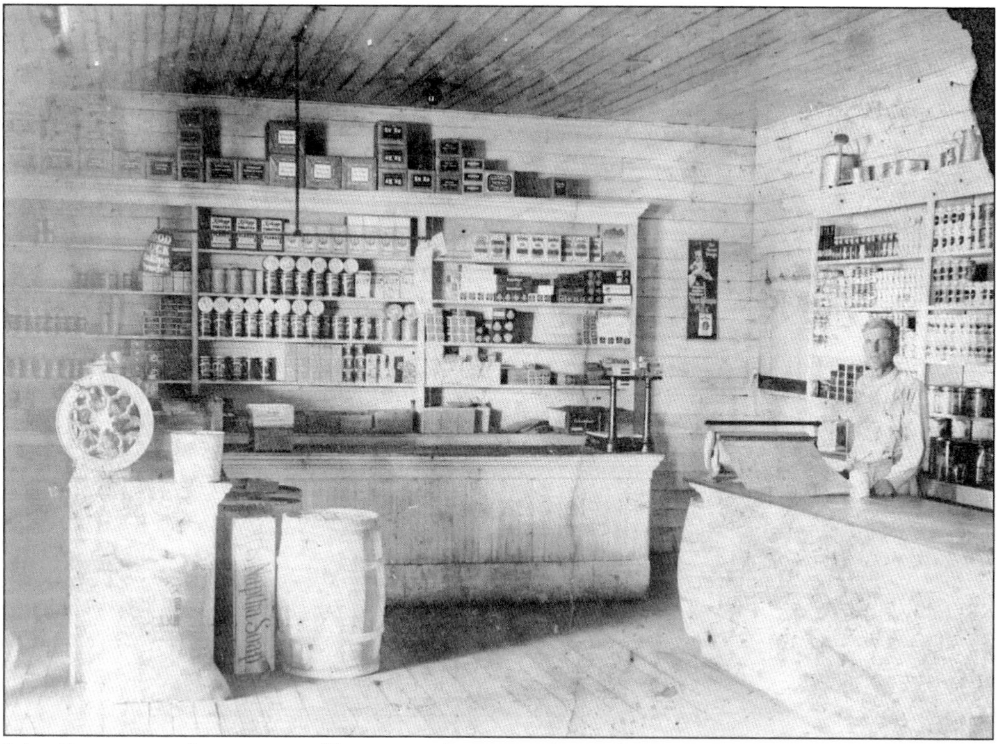

John Epps mans the counter of his general store in the early 1900s. The display of Fels-Naptha was a brand of bar laundry soap used for pretreating stains on clothing and as a home remedy for exposure to poison ivy and other skin irritants. Seen below, the Wayside filling and service station, offering refreshment and fuel, was a welcome sight to travelers coming through central Florida in the 1920s. Crown gasoline and Polarine motor oil—trademarks of Standard Oil—were the fuels of the period. The Wayside was located on the shores of Lake Tutuola. (Above BJM, below DS.)

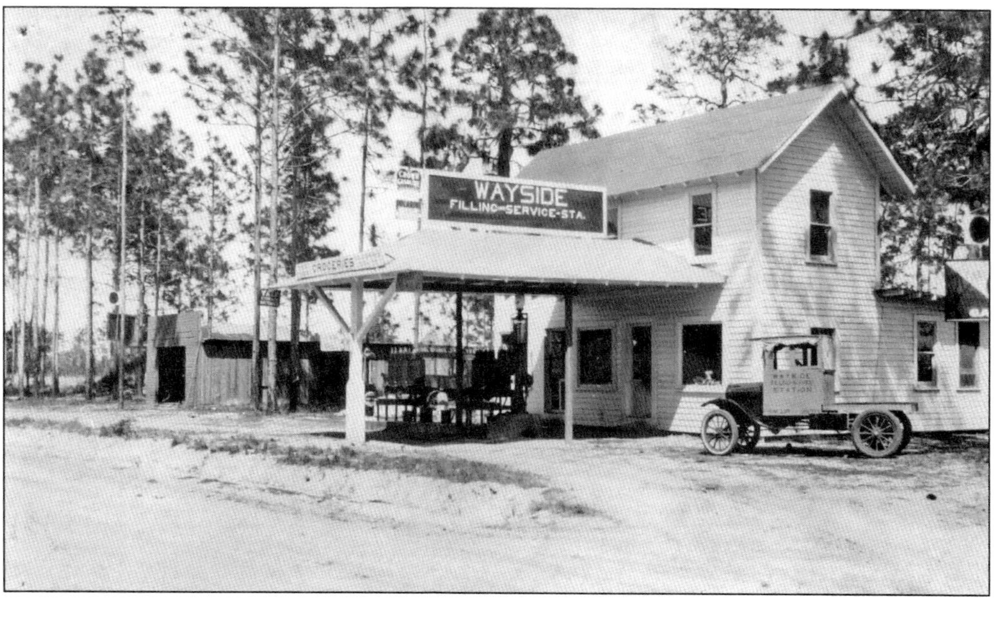

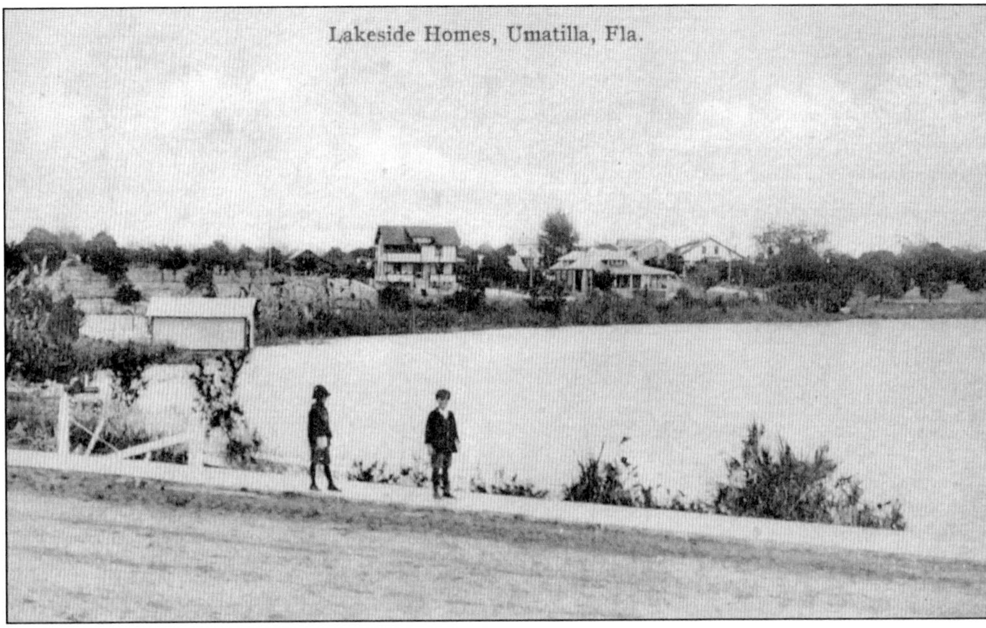

Beautiful homes were built throughout Umatilla. Seen above in the late 1800s are homes along the shore of Lake Umatilla, with surrounding seedling orange groves. The Richmond Home on Trowell Avenue is pictured below in 1913. The sandy road out front had some pine needles for traction, but the deep ruts show the difficulty faced by cars traveling along roads more suited for horses and carriages. Umatilla began improving its roadways and by 1940 boasted miles of paved roads. (Above CB, below EAS.)

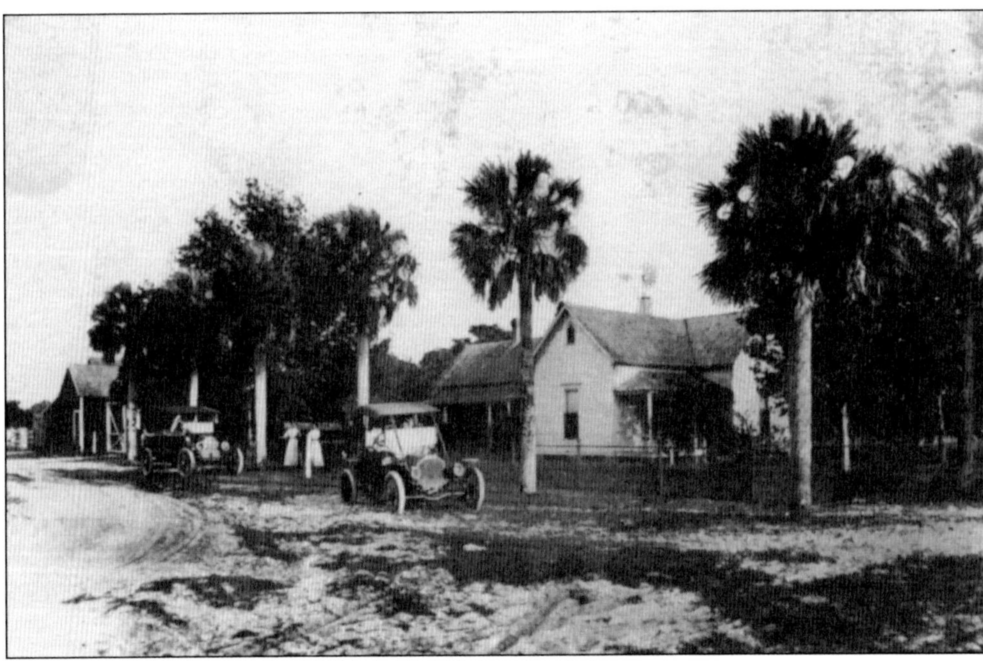

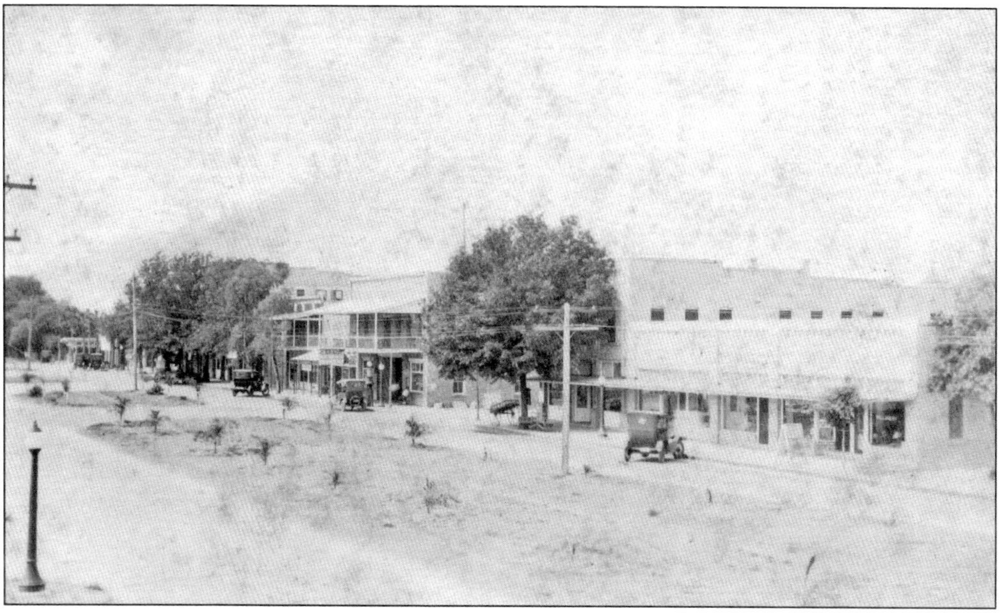

The photograph above of downtown Umatilla facing south was taken between 1915 and 1920. New palm trees were planted along the railroad tracks. Shown on the next block is the post office with the mail cart out front, and a filling station. Upstairs was the meeting hall for Umatilla Mason Lodge No. 65, F. and A. M., dating back to 1873 when the lodge met near Fort Mason and was called the Fort Mason Lodge. This building replaced the original meeting hall that was consumed by the 1899 west side fire, in which all records were lost. Tibbals Drugs, Quality Grocery, the Millinery Shoppe, and the Whitley Inn are visible also. The photograph below, taken nearly 40 years later, shows the palm trees have matured along the railroad tracks. The Tennessee Apartments have replaced the Whitley Inn, Umatilla State Bank has replaced the filling station, and new businesses reflect Umatilla's good fortune and success. (Above, CB, below BJM.)

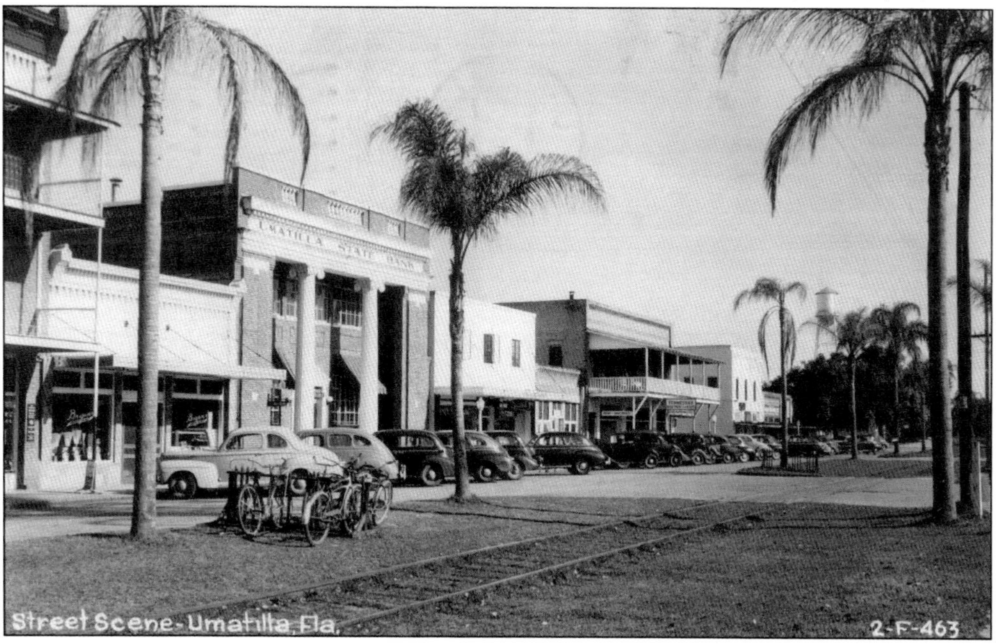

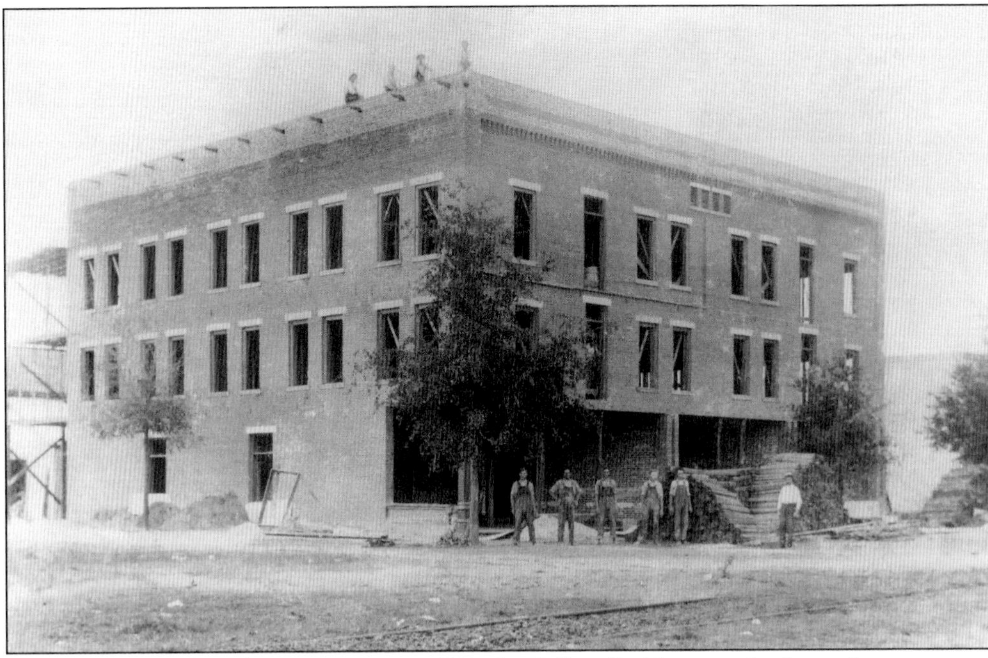

Photographed while under construction in 1912, the Collins Building was the first to be constructed downtown in more than 15 years. The economically devastating big freeze of 1895, followed a few short years later by the Alliance fire in 1899, left most of business section on the west side of downtown vacant. Umatilla was entering a period of prosperity and growth as the citrus industry matured and opportunity abounded. By 1920, Umatilla began providing water and lighting services for itself. A diesel generating plant was built and water and sewer systems were constructed. The generating plant was later sold to the Florida Public Service Company, now known as Florida Power and Light. By 1929, Umatilla was listed as having property values of $3 million. (Above MG, below CB.)

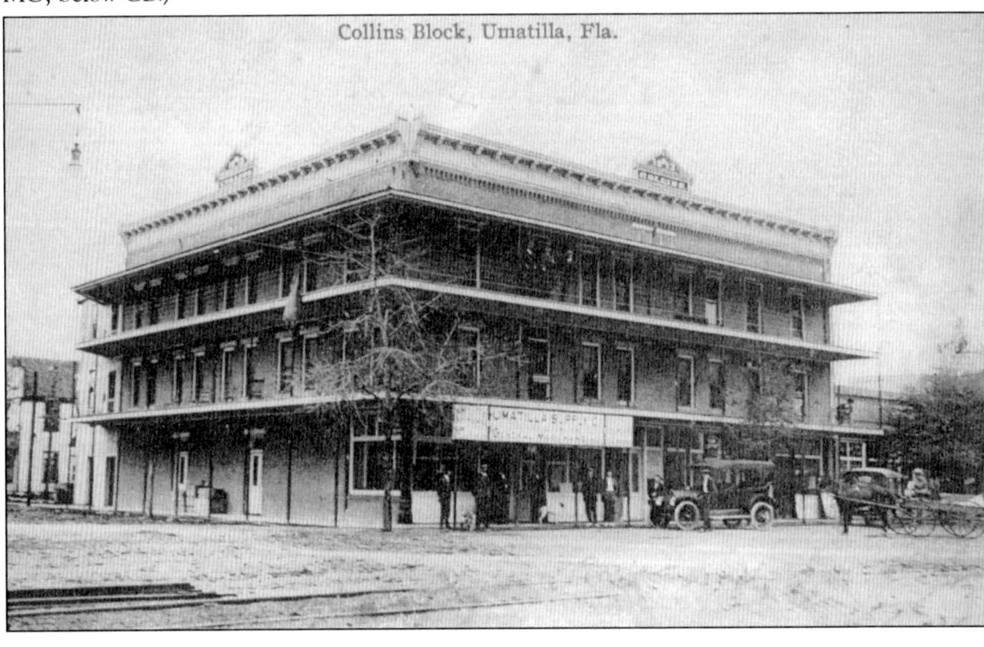

Guests of the Colonial Hotel pause to be photographed in 1916, while their suitcase sits on the running board of the car. The hotel occupied the second and third floors of the Collins Building. Seen below, Robert Lee Collins (who owned the Collins building) and his son Harry Lee do a little bench warming out front in 1920. From his humble start, Collins was instrumental in the development of Umatilla into a prominent citrus community. His service to the community extended beyond his groves and business interests. Collins was an investor and director in the Bank of Umatilla, and director of both the Lake County Growers Association and the Lake County Citrus Exchange. (Right CB, below BJM.)

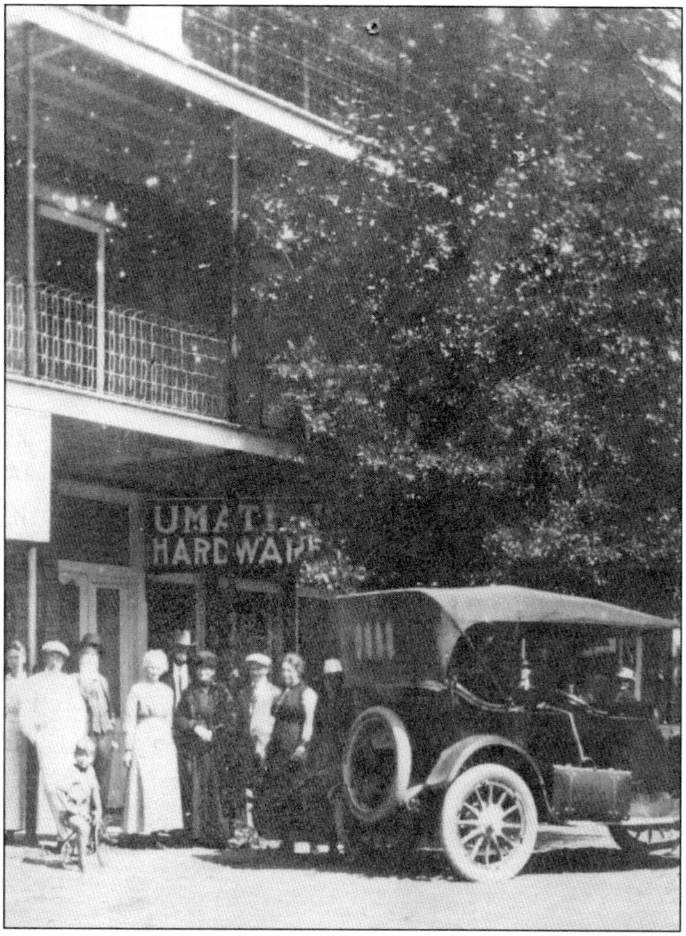

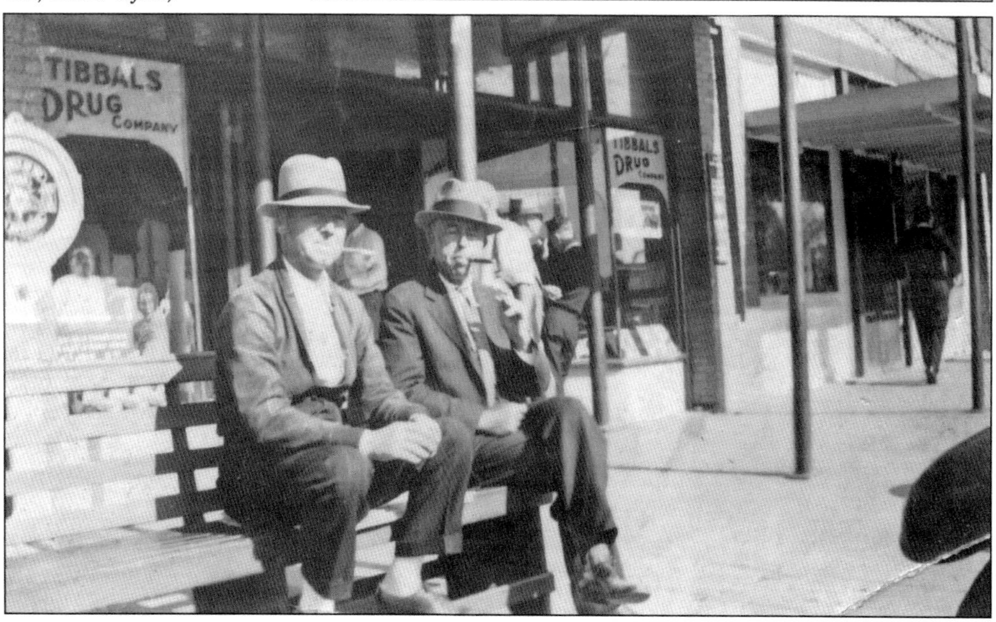

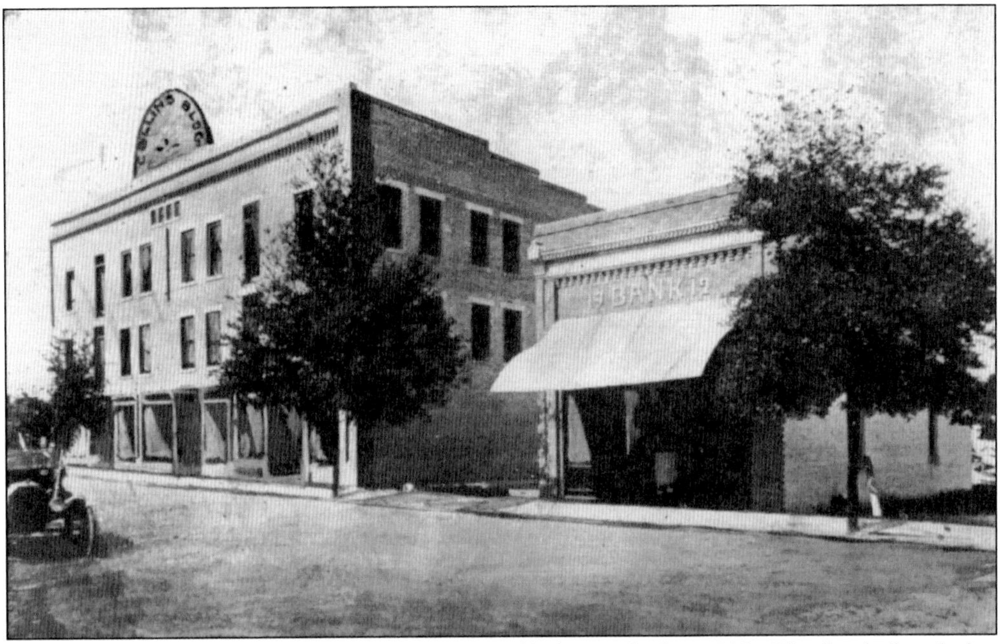

The Bank of Umatilla is pictured above in 1912 and below in the late 1920s. This bank closed after the stock market crash, and Umatilla had no bank until the Umatilla State Bank was chartered in 1937. As Umatilla State Bank continued to grow and branch banking was approved, the bank began opening branches in 1977. The directors formed a one-bank holding company and changed the name to United Southern Bank, retaining the trademark initials USB, in 1986. Today, with 11 offices in the Lake County area and 65 years of community banking, United Southern Bank still puts a premium on building strong customer relationships. (Above CB, below LCHS.)

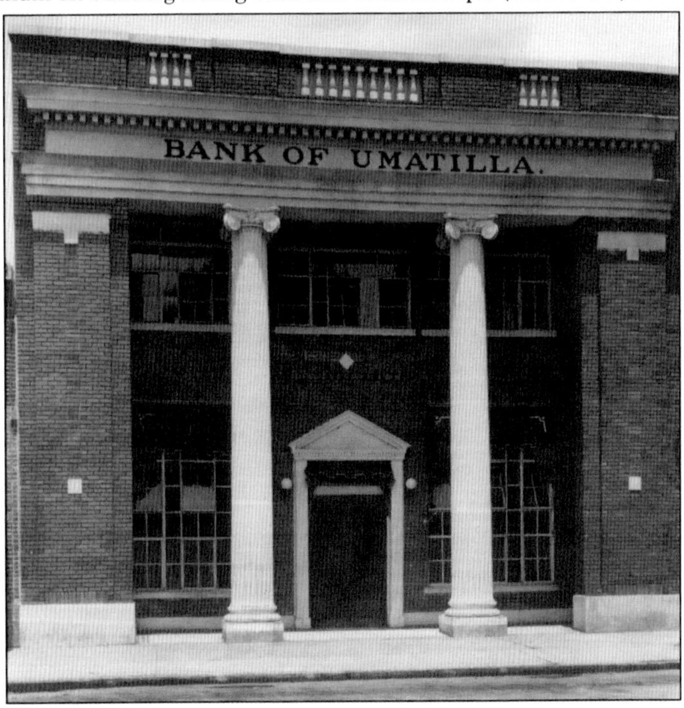

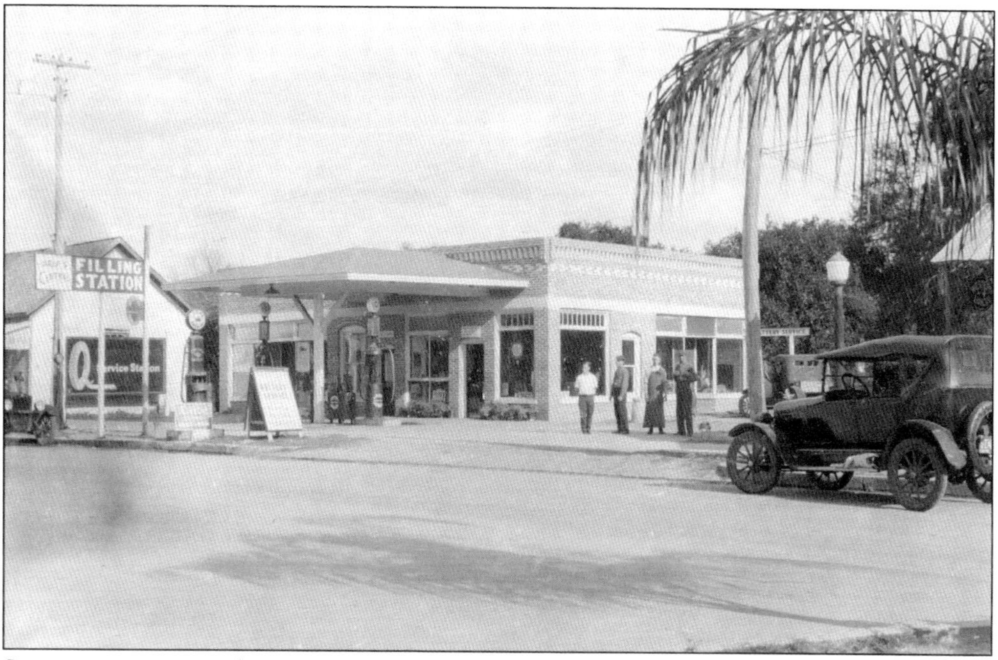

Service stations started popping up as automobiles became the common form of transportation. This photograph shows Self's Central Filling Station on Central Avenue taken in 1920s. The car on the street apparently has been parked long enough for the dog take a nap on the running board. Road improvements were left to locals and the sign markers used were as colorful as some of the promoters. All that was really needed to run an auto trail was a couple buckets of paint and a knack for self-promotion. Trail markers were occasionally posted as independent signs, but more often were posted by painting them on utility poles, bridge abutments, and fence posts. Pictured below is the post office built to replace the original post office that burned in the 1899 fire. The Masonic lodge met upstairs in the Masonic temple. (Both photographs MG.)

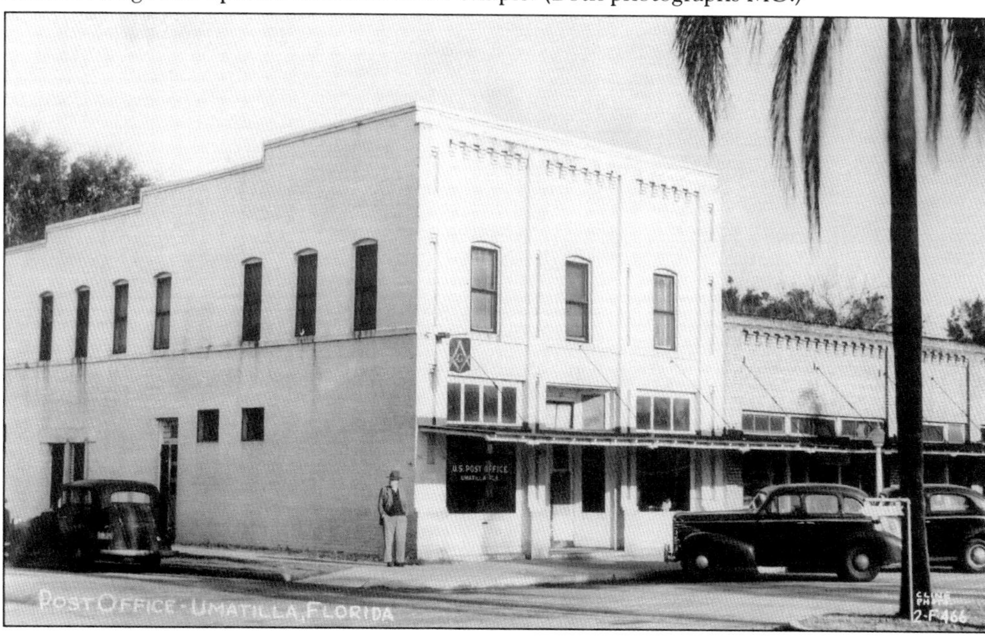

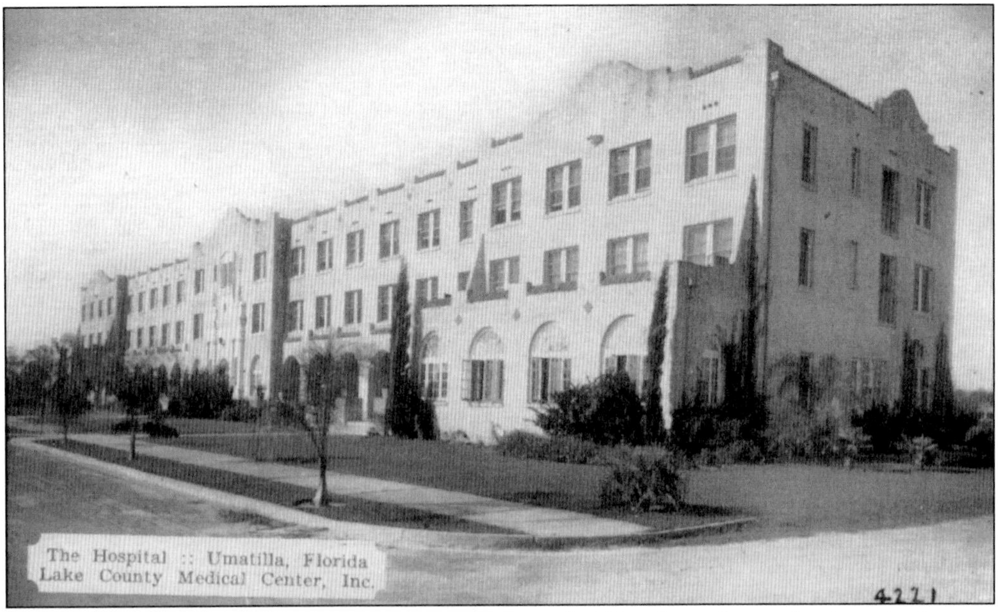

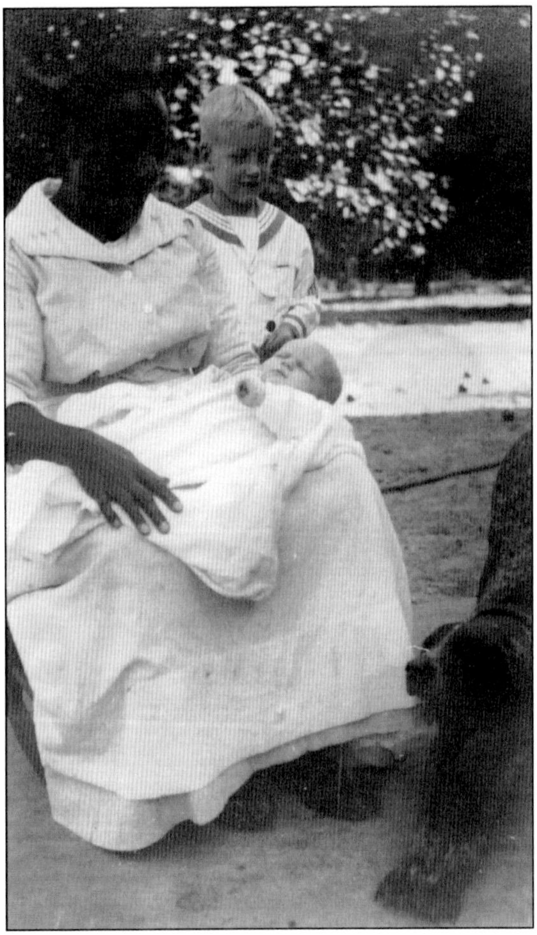

In 1931, the polio epidemic arrived and there was no provision for caring for the sick in the county. Hospitals of adjoining counties were full and unable to take cases from Lake County. Seen here, the Lake County Medical Center opened in January 1933, in Umatilla's vacant Rowebuilt Hotel, with 18 beds and six bassinets. The Florida Elk's Association Home for Crippled Children initially occupied the south wing of the hospital. The Harry-Anna Crippled Children's Home later moved into the entire building when the hospital relocated to the Fountain Inn of Eustis in 1938. That building was owned and sponsored by Frank Waterman, of fountain pen fame. Today the hospital is known as Florida Hospital Waterman Medical Center and is located in Tavares. Until these hospitals opened, midwife Maggie Evans, seen here in 1921, attended many of Umatilla's home births. (Above UHS, Left RBD.)

In 1933, Anna and Harry Miller are pictured signing the deed to the Rowebuilt Hotel over to the Florida Elks. The Rowebuilt became the Harry-Anna Crippled Children's Hospital, seen below. Miller acquired the hotel through a mortgage held on the furnishings, and ownership passed to him when the hotel was foreclosed upon following the stock market crash. Money to open the hospital was raised by the Hialeah Park Race Track in Miami, who donated a day's receipts, which amounted to $34,500, to the hospital. Dr. W. L. Ashton, who later became medical director of the hospital, went to Miami and brought the funds back in a satchel. The operating funds for the hospital were augmented each year, beginning in 1953, by the Tangerine Bowl football game in Orlando. (Right LCHS, below CB.)

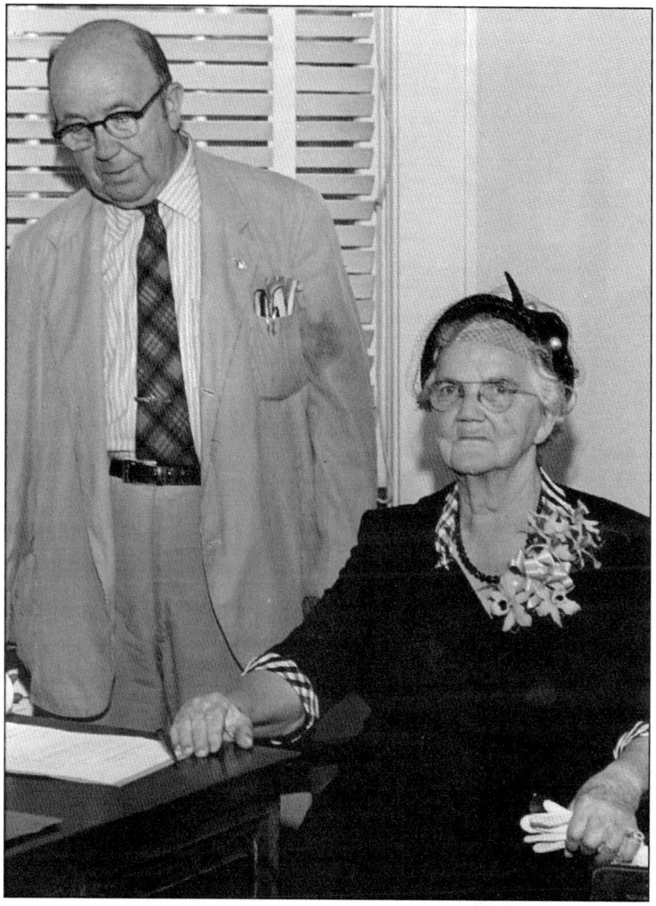

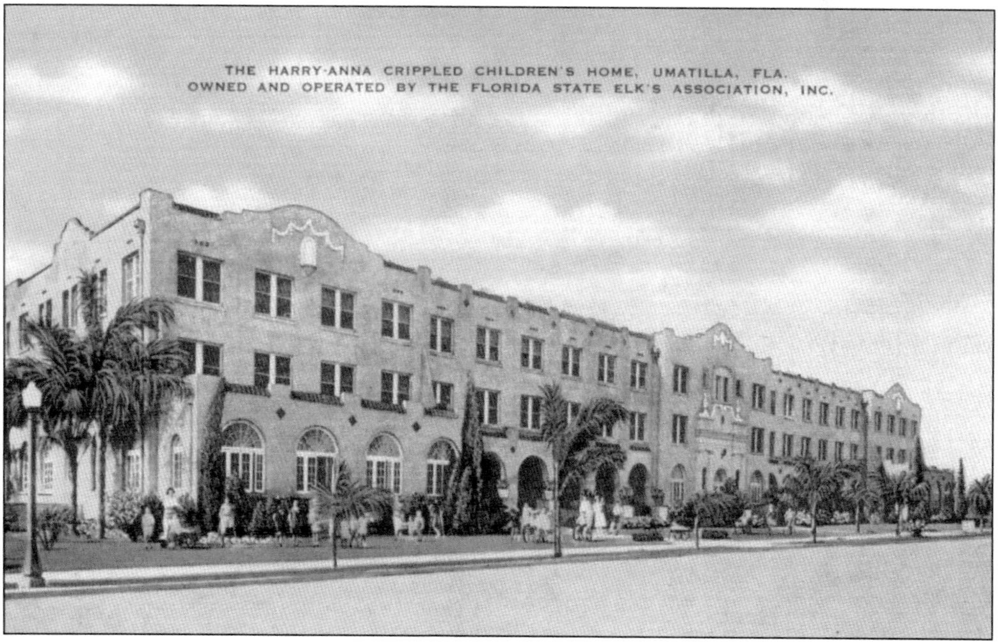

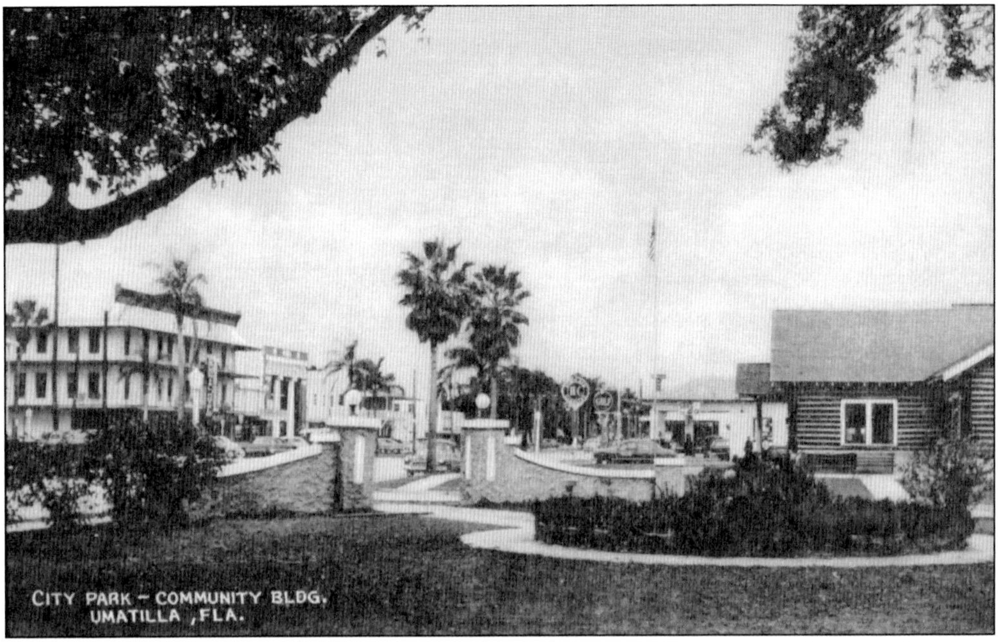

Umatilla City Park is pictured above in 1940. The park became the recreational center of town in the 1920s with horseshoe pitching, croquet, tennis, and a playground for children. A magnificent electric fountain was admired and known far and wide over the state. Shuffleboard courts were added in the 1930s and were often crowded with players. Tournaments, complete with trophies and prizes, were a major competitive activity. The entry to the park was a familiar subject for picture postcards. Pictured below is the Umatilla High School band during a 1942 performance in the park. (Above CB, below RBD.)

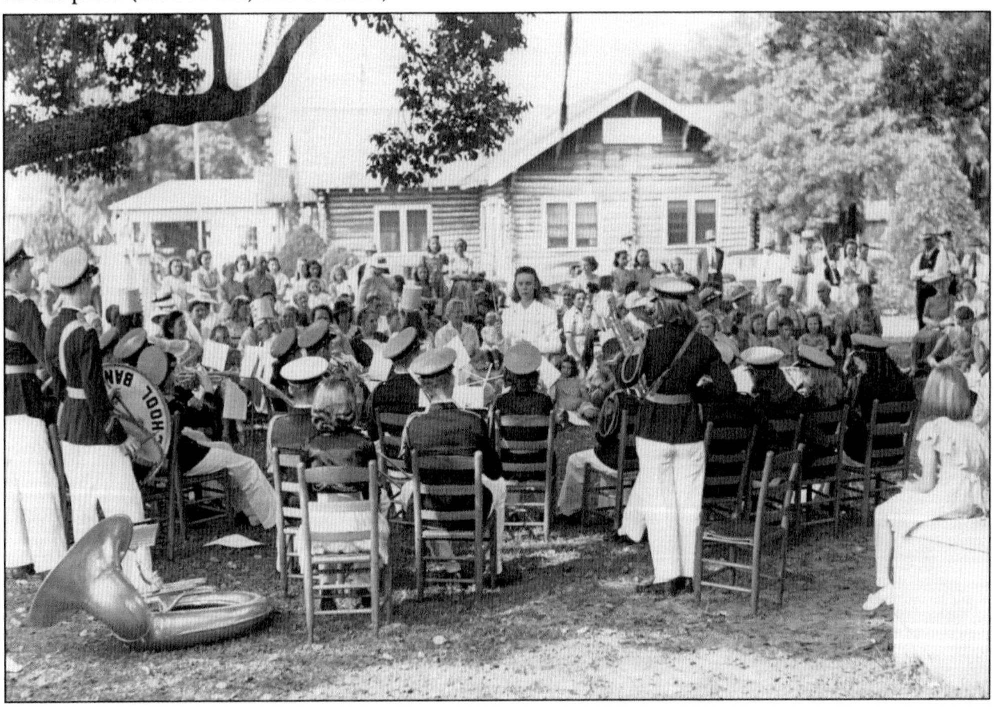

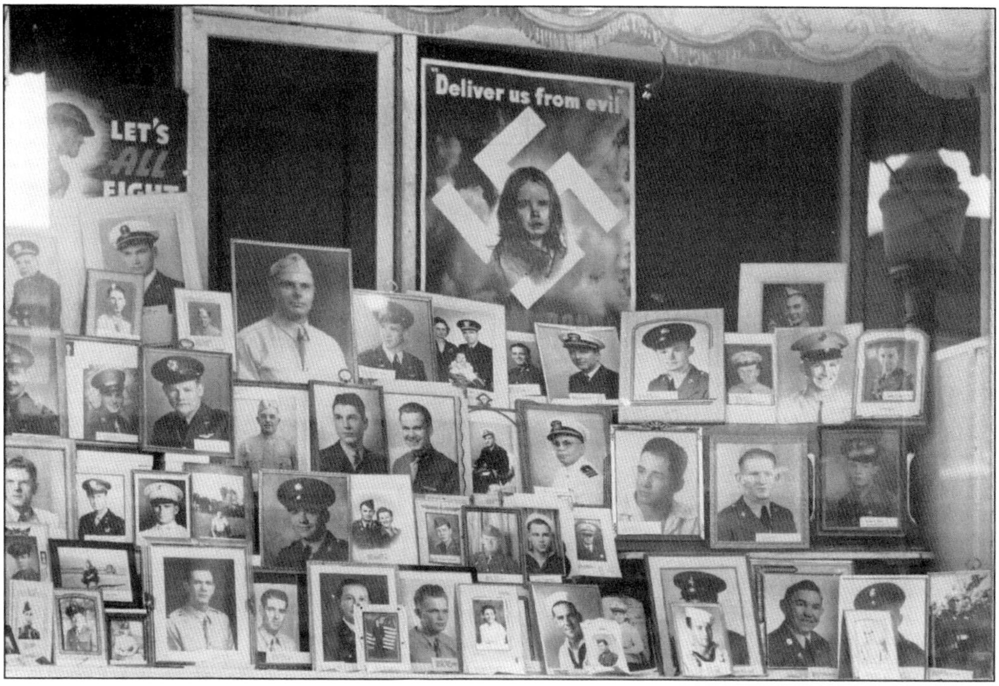

Displaying community support for men and women serving during World War II, Lillian Feigan's storefront, shown in the above photograph, displayed pictures of loved ones away at war. Umatilla played its part when residents—many of them women—manned a watchtower and reported every plane. When World War II erupted, soldiers arrived by rail and convoys of military vehicles in Umatilla to train as members of searchlight brigades. Their job was to install a ring of searchlights, and then someone simulating enemy aircraft would fly a plane over at night. The searchlight brigade's job was to find and illuminate the plane, just like in the movies. On the right, Hubert Collins and Bena Allen share a meal with soldiers at the training base just north of town, by the present-day American Legion Hall. (Above UHS, Right EAS.)

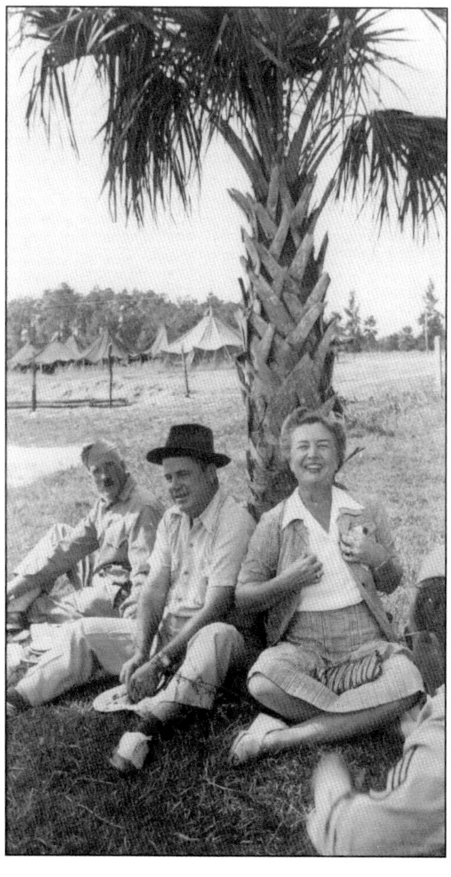

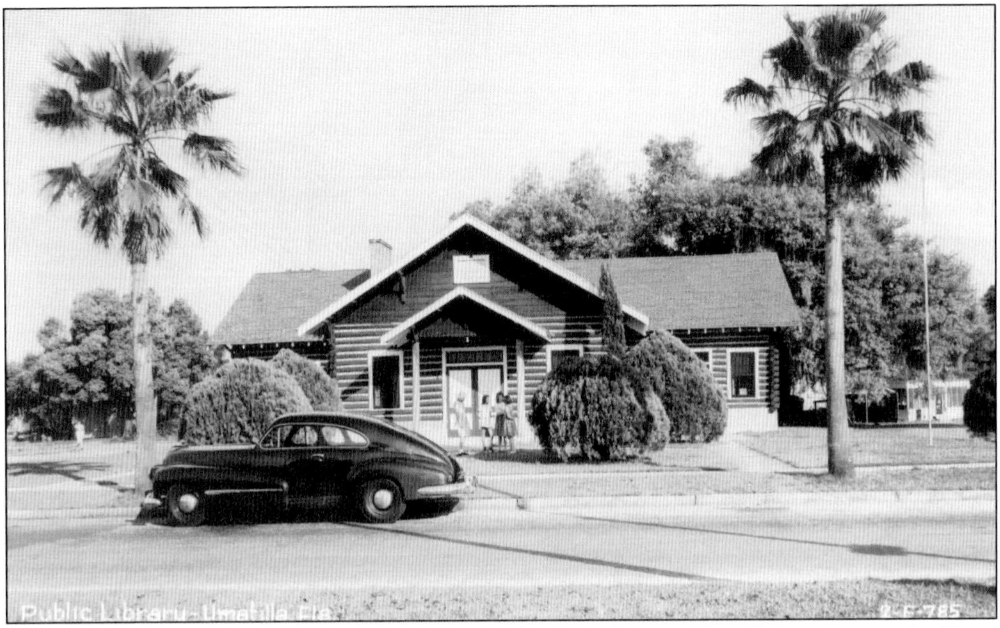

Built by the Works Progress Administration in 1940, this log cabin was Umatilla's community building. Along with housing the municipal administration and the library, it provided a modern kitchen and large auditorium as a meeting place for Umatilla's progressive Women's Club, the community club, the Kiwanis, and other social gatherings. A fire in January 1959 destroyed the community building as well as many of Umatilla's historical and official records. (CB.)

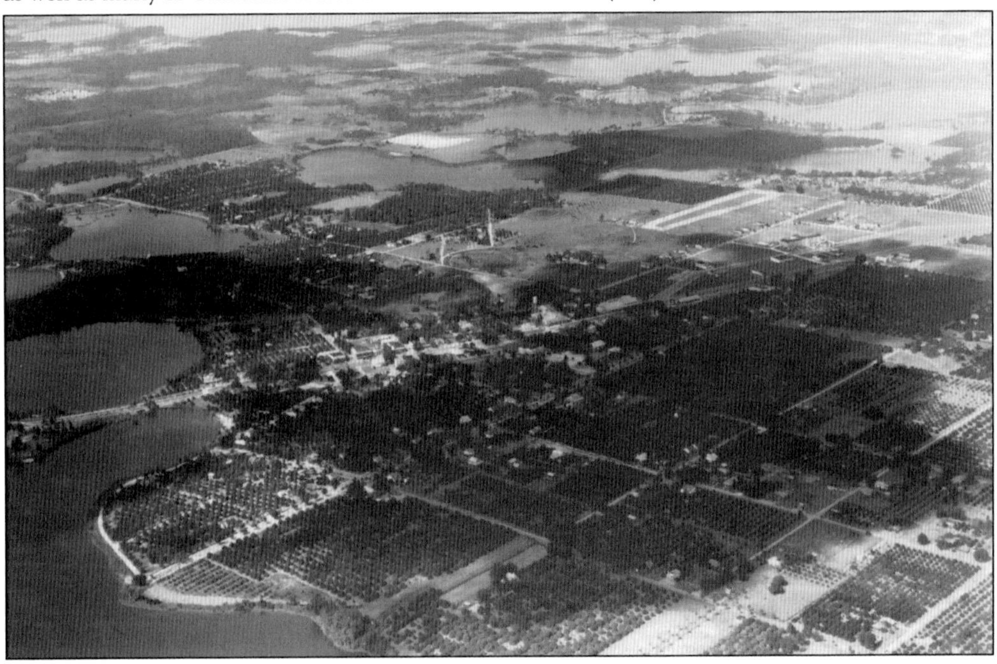

An aerial view from the 1930s shows Umatilla is more groves than town. State Highway 19, running through Umatilla, earned the nickname "The Velvet Highway" for the view of mile upon mile of citrus groves appearing as a velvet landscape. The citrus industry peaked in 1969, when 144,000 of Lake County's 650,000 acres were in grove land. (LCHS.)

Eight

Historic Citrus, Logging, Farming, and Turpentine

The first orange trees cultivated were all of seedling type, growing high off the ground. Pioneer citrus growers had little or no commercial fertilizer, and cattle were brought in for a few days twice or more a year to fertilize the groves. The high limbs of the trees protected the foliage from cattle that roamed the interior of Florida free range through the mid-1900s. Until 1895, Florida's citrus industry was confined within a 125-mile radius of St. Augustine.

The area was forested with longleaf yellow pine, and there was practically no market or way to move the timber being cleared for citrus groves and farming. Trees were cut and rolled together in heaps and burned until mills began operating in the forest and turpentining in the vast pine stands.

The Big Freeze of 1894–1895 virtually destroyed every grove and agricultural crop in Florida. Only a few short years later, on July 2, 1899, a fire broke out in Umatilla's Alliance store; with no firefighting equipment, the entire business section on the west side of town was destroyed. Many had no choice but to leave Florida altogether. Those who remained managed to eke a living from lumber, cattle, and vegetable farming.

The Hodges Lumber Company operated a large mill in Umatilla, with logging trains and a 25-mile track. Log trains hauled timber to the mill and to the St. Johns River to be rafted downstream. The train also carried out fertilizer, building materials, and supplies to farmers in the hinterland and brought in watermelons and other produce to the commercial railroad.

Growers originally operated their own packinghouses. By the mid-1920s, eight packinghouses were established; the largest were the Umatilla Fruit Company owned by the Turner family, and the Umatilla Citrus Growers Association—a farmers' cooperative. Watermelon, cotton, and peach orchards produced crops through the 1950s. The "Hundred Year Freezes" of the 1980s forever changed Umatilla's "velvet" landscape, but each spring, simply breathing the intoxicating fragrance of orange blossoms stirs old memories and creates new ones.

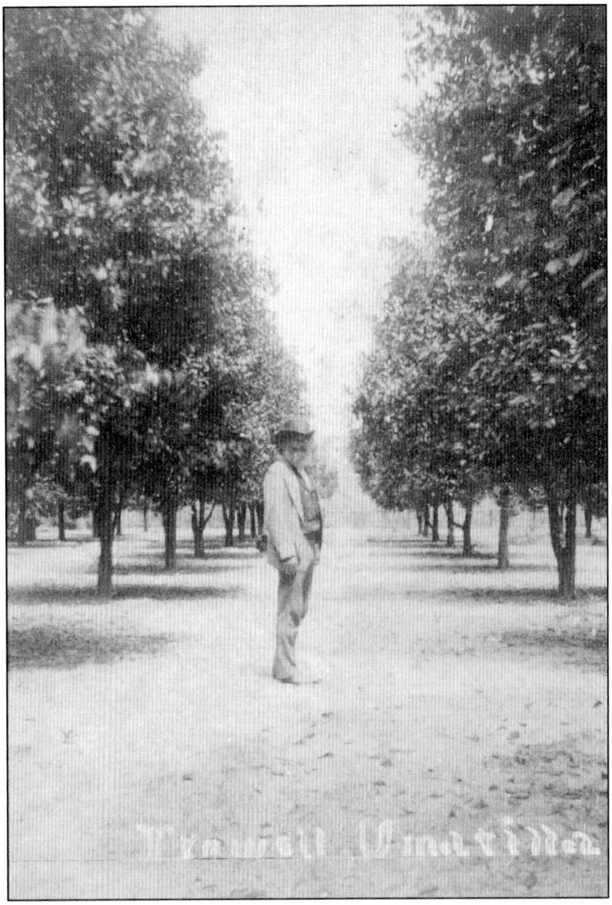

Nathan Trowell is pictured on the left in one of his seedling groves in 1880s. Citrus grew in Florida hundreds of years before many New World settlers had ever seen the countryside. Spanish conquistadors who founded St. Augustine shared with Native Americans citrus seeds brought from Spain. These trees produced mostly sour oranges, but some were sweet and became the predecessor of the orange we know today. White settlers cultivated the trees and planted others that would become the backbone of one of the world's largest citrus-growing regions. Packers would ship fruit up the Ocklawaha River to the St. Johns River to Jacksonville. The railroad really put the industry in business when transportation across the state opened Umatilla to larger ports. Seen below, R. L. Collins is with the harrow patented in the 1920s. (EAS.)

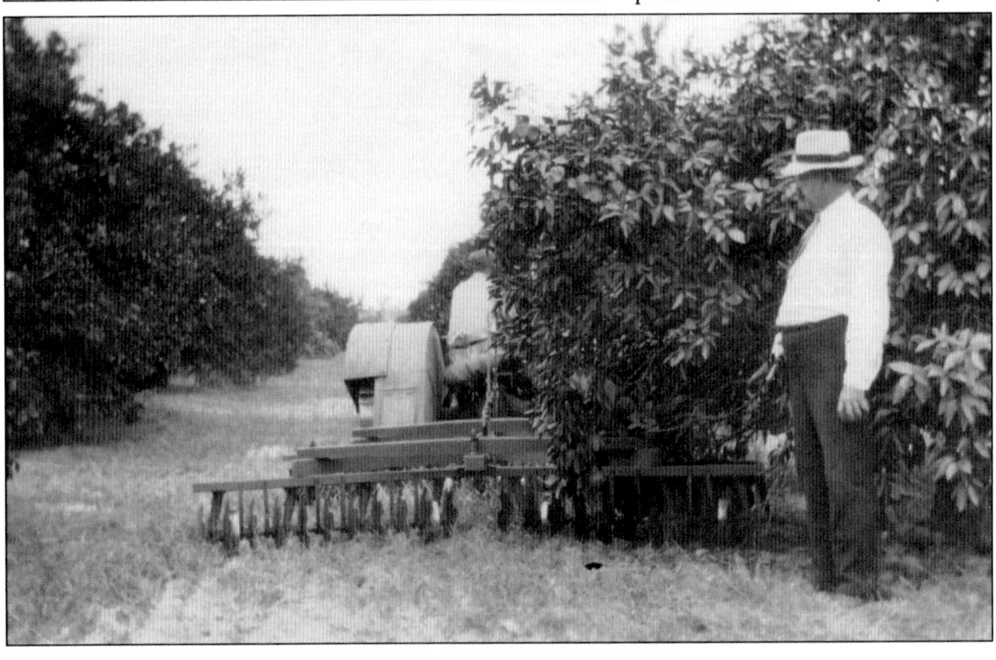

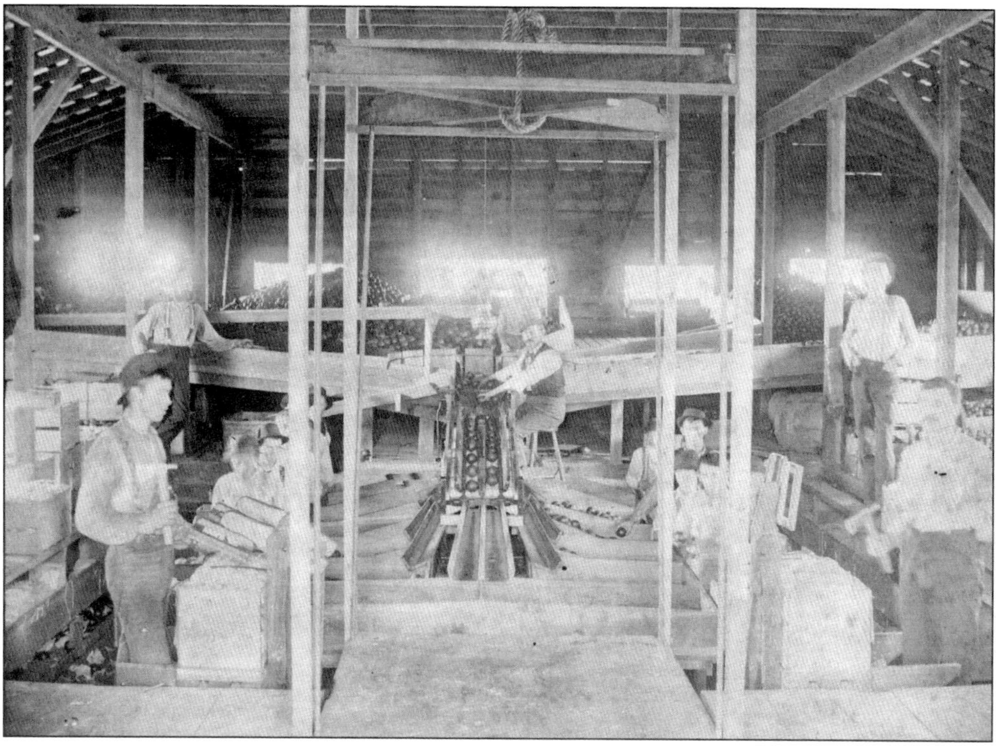

The George V. DeVault packinghouse, Umatilla's first, is pictured around 1907. Though modern for its time, this packinghouse could handle only a few hundred boxes a day. By 1949, an average of 700 freight car loads of citrus shipped from Umatilla. At least as much citrus went out by truck and another 11,000 pieces of express citrus went out of the little express office in town. During the season, deposits at the bank ran $30,000–$50,000 every day. In the 1950s and 1960s, the industry employed 20,000–30,000 workers a year. Packinghouse workers are pictured below while at work. Crates were bound with thin metal straps, and open crates glow with Umatilla's golden fruit. (Above UHS, below LCHS.)

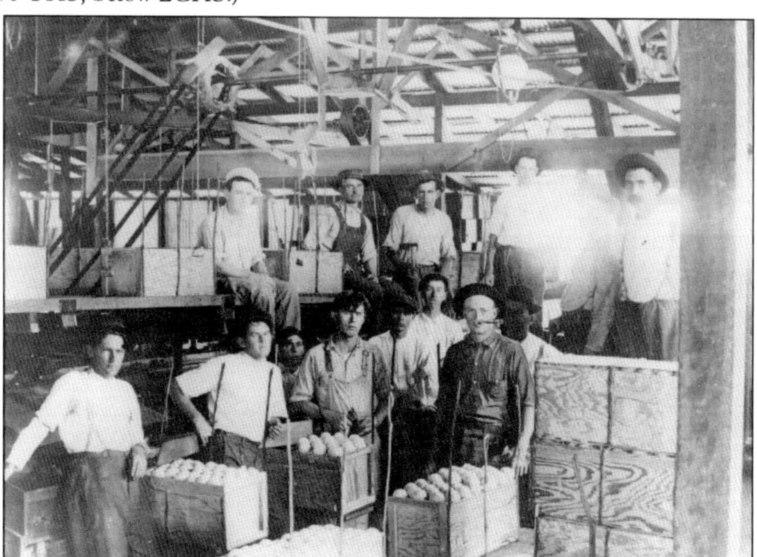

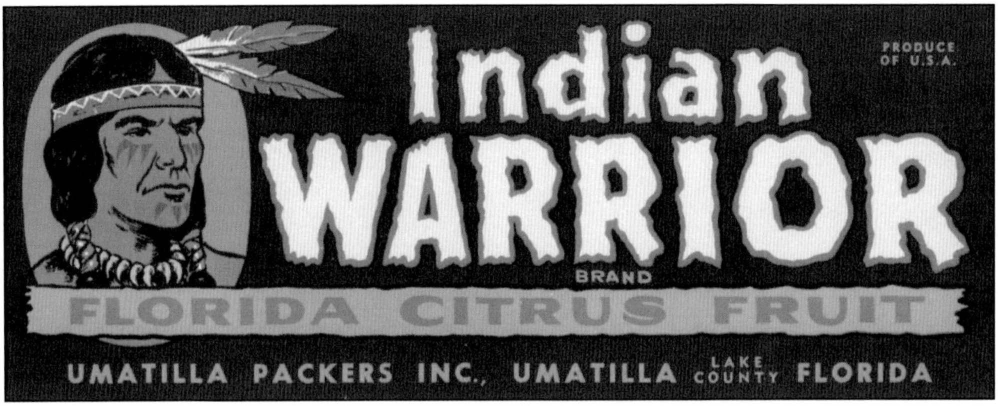

Colorful relics of a bygone era, citrus packing labels once adorned every wooden box of oranges shipped to market. The practice of pasting paper labels on boxes began in the 1880s to identify and advertise citrus fruit. Easily recognizable with catchy brand names, the labels helped growers, packers, and shippers market their products. Shown here are citrus labels from some of Umatilla's packinghouses; above, the Indian Warrior brand of Florida citrus fruit was used by Umatilla Packers, Inc., and is one of the most familiar brands of citrus. Below, the Umatilla Belle brand was packed and shipped by the Umatilla Citrus Growers Association, a cooperative of growers. (RBD.)

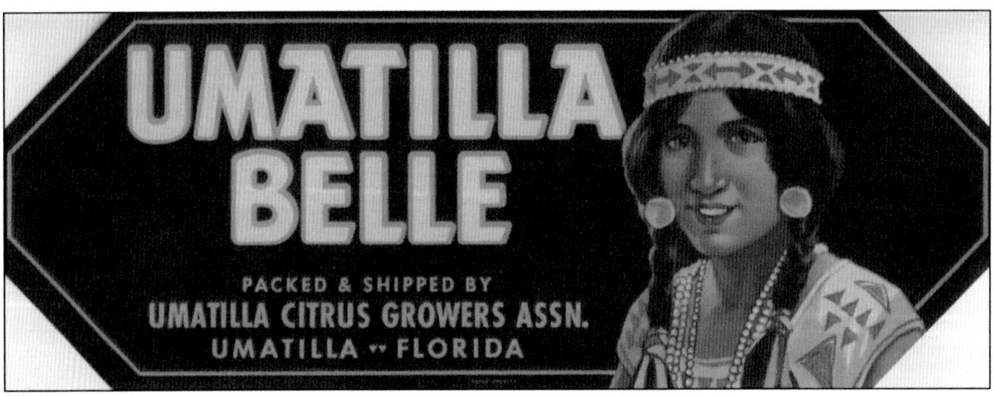

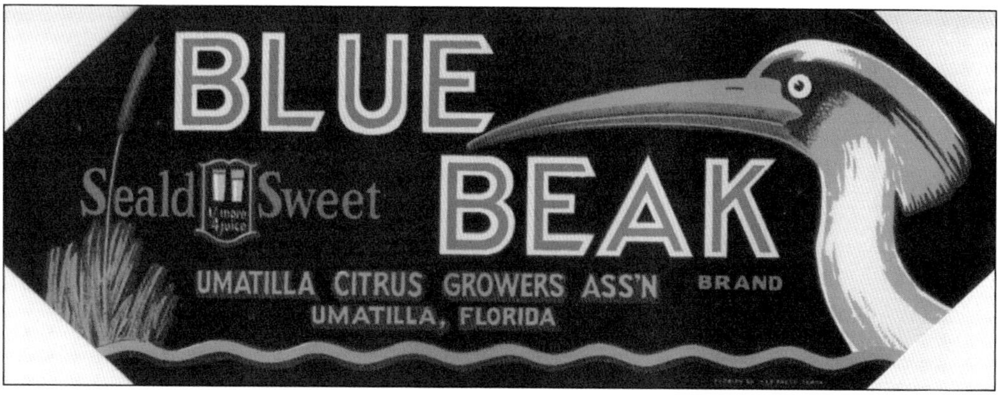

The age of labels came to an end during the 1950s when the traditional wooden box gave way to the preprinted cardboard carton. Thousands of citrus labels were destroyed, leaving just a few pieces of vintage art to remind the world of a uniquely American marketing tool. Those labels that have survived are collectibles. One of the most collected citrus labels, Blue Beak brand, was packed and shipped by the Umatilla Citrus Growers Association and associated with the Seald Sweet brand, which claimed a quarter cup more juice than its competitors. Below, the LACO brand label features citrus groves in and around Umatilla. The LACO brand belonged to the Umatilla Citrus Growers Association. (RBD.)

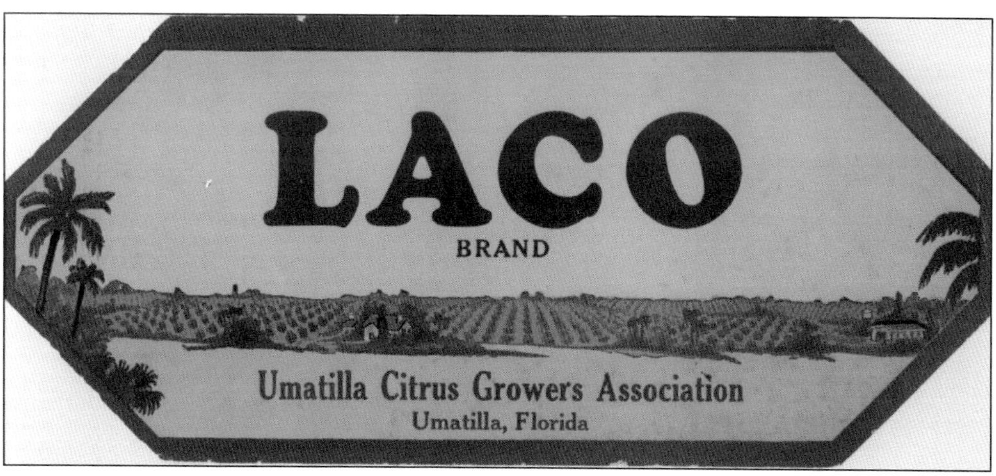

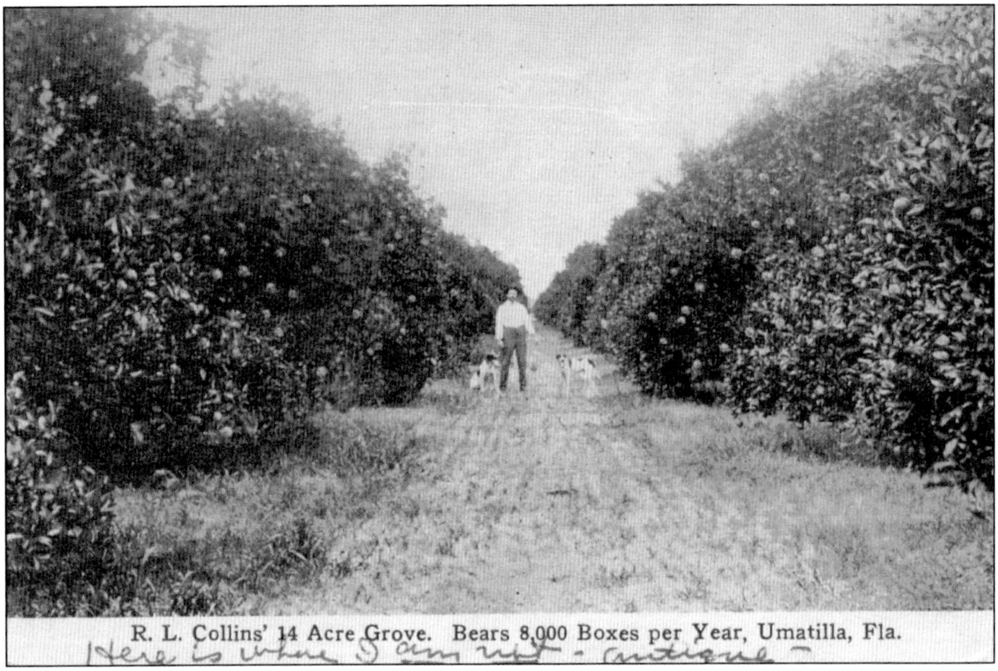

Above, Robert Lee Collins stands with two of his hunting dogs in a 14-acre grove that produced 8,000 boxes of oranges a year. A 1913 promotional brochure reported it would take "an estimated $1850 to start a citrus grove, including $500 for 10 acres of land, and $700 for 700 'first class' trees. The investment thereafter ran $250, $350, $400 a year. At the third year, some fruit will show up; at the fourth year enough fruit to pay the expenses; and the fifth year's crop after paying expenses would leave satisfactory surplus." Pictured below, Collins appears in a grapefruit tree in one of his groves. (RBD.)

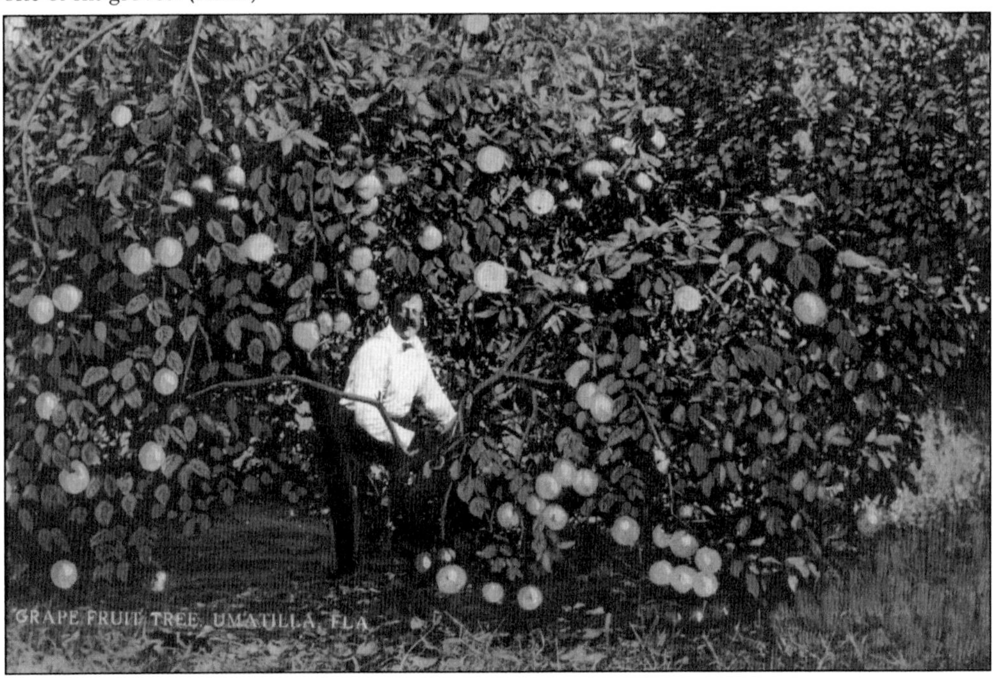

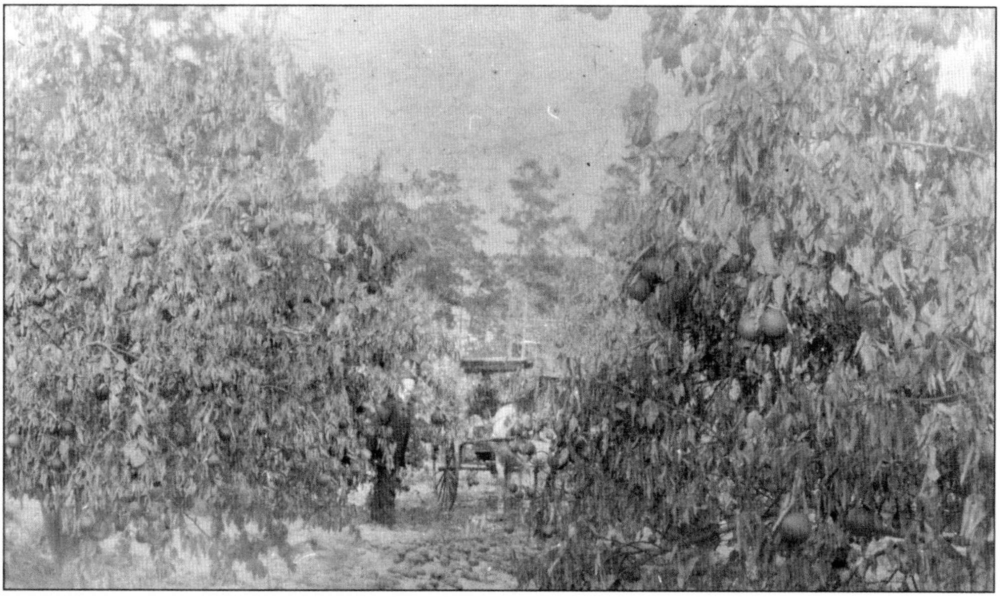

The Big Freeze of 1895 killed 99 percent of the area's citrus trees when temperatures plunged to 14 degrees Fahrenheit. In the above photograph, a grower with horse and carriage surveys the damage in his grove. The crop was a total loss, and the curled leaves indicated tree damage. Pictured below, a few months later, trees are trimmed of barren branches in the hope that some trees would survive. Snow fell as far south as Bradenton and Tampa and stayed on the ground in Tallahassee for three days. In March a second freeze arrived. For years afterward, growers showed little interest in replanting. By 1920, citrus had made its comeback with more than 250,000 trees growing. Three years later, Lake County had 30,000 acres of grove land. In 1925, the average grove worker's salary was $20 a week. (CB.)

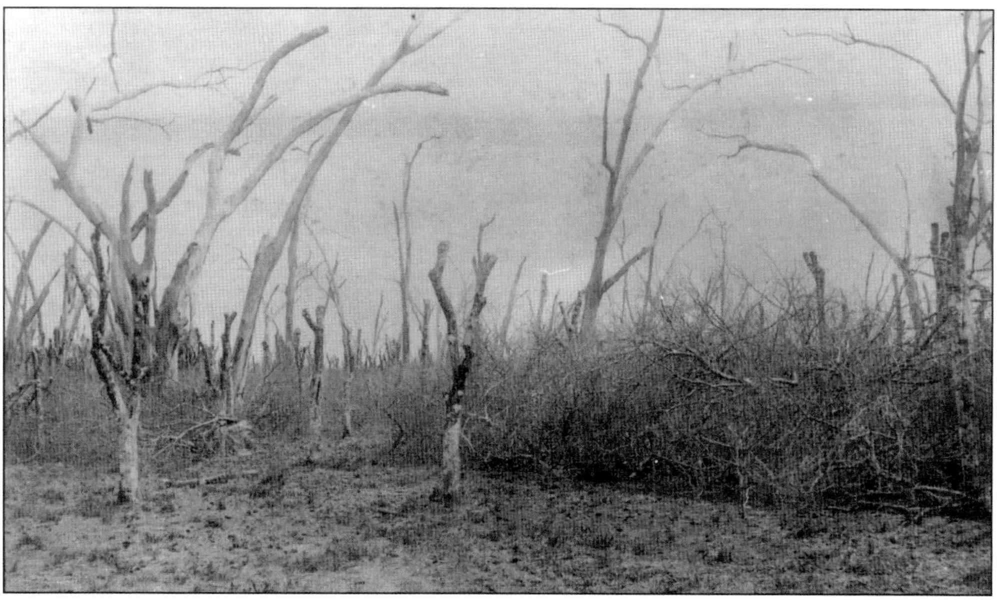

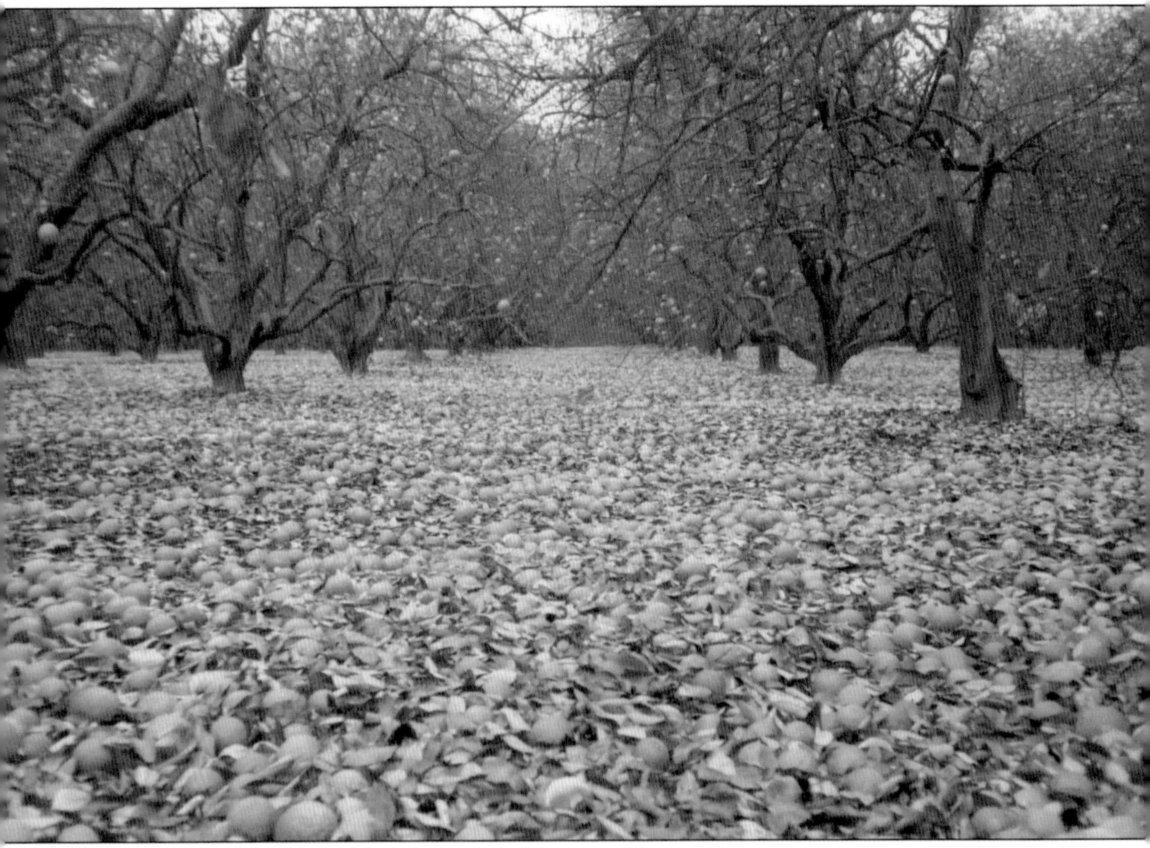

"The history of citrus is, by and large, the history of Lake County," said John Jackson Jr., Lake County's agricultural agent, who spent his life working in the citrus industry. The one-two punch of the 1895 Big Freeze was repeated on Christmas Day 1983, when the temperature fell to 14 degrees for more than eight hours. The second freeze came on Super Bowl Sunday in January 1985. In this photograph, a frozen grove has dropped its fruit following the 1983 freeze. After several more freezes during the 1980s, Lake County was left with only 13,500 acres of groves, which was only 11 percent of the more than 120,000 acres that stood in 1980. Approximately 60,000 acres were eventually replanted, but the local economy, dependent on citrus, suffered a tremendous blow. (DR.)

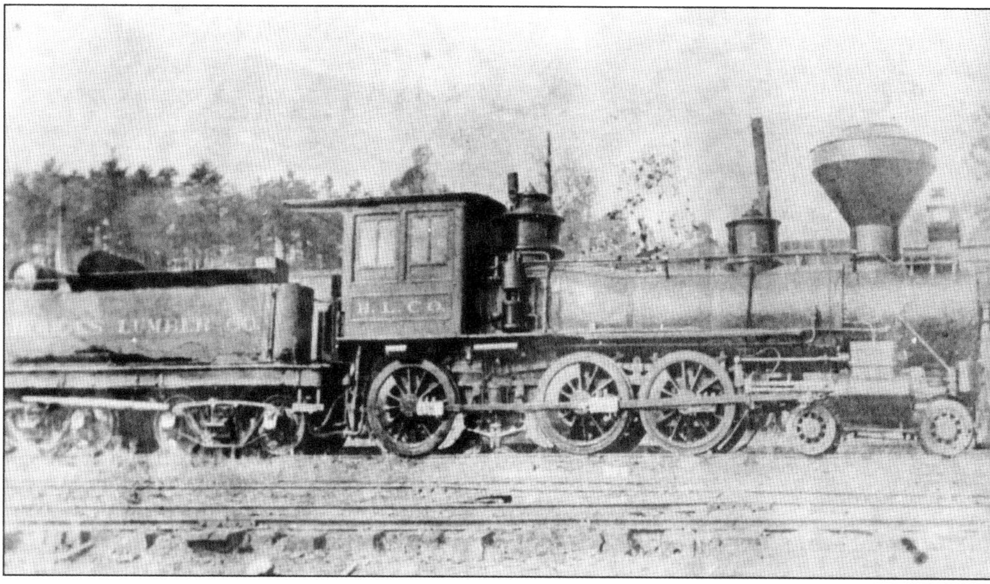

The train seen here belonged to the Hodges Lumber Company, which operated 25 miles of track for its large mill near Umatilla. The Atlantic Lumber Company, the Bradford Lumber Company, and the Wilson Cypress Company also had log trains hauling timber to the St. Johns River to be rafted to mills downstream. Supplies for farmers, building materials, and fertilizer were hauled on company trains to farmers out in the country, and watermelons and other farm produce were brought in to the commercial railroad. The photograph below shows the Hodges sawmill in operation. Benjamin C. Yancey also owned and operated a large lumber mill and syrup mill in Umatilla. (MG.)

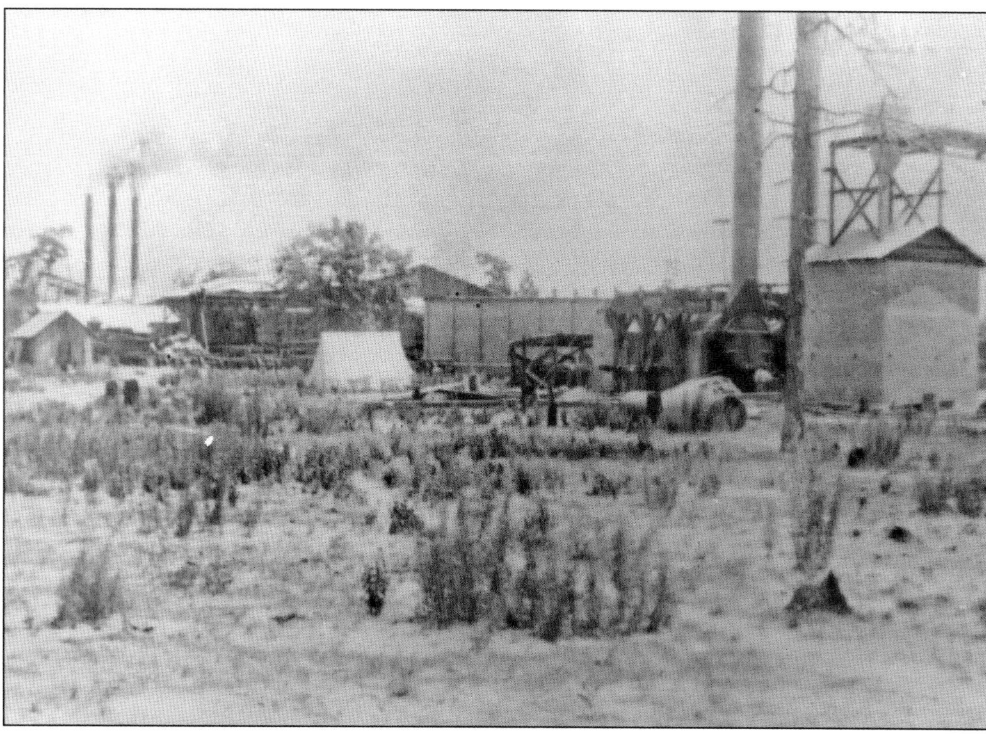

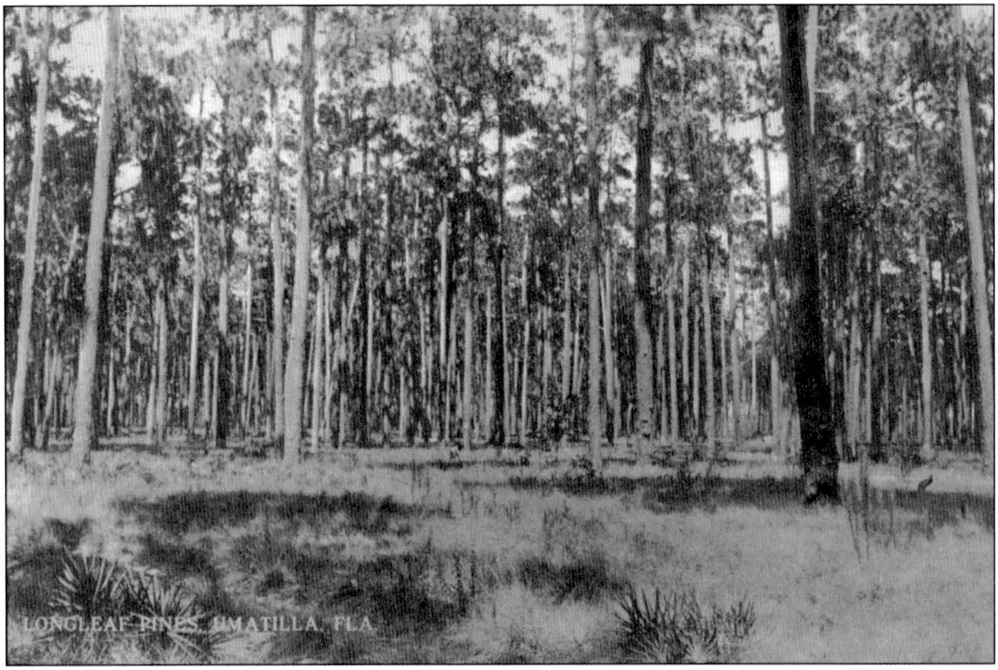

Virgin pine covered thousands of acres surrounding Umatilla. By 1913, Umatilla's lumber mills were producing 50,000 feet per day and the turpentine industry had come into the area to tap the vast forests. Seen below, pitch was harvested from the standing tree by slashing through the thick outer bark in a V-shaped groove, at the bottom of which an earthen pot was placed to catch the thick liquid. When filled, the crocks were collected, placed on mule wagons, and carted to the mill to be processed over high heat, much in the manner of sugar cane. (Above DS, below CB.)

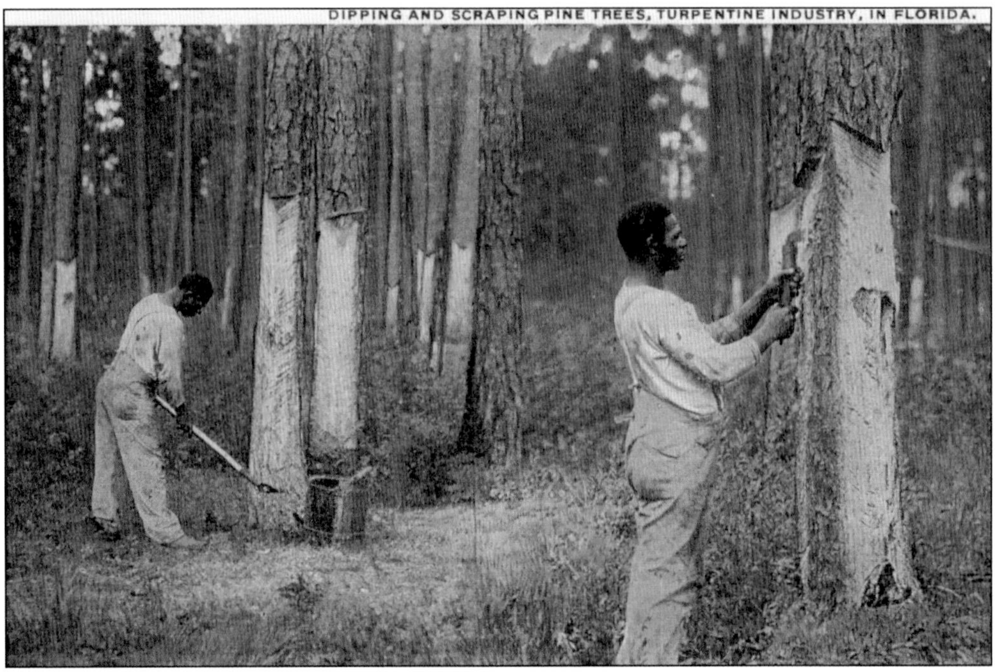

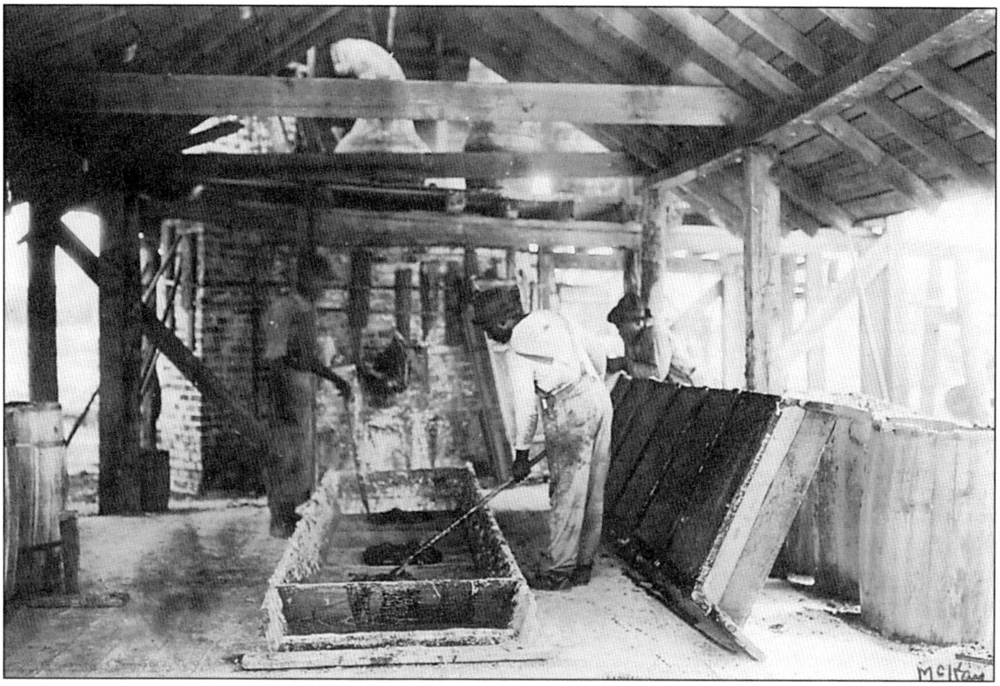

In this photograph, thick pine sap is being cooked over an open fire inside the mill. Turpentine was distilled from the sap, and a by-product, hard resin, was used chiefly by musicians for stringed instruments. In the image below, wooden barrels are being manually filled. They were then hauled to the railroad siding in Umatilla, which was the place where barrels of distilled gum and turpentine began their journey to Palatka. Otherwise, still products had to be hauled by mule train or truck to the St. Johns River at Crows Bluff and hence by boat to Palatka. (LCHS.)

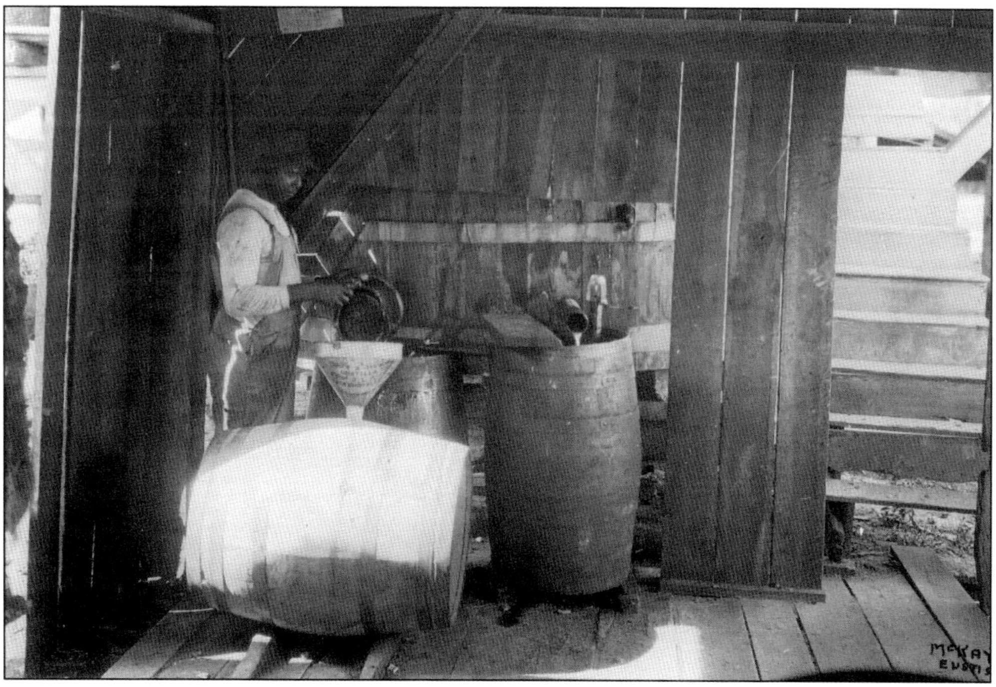

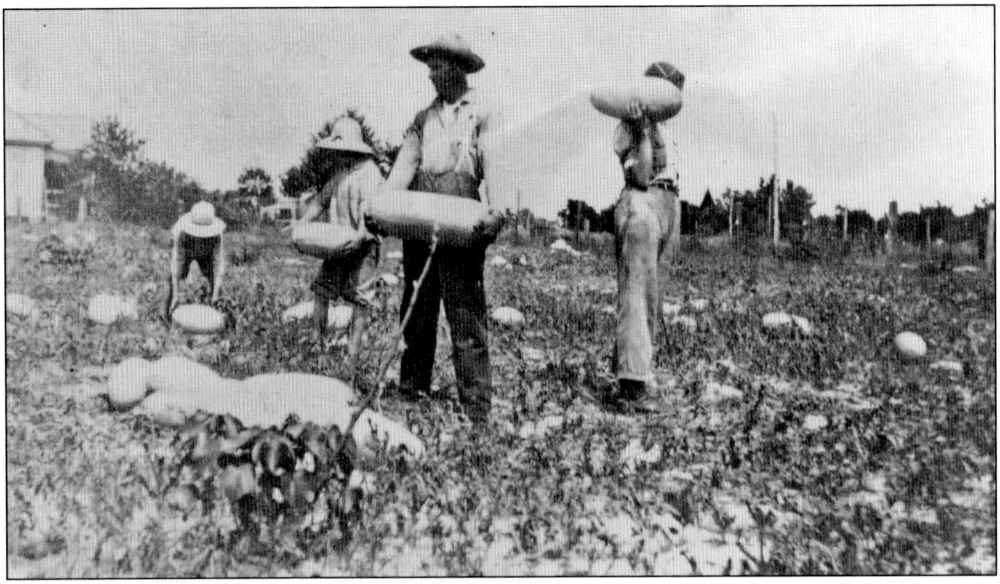

Pictured above, Gus Smith oversees his watermelon crew in 1911. By 1949, Umatilla growers were shipping an average of 500 railcar loads of watermelons a season. As many more were shipped by truck. Watermelons were farmed by Native Americans in Florida by 1664 and were a major agricultural crop in Umatilla, second only to citrus. Until the 1940s, it was hard to find watermelons in good condition in grocery stores. Melon lovers had to grow their own or purchase them from local stores or roadside produce stands. Radford Collins is pictured below in the watermelon field carrying home two fine specimens for his family's enjoyment. (Above UHS, below JCG.)

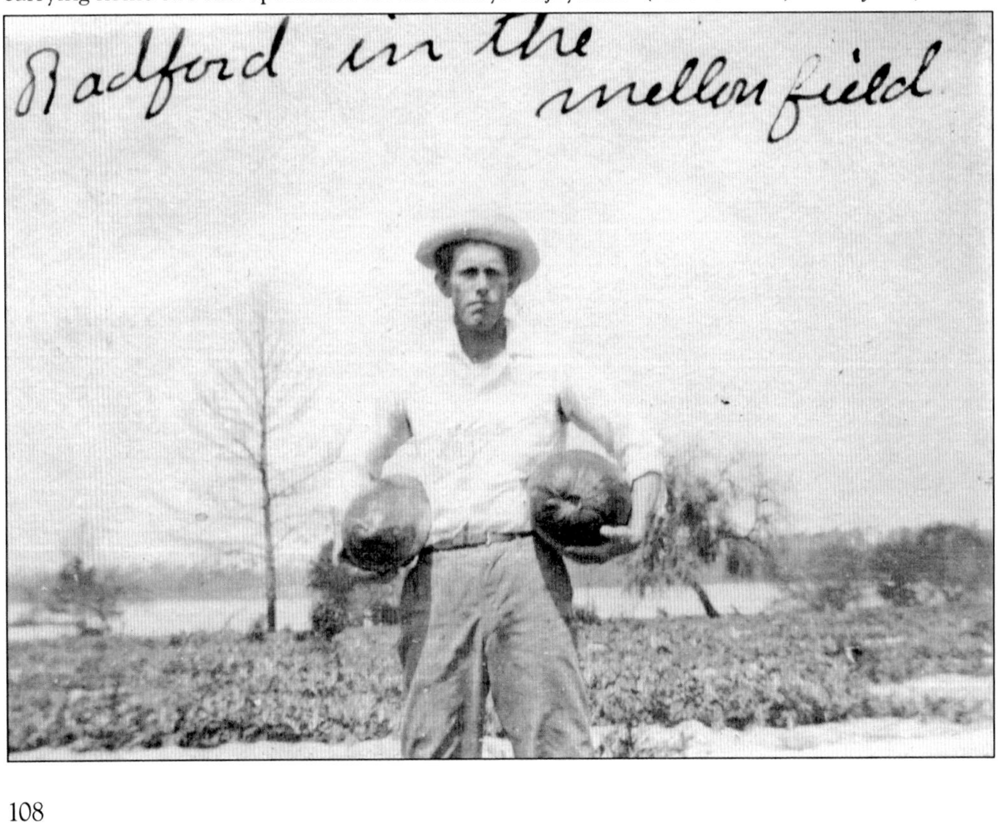

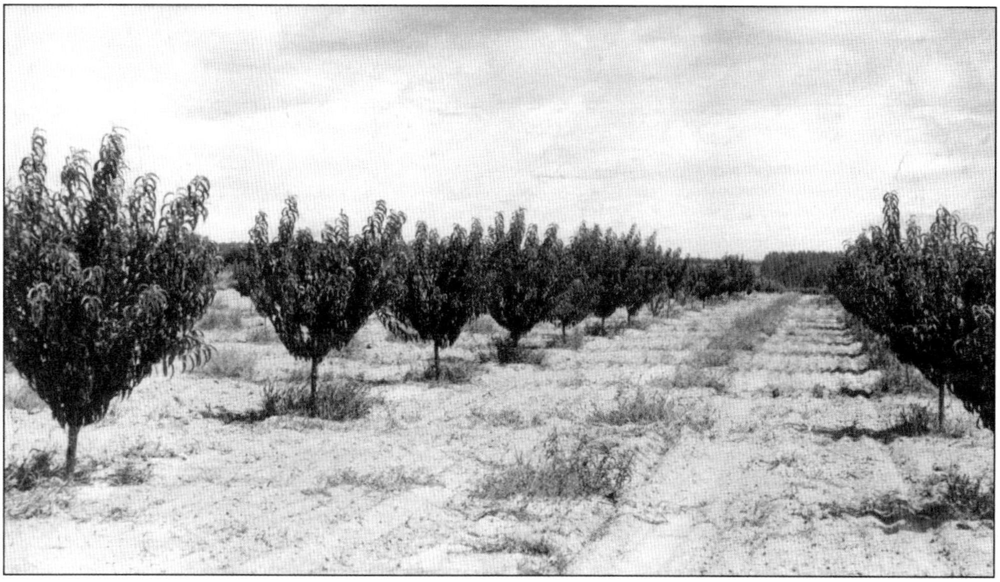

This photograph of Dr. Charles Demko's peach orchard in nearby Altoona was taken in the 1960s. Peach orchards had been cultivated in the area since settler days, but by the mid-20th century citrus had all but replaced peaches as an agricultural crop. Demko also had a vineyard and was the author of *Growing Grapes in Florida*, published in 1959 by the Florida Department of Agriculture. Demko served as president of the Florida Grape and Peach Growers Association. Demko is seen below at his roadside produce stand in Umatilla in 1964. The above photograph of the peach orchard is also hanging behind Demko in the photograph below, under the telephone. (UHS.)

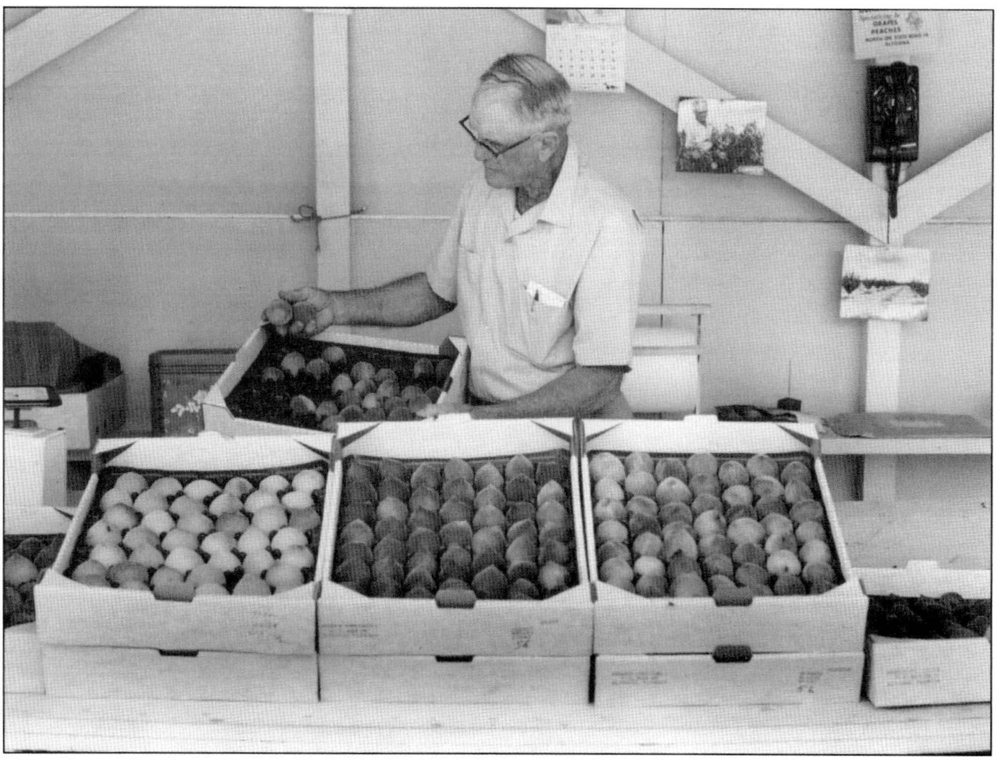

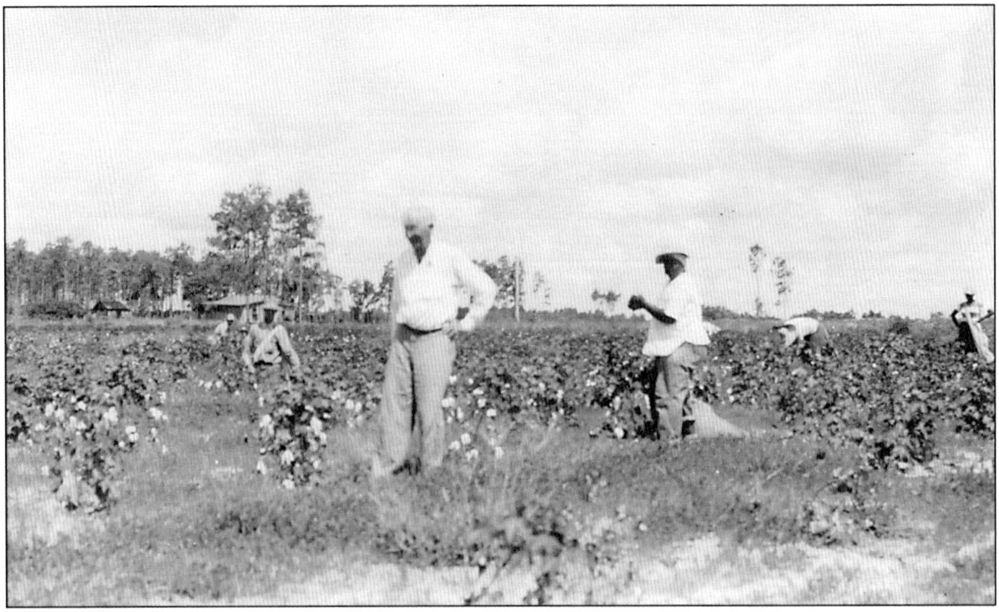

Pictured above during cotton-picking time, Hartley Hethcox surveys his 15-acre Sea Island long-staple cotton field in 1940. Cotton had been grown in the area since Umatilla's founder Nathan Trowell first planted cotton and built a gin in Umatilla in the 1860s. Hethcox's cotton crop had to be shipped to Leesburg, where the Central Florida Cotton Association built a ginnery in the 1940s, near the Leesburg Municipal Airport. Pictured below, seated from left to right, are Mattie, Mary Ann, and Hartley Hethcox with field hands in the cotton bolls harvested in 1940. (UHS.)

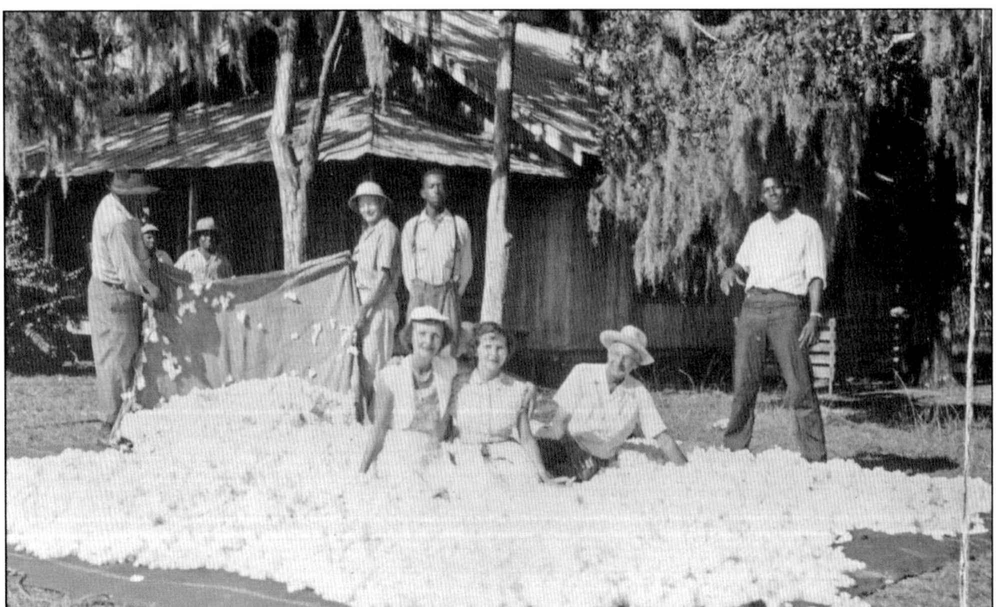

Nine

The Lake Region and the Highlands of Florida

Kindle the love of Nature in the minds of coming generations, the lack of which will inevitably increase the current deterioration of our planet as a place in which to live.

—Dr. Thomas Carr, January 24, 2009

What does the country look like? Umatilla is in the Lake Region—the Highlands of Florida. There are more than 1,400 named lakes in Lake County, some of them 5 to 35 miles in expanse, and they are among the highest elevations in Florida. The shores are not swampy and unapproachable, but gradually sloping down to the water's edge, with bottoms of hard white sand, and sparkling blue waters teeming with the best varieties of edible fish—mostly largemouth bass, the delight of the sportsman. The green forests, sparkling lakes bordered with their semitropical growth, high hills from which magnificent views may be had, and the lovely orange groves tucked away in nooks and crannies and appearing in the most unexpected places all afford unending interest and charm.

Today in Umatilla, beyond bountiful hunting and fishing, visitors can hike the scenic Florida Trail, enjoy sites on the Great Florida Birding Trail, and attend the annual Black Bear Festival—one of Florida's most important wildlife education events. Umatilla is the historic site of the Florida Horsemen's Association's three-day, 100-mile competitive trail ride, and home to Rocking Horse Ranch, a mecca of Florida horsemanship and the selected site of equestrian selection trials for the 1995 Pan American games, 1989 World Championship, and 1988 U.S. Olympic team.

In 2007, the U.S. Forestry Service of the Ocala National Forest received a gift of inestimable value from Dr. Tom Carr: the Carr family cabin and the 46 acres on the northwest shore of Lake Nicotoon. The cabin and its environs are being restored for broad-based appreciation of nature, contemplation, and to pass Dr. Archie Carr's conservation ethic to future generations.

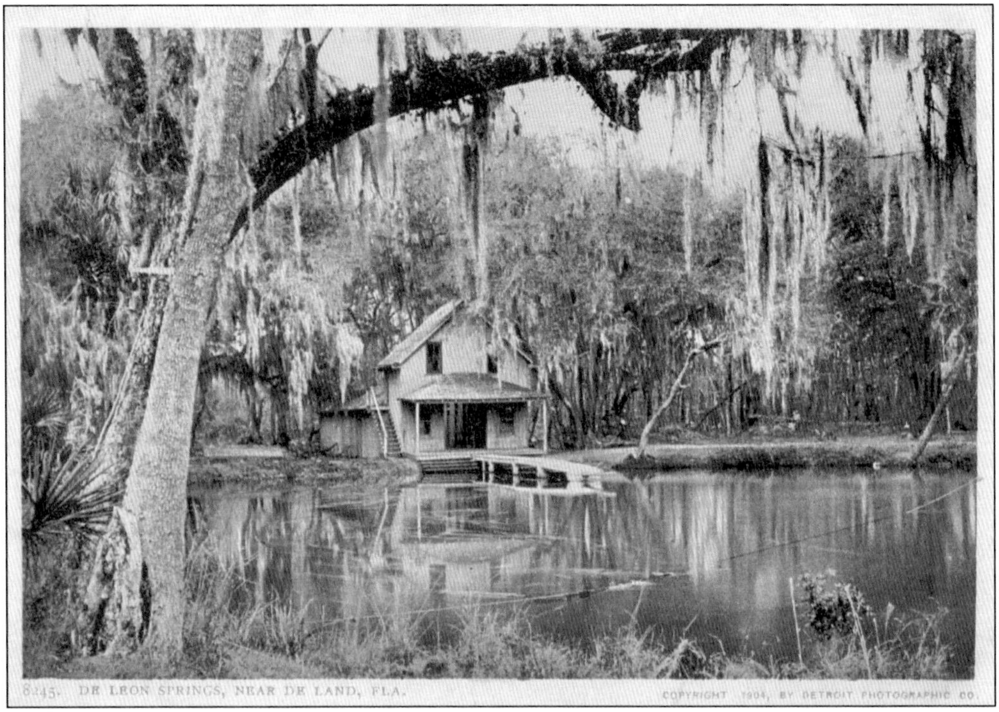

The sugar mill at de Leon Springs is pictured above in 1904. In the late 1800s, de Leon Springs was utilized to refine sugar and crops by way of the sugar mill. The mill was powered by the springs' strong outflow of water and was burned down twice by Union soldiers during the Civil War. Juniper Springs, seen below in the 1930s, is one of Florida's 33 first-magnitude springs. The health of Florida's ecosystems depends on dynamic natural processes. Hidden in the forests, the spring ecosystem is one of a few natural places in Florida where a visitor may encounter manatees, alligators, otters, deer, largemouth bass, turtles, eels, ospreys, and snails, all in a single visit. (Above RBD, below MG.)

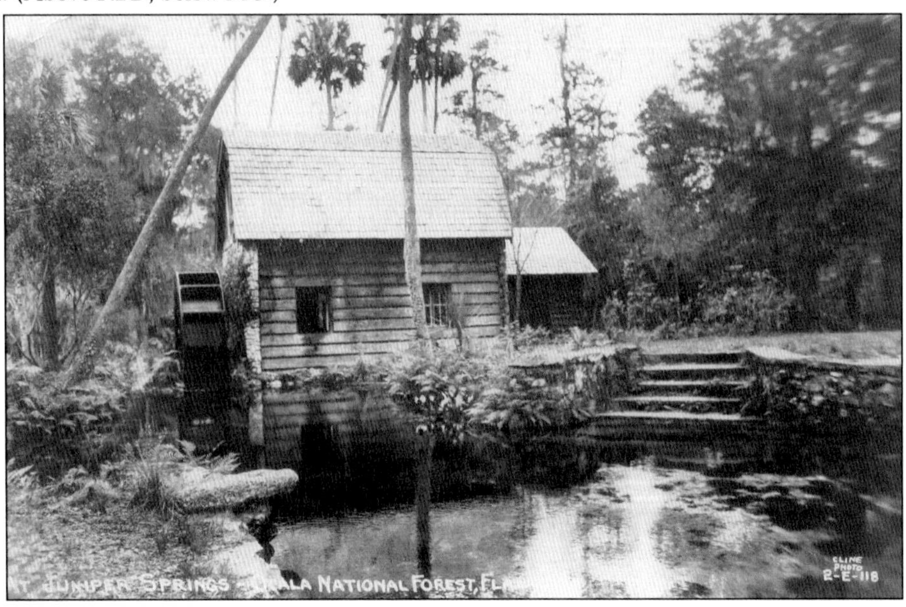

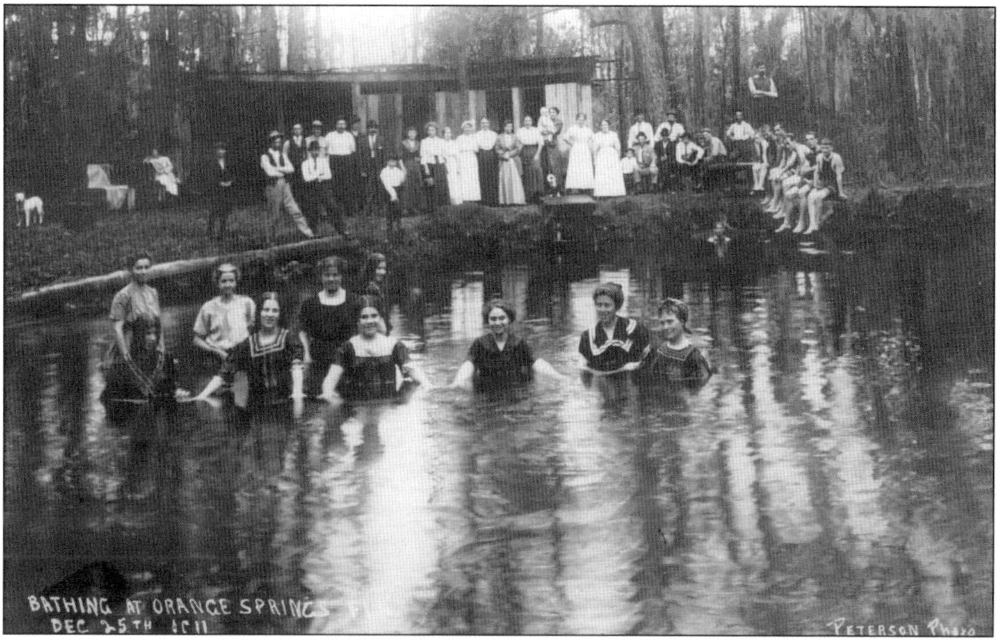

Florida springs average a temperature of 72 degrees, naturally warm enough for these bathers photographed in Orange Springs on Christmas Day, 1911. Water is Florida's most abundant natural resource, a place of recreation and renewal, as well as a vital food source. From Florida springs flow the purest, clearest, and freshest water in the world with underwater views that are absolutely breathtaking. Below, this group wades in Alexander Springs, one of four first-magnitude natural springs located in the Ocala National Forest (along with Juniper, Salt, and Silver Glen Springs). Access for hikers to and from the Florida Trail is provided at Salt Springs, Juniper Springs, and Alexander Springs recreation areas. Springs are excellent scuba diving, cave diving and snorkeling locations; some are over 200 feet deep and can be explored to a depth of a mile underground. (Above DS, below RBD.)

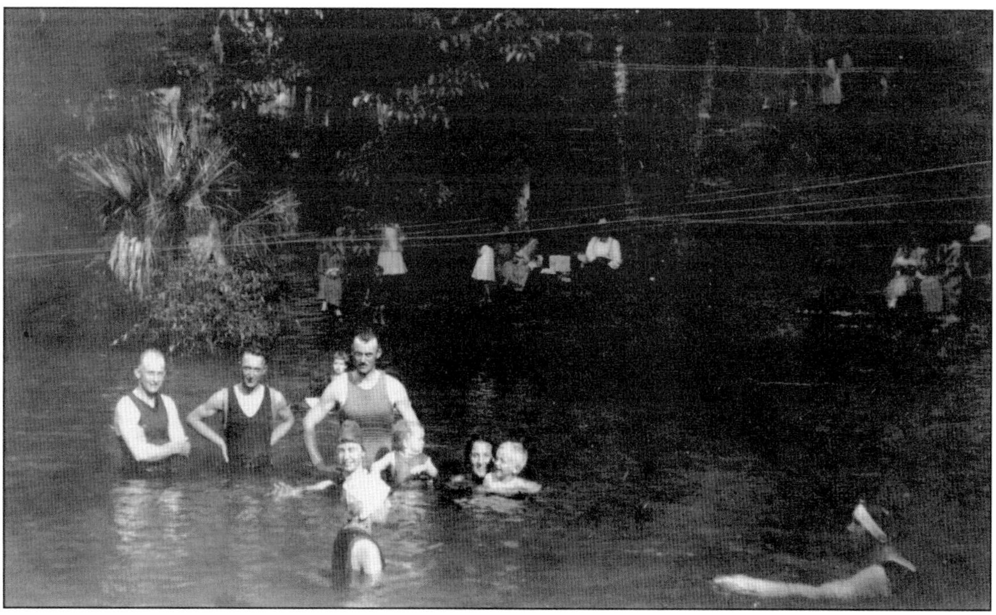

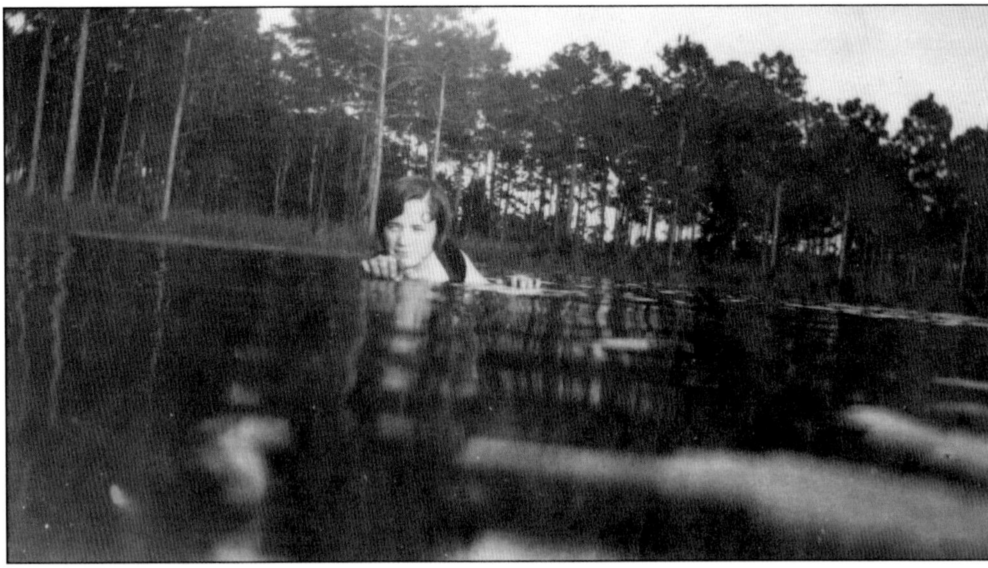

Louise Vaughn is photographed from a unique perspective, while swimming in Lake Umatilla in the 1920s. Seen below, Lucille Little, Bena Allen, and Lucy Collins pose in a rowboat, enjoying the setting in 1923. A local historian, Wass de Czege, described Umatilla's surroundings with these words: "The majestic flight of the bald eagles, the cry of the osprey, the silvery white of the egrets along the lush, green shoreline, the silent marshes where the sand hill cranes nest, the clear, cool water of enchanted creeks . . . where the air smells of maple buds and sundrenched hammocks will be here for those whose souls are yearning for a world created by God and not yet spoiled by man." (Above IV, below EAS.)

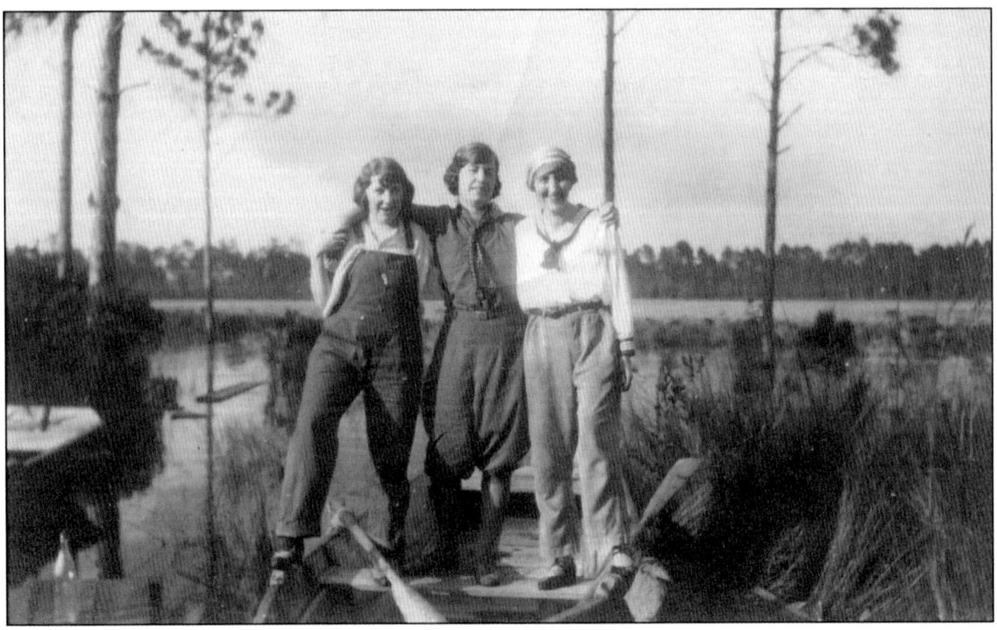

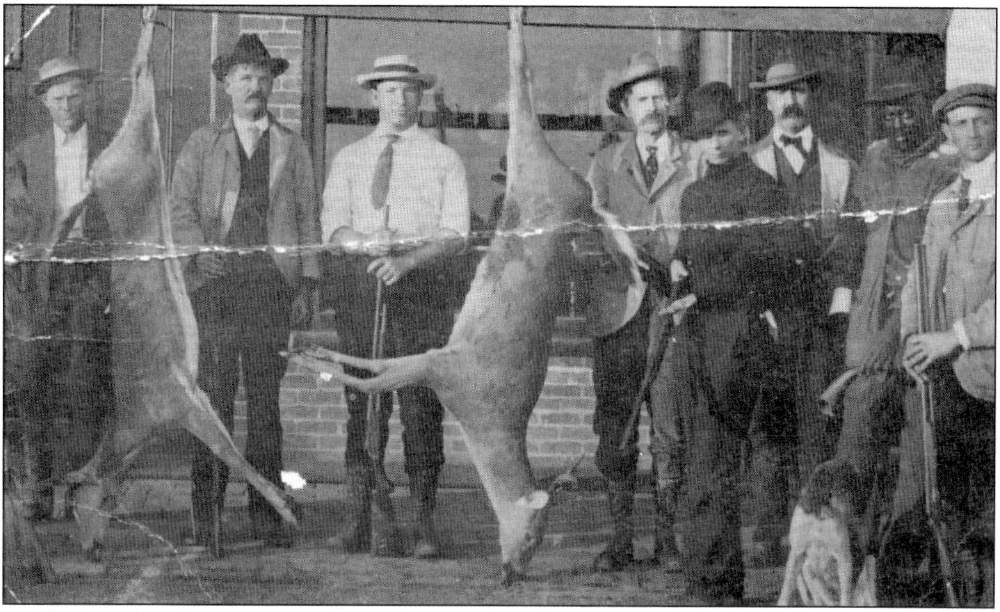

The big scrub is a hunter's paradise, with deer, hogs, doves, quail, ducks, and turkeys to be hunted for sport. In 1908, Pres. Theodore Roosevelt proclaimed 240,000 acres of the "Big Scrub" as the Ocala National Forest. It is the southernmost forest in the United States, located between the Ocklawaha and the St. Johns Rivers with Umatilla as its southern gateway. Photographed in 1912, hunters display their deer in front of a store in Higley, only C. A. Vaughn, on the left, is identified. In the image below, Robert Lee Collins sits high in his saddle while carrying home a deer from the forest. An unidentified friend on foot, carries his deer bound over his shoulder. In the pioneer days, alligators, panthers, black bear, lynx and bobcats were hunted from every vantage, nearly to extinction. (Above IV, below EAS.)

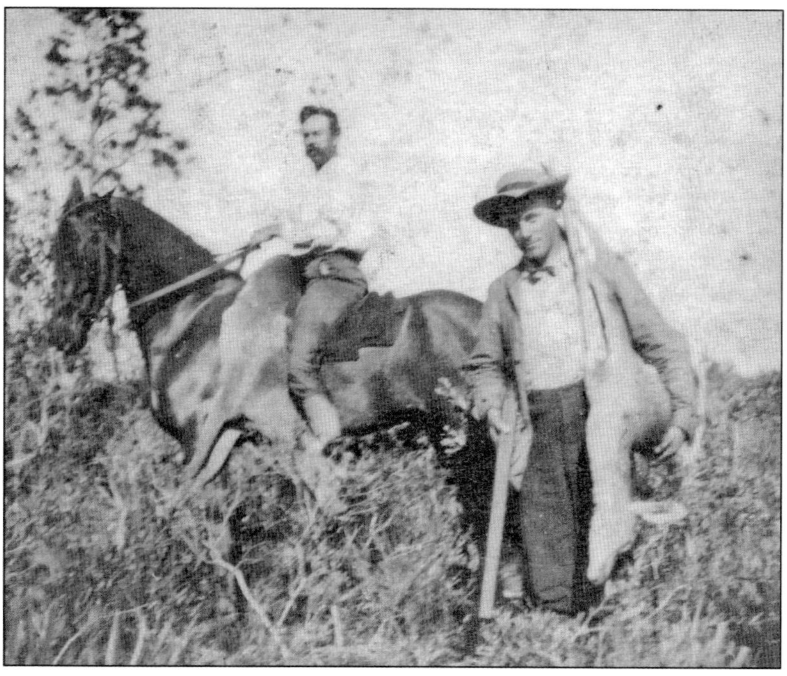

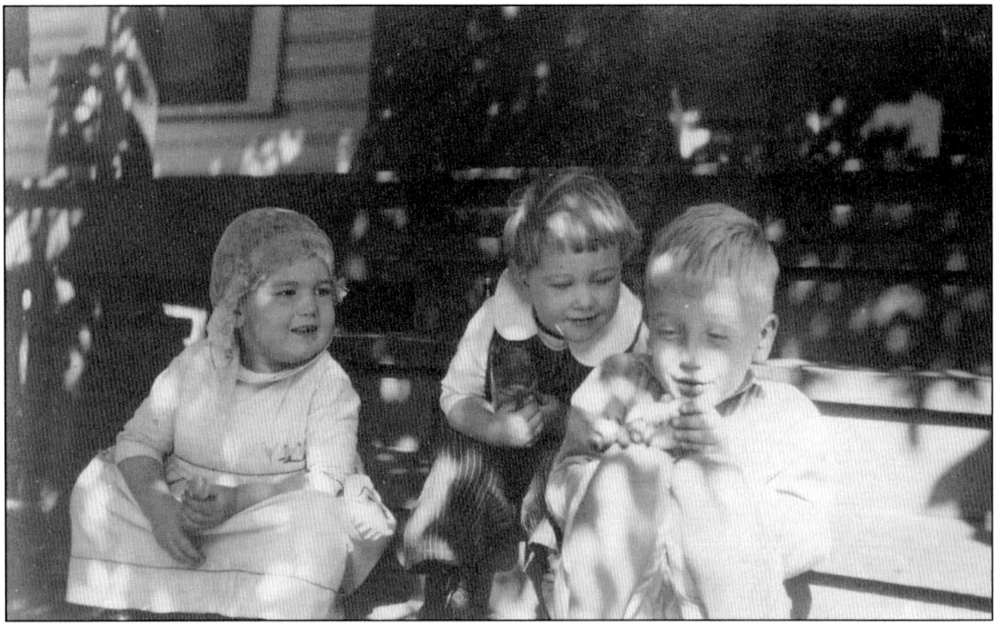

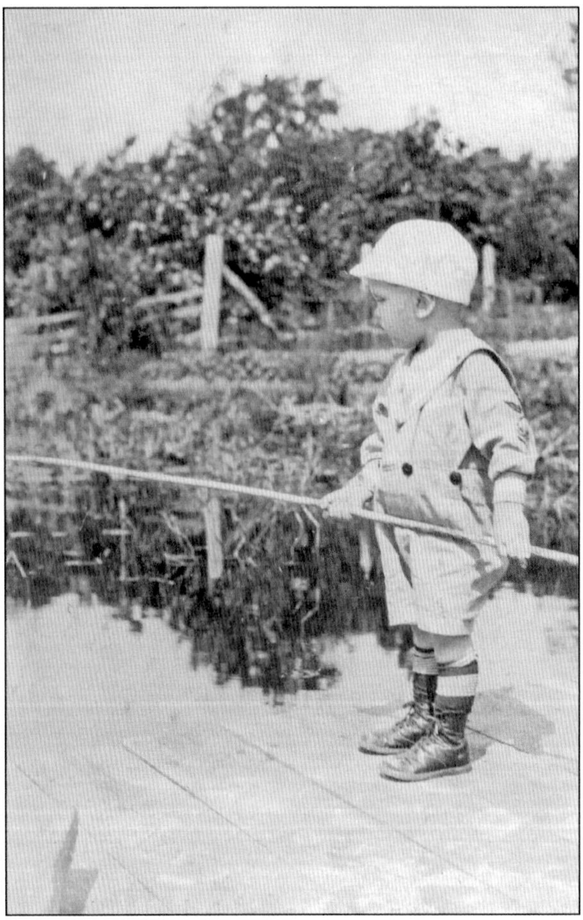

Carolyn, Mary, and Bobby Collins take delight with a bird in hand in this 1921 image. Children learned lifelong lessons through daily encounters with Mother Nature, the best teacher of all. Time spent in an unspoiled and largely undeveloped natural setting made the woods and countryside as familiar as home to Florida's early generations. In 1924, young Harry Collins Jr. is pictured below cane pole fishing from the family dock. Passion for the great outdoors was cultivated at an early age and became second nature to children raised in Florida's outdoors. (RBD.)

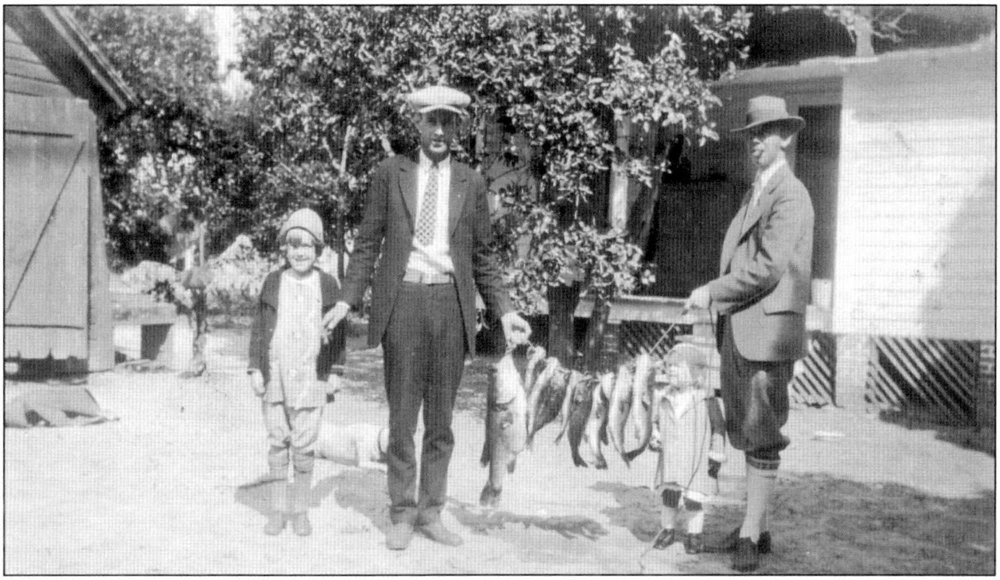

Carolyn and Virginia Collins admire an impressive string of fish held by their father and a friend in 1927. Children in Umatilla practically grew up with a pole in hand. Pictured below in the 1930s is Bob Vaughn with a bass he caught in Lake Umatilla. Bass fishing historically lured enthusiasts to Lake County, and the area became a popular location for tournaments beginning in the 1920s with the Florida Bass Tournament. Tournaments held on the Ocklawaha Chain were notorious for the supreme largemouth bass and fighting black crappie. Topping the list for best statewide fishing sites in 2005 are the St. Johns River and Lake George. Today there are numerous bass clubs in the central Florida area, including BASS Federation affiliation for competitive fishing enthusiasts. (Above RBD, below IV.)

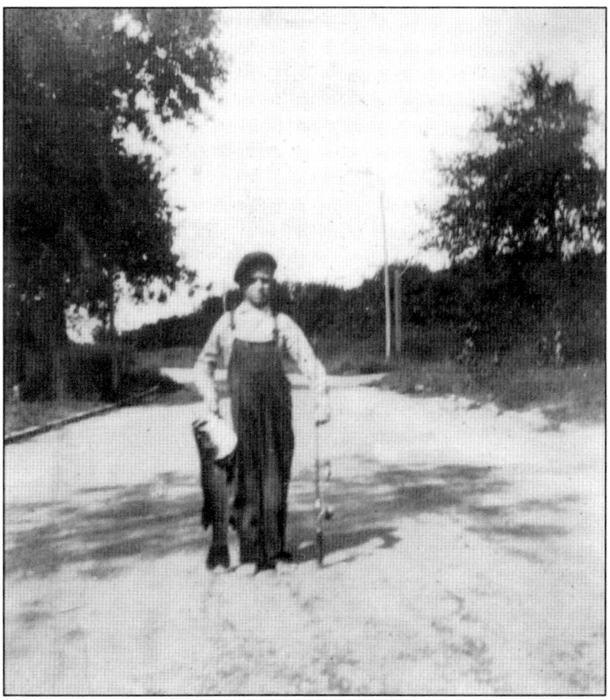

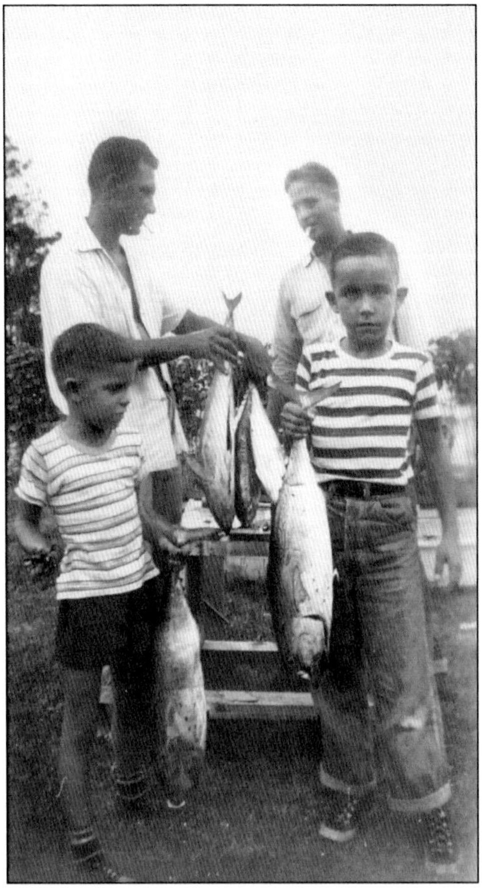

Early settlers primarily spent time in the forest hunting and fishing. Today camping, hiking, and birding are the basis of ecotourism in Florida. The boys in the image on the left, Dan Smith (left) and Warren Smith, take pride in their catch from a successful day of fishing. The men in the background are Warren Smith Sr. (left) and Jack Robertson. The group most likely caught these saltwater fish in the Banana River. Florida's National Scenic Trail stretches more than 1,400 miles across the state, from the sawgrass prairies of Big Cypress National Preserve at the edge of the Everglades to historic Fort Pickens at Gulf Islands National Seashore at Pensacola Beach. Part of the National Scenic Trail, the Florida Trail, with a trailhead near Umatilla in the Ocala National Forest, provides opportunities for both short hikes and extended backpacking trips. The Florida Trail crosses the Ocklawaha River, seen below in the early 1900s as it exits the Ocala National Forest on the north. (Left DS, below CB.)

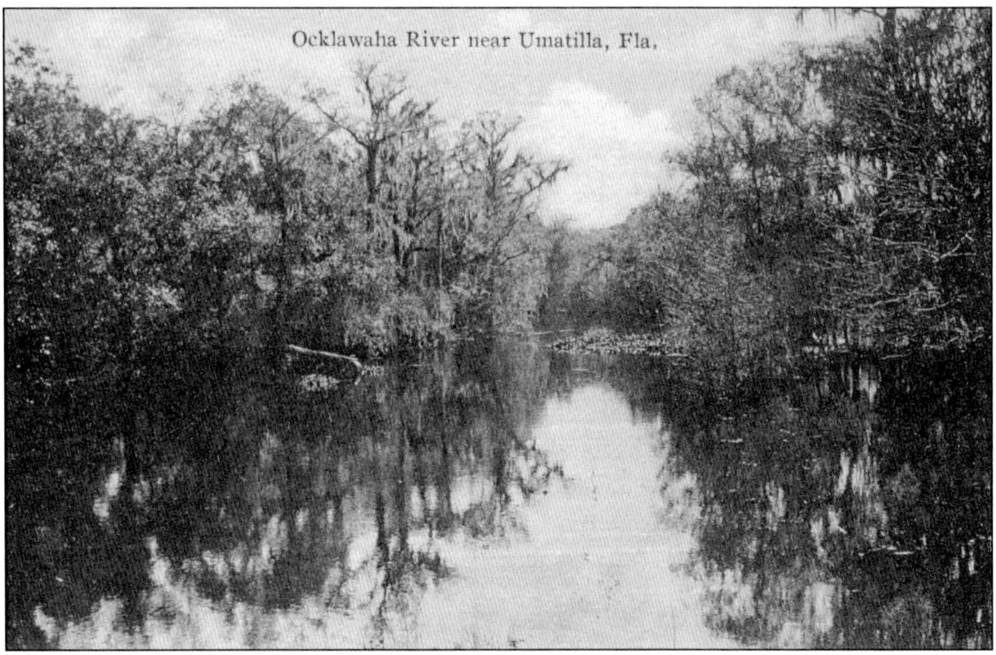

At right, Leonard and Jack Robertson pose with their catch of the day in 1940s Umatilla. Pictured below, Virginia "Smitty" Robertson holds her backyard catch in 1945. Large bass began to decline in number and around 1990, the BASS Federation held a disastrous national tournament on the Harris Chain, setting a record for the lowest average catch rate of any national tournament. This tournament created ripples throughout bass fishing circles, eventually culminating in an article in the December 1992 issue of *Bassmaster Magazine,* which detailed many of the problems. The causes were reported as overenthusiastic weed spraying, locks, mysterious bass viruses, and a dozen other causes. Restoration efforts begun in the 1990s successfully replenished these waters, which produce five fish tournament limits of over 20 pounds on a regular basis. Bass weighing 9 to 11 pounds regularly anchor most of these catches. (Right DS, below RBD.)

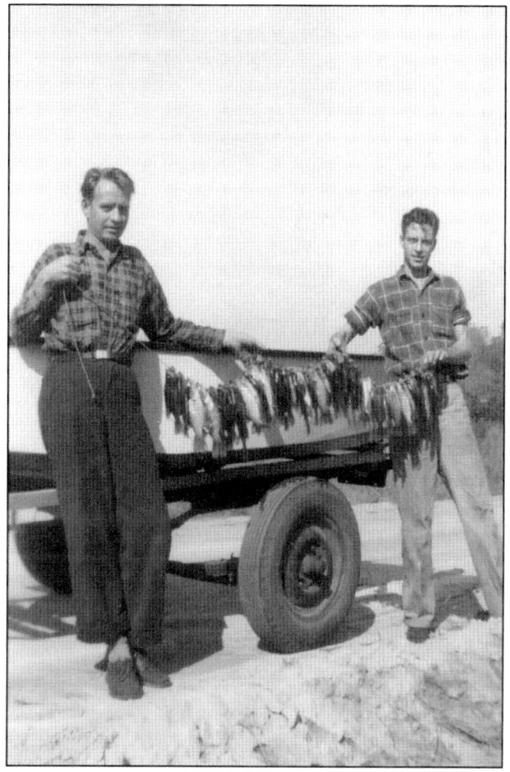

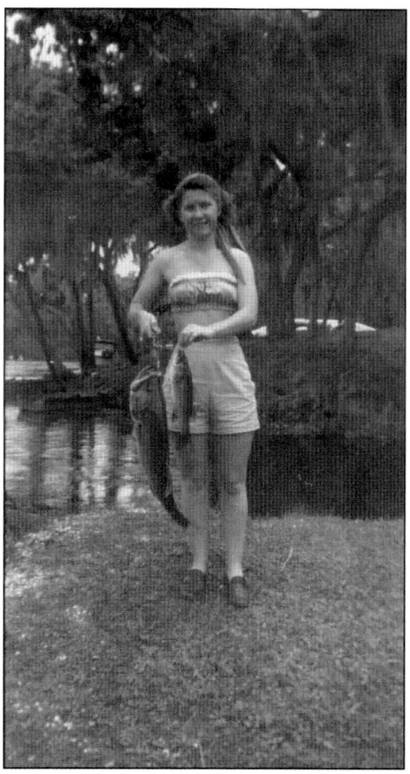

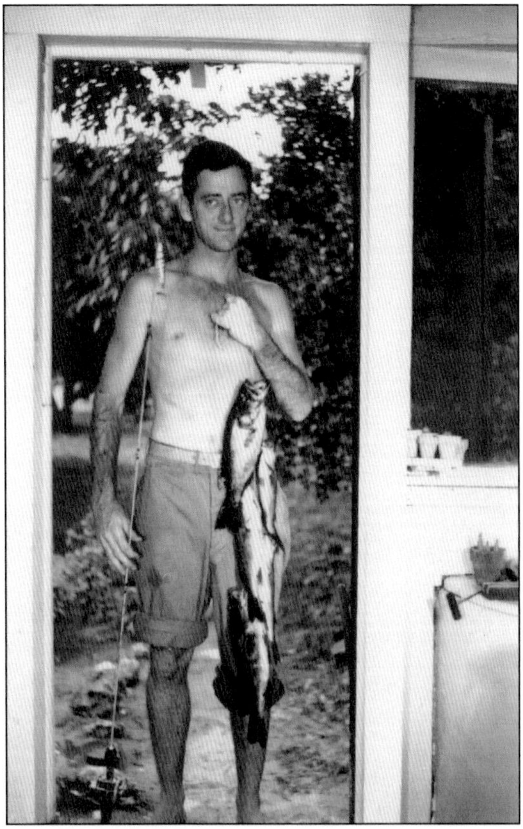

Tom Carr, pictured in the 1930s, brings home his bass caught in Lake Enola for preparation as dinner. Below, Grover Bryan kneels with an impressive string of bass caught in Lake Yale in the mid-1940s. Florida implemented a daily limit of five bass at least 14 inches in length that went a long way to improve the overall success of Florida bass anglers in the 1990s. Catch and release caught on with anglers and guides. In 2001–2002, a severe drought created an artificial draw down that regrew miles of eelgrass, pads, and shoreline cover. Game officials and residents replanted acres of beneficial reeds in large areas of the Harris Chain, and water levels have returned to normal. The Harris Chain is producing good numbers of bass, and many 10- and 11-pound fish are caught each spring, along with an occasional giant in the 12–13 pound range. (Left TC, below RBD.)

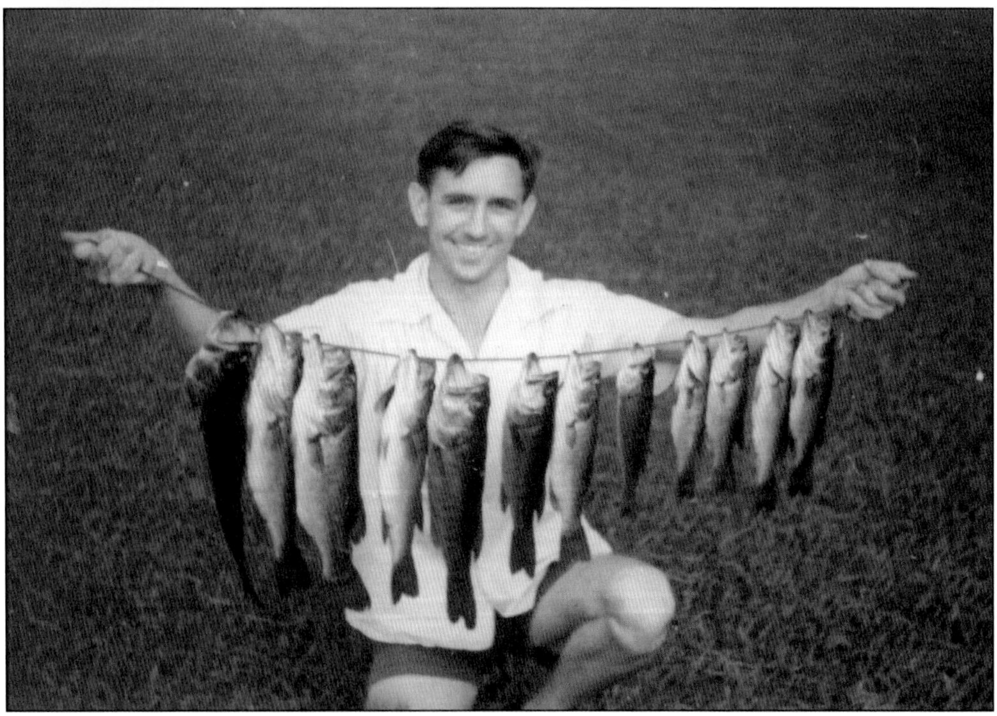

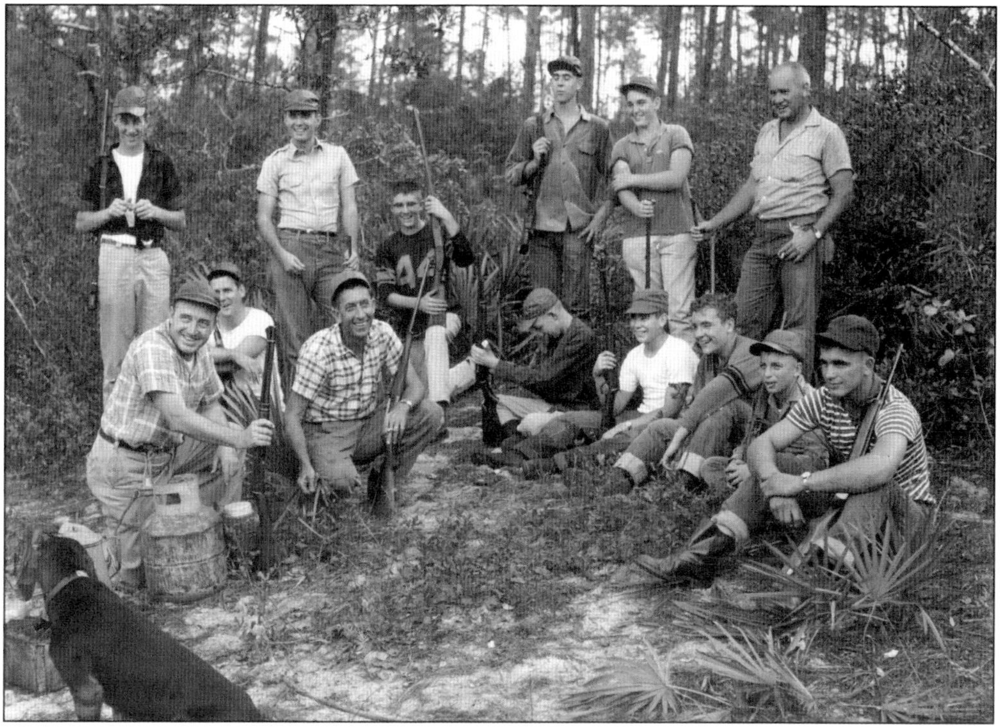

The hunting party pictured above included, from left to right, the following: (kneeling and sitting) Clyde Marteeny, Don Hampton, "Doc" F. P. Hatfield, Mike Hatfield, Ike Vaughn, Grable Parker, Johnny Webb, Buddy McTureous, Jack Austin; (standing) Roger Johnston, Jerry Brown, Leon Stricklen, Dick Collins, and Wilbur "Sonny" Parker. The Florida Trail in the Ocala National Forest is certified as a Florida National Scenic Trail, and has been called the "crown jewel" of the Florida Trail system. The trail traverses a range of natural communities, including extensive stands of longleaf pines and scattered communities of sand pines, and skirts open prairies and ponds that are excellent for viewing wildlife. Below, a group of unidentified young men display their fish along the shore. (Above IV, below EAS.)

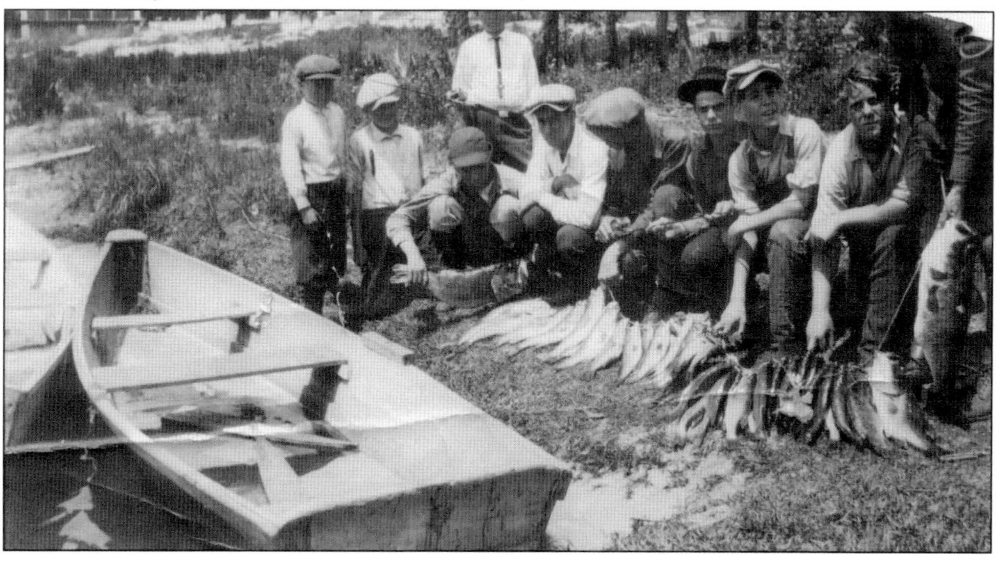

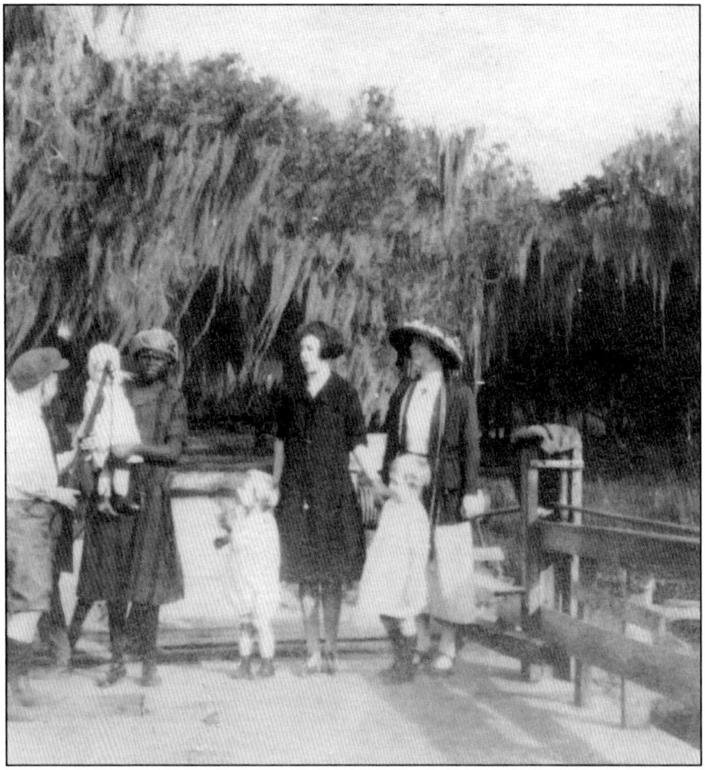

Photographed crossing on Fort Gates Ferry in 1923, are, from left to right, Bill and Harry Collins, unidentified, Mary, Carolyn, and Evelyn Collins, and Bena Allen. The Fort Gates Ferry is the last ferry operating on the Saint Johns River, and crosses the river just north of Lake George between Fruitland on the east and Salt Springs on the west. The ferry is still operating with the original barge. (RBD.)

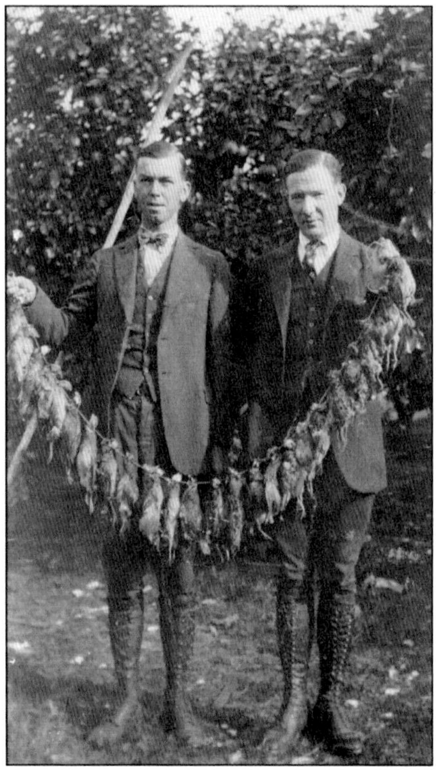

Harry Collins and Jim Dickinson (right), dressed in gentlemen's hunting wear and snake boots, proudly display a string of quail from a hunt in the scrub. The excitement of pursuing bobwhite quail, with the sight of pointing dogs lacing back and forth across expansive fields, and the suspense of walking into the feathered whirlwind of a rising covey, makes quail hunting a favored sport. (RBD.)

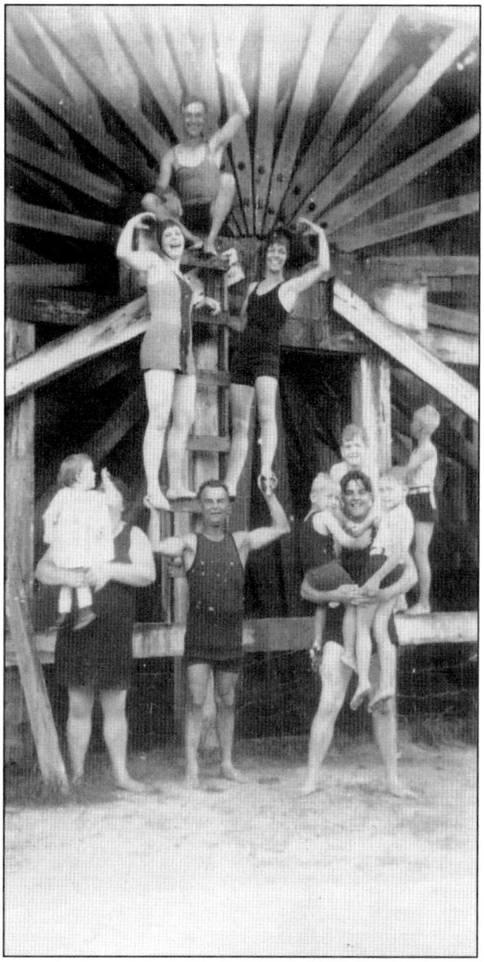

A mighty show of muscle, in a mock strongman circus performance, is displayed in this photograph from 1925, with the Juniper Springs gristmill water wheel as a background. The children are the only "performers" whose identities are known. They are, from left to right, Virginia, Harry, Carolyn, Mary, and Bobby Collins. Photographed below in 1926, rolling in fun, these children take turns on the waterwheel at de Leon Springs. Florida's springs and waterways were the first playgrounds for residents, and a popular attraction for visitors. The cool waters were nature's air conditioning and relief from Florida's long, steamy summers. (RBD.)

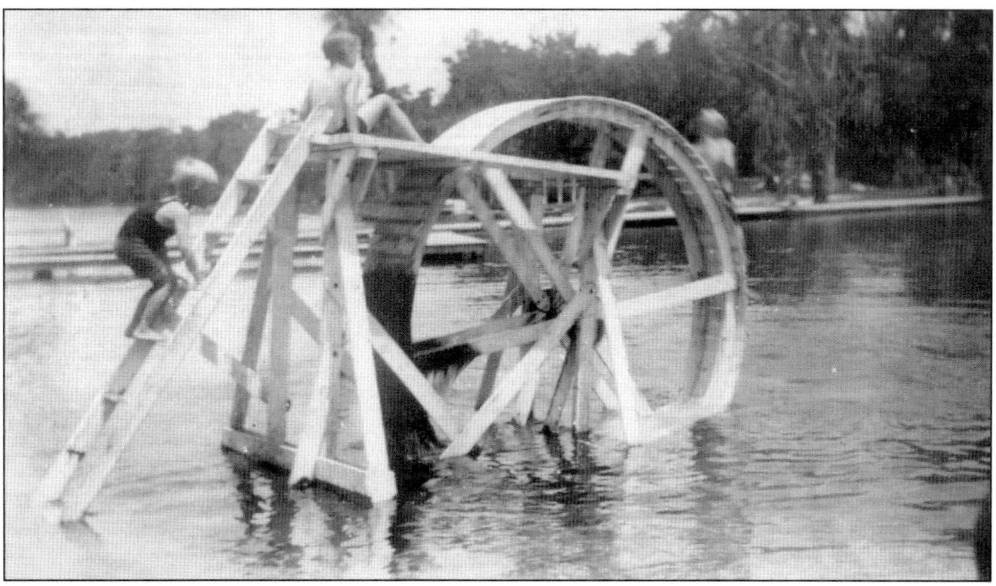

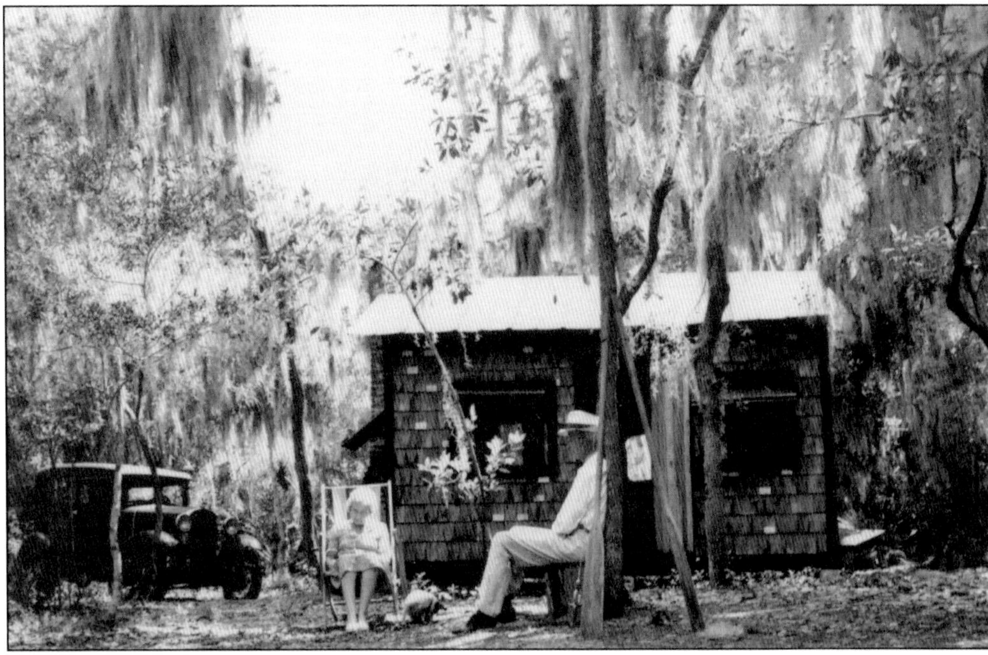

Louise and Dr. Archibald "Parson" Carr are photographed on the grounds of their lakeside cabin. Carr liked fishing and hunting and bought a bit of land on the edge of the Ocala National Forest, where he built this small cabin in 1938. The cabin, seen below, played a key role in the development of the conservation ethic of the Carr family. It was a family affair, where observations were made and ideas were exchanged and passed among the three generations of Carrs who escaped to interact with a natural, unspoiled Florida. The cabin provided a full immersion experience in the Florida landscape for family and friends. Today Archie Carr Jr. and his wife, Marjorie, are remembered for the courageous work they accomplished in Florida—Archie with sea turtles, and Marjorie instrumental in stopping the construction of the Cross Florida Barge Canal. (TC.)

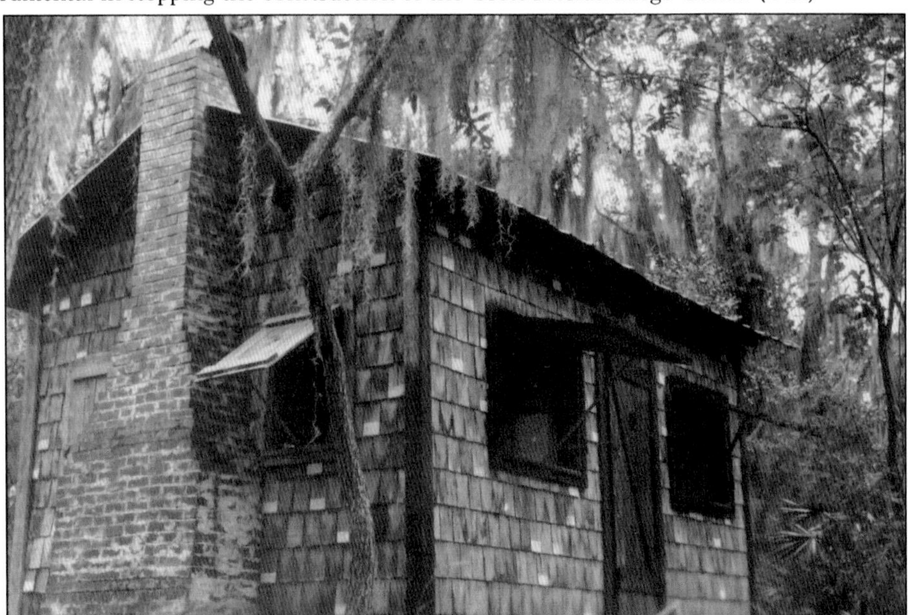

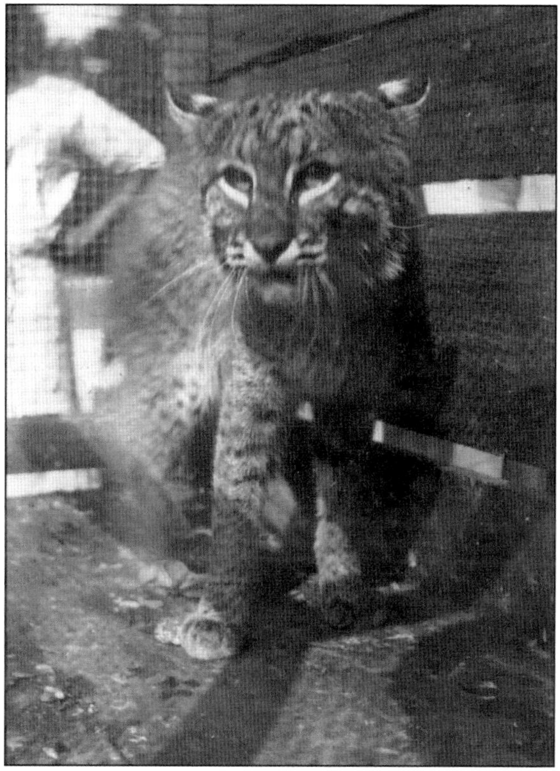

Ever the naturalists, the Carr boys Archie and Tommy kept a "pet" lynx, captured in the scrub around 1930. The wildcat proved a poor pet and was released soon after this photograph was taken. Pictured below in 1935, Tommy Carr sits in his rowboat-turned-sailboat on Lake Enola. During the Depression, sail cloth was too expensive to buy, so Louise Carr sewed flour sacks together to make his sail. Carr took his little boat out on Lake Enola during a hurricane in 1935, just to see how fast it would sail. Carr remembers the tropical winds blew that little boat clear to the far shore in no time, and unable to sail back, he had to walk the distance back home during the storm. (TC.)

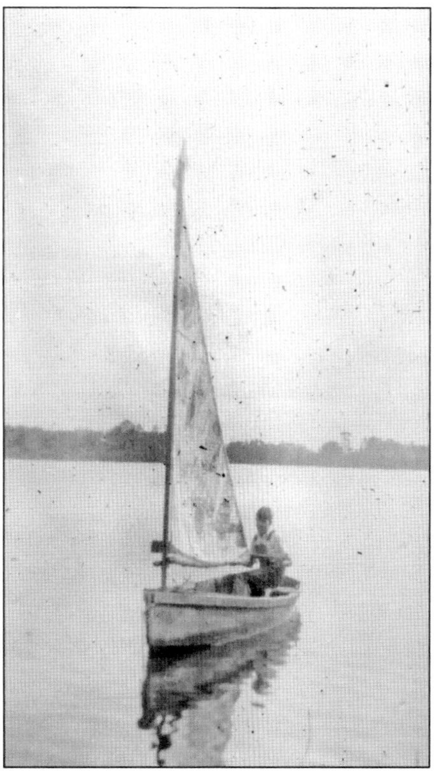

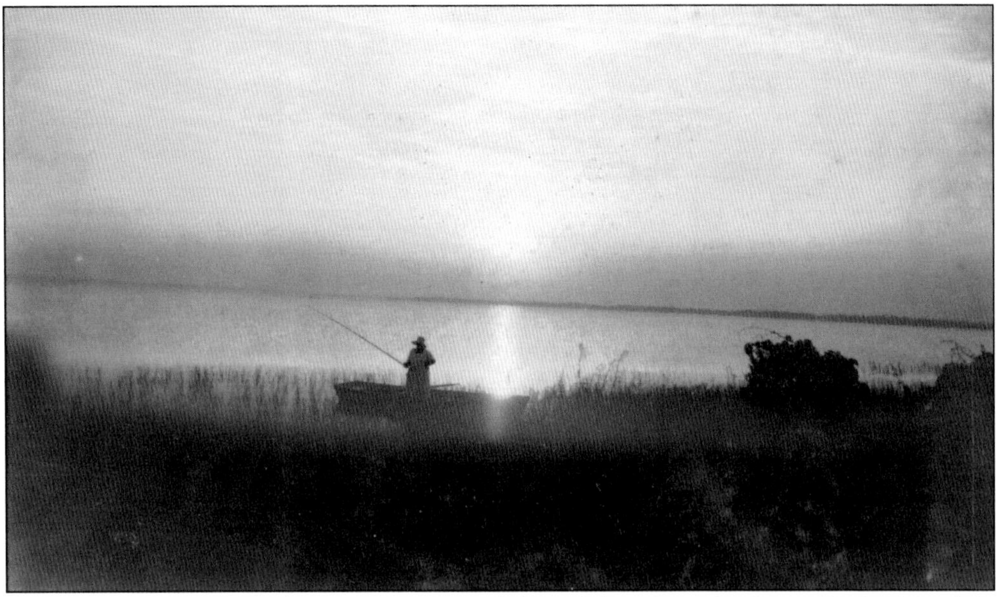

Living the abundant life, a lone woman pictured above fishes along the shore of Lake Yale while a Florida sunset paints the sky in the 1920s. Life in Umatilla is abundant living, just as advertised in this 1940s chamber of commerce promotion. Before time was recorded, Florida's abundant natural resources made provision for every human need—a fertile earth for crops and groves, fish and wildlife for sport and food, restful places where body and soul are restored, mystical views of fauna and flora—all nature's gift. Stewards of Florida's abundance continue to preserve and pass on to future generations the same beauty and bounty. (RBD.)

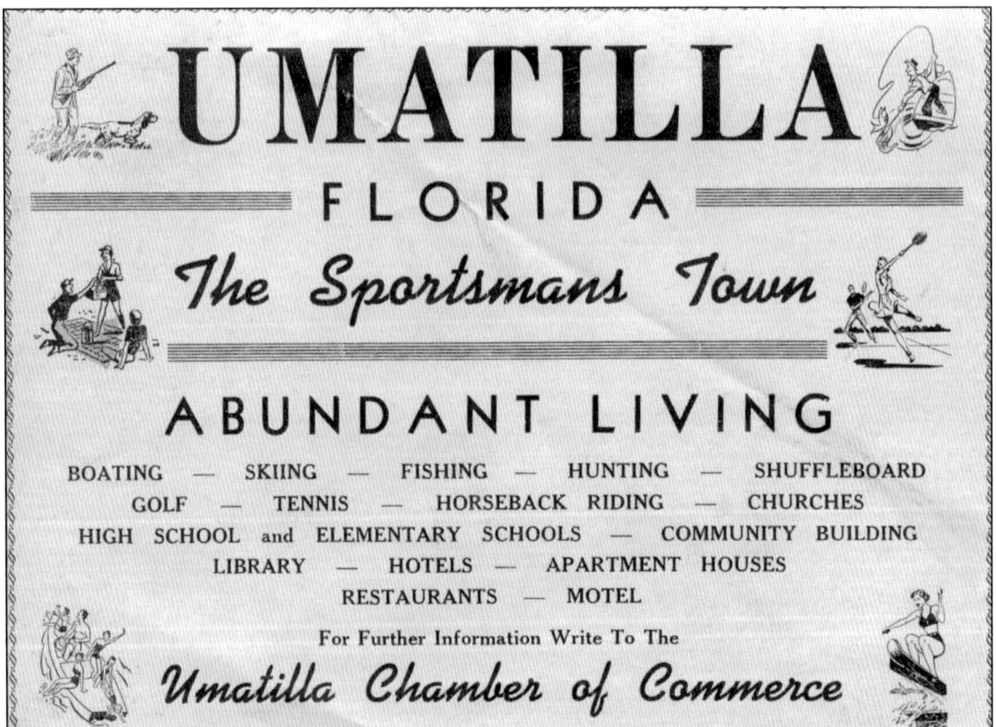

Bibliography

Bains, Larry. "Umatilla History: Turner Family and President's Son." *Orlando Sentinel.* July 4, 2004.

Burdette, Dick. "Rails Sing No More But Melody Lingers." *Orlando Sentinel.* November 30, 1980.

files.usgwarchives.net/fl/lake/bios

Kennedy, William T., ed. *History of Lake County, Florida.* 1929.

Lamm, Greg. "As an Industry Grew, So Did Lake County." Souvenir Edition, Leesburg Commercial. May 20, 1987.

Reed, Rick. "Umatilla's History." *Orlando Sentinel.*

Seabrook, Sue Yancey. "Yancey Family Comes to Umatilla." Lecture, Lake County Historical Society, April 23, 2004.

The Umatilla Progress. January 27, 1894.

"Umatilla: Its Story." *Quill and Scroll.* Umatilla, FL: Umatilla High School. c. 1951.

"Umatilla History." *Triangle Shopping Guide* supplement. June 28, 1989.

www.americantowns.com/fl/umatilla/organization/umatilla_public_library

www.astorflorida.com/history.htm

www.fhadistanceriding.com

Yancey, Fred D. "A History of the Umatilla Area of Lake County, Florida." *Lake County—Then and Now.* Lake County Historical Society, January 1966.

Yancey, Lucy E. *A Century of Vision, History of First Presbyterian Church, Umatilla, Florida 1886–1986.* Eustis, FL: Southern Print Co., 1986.

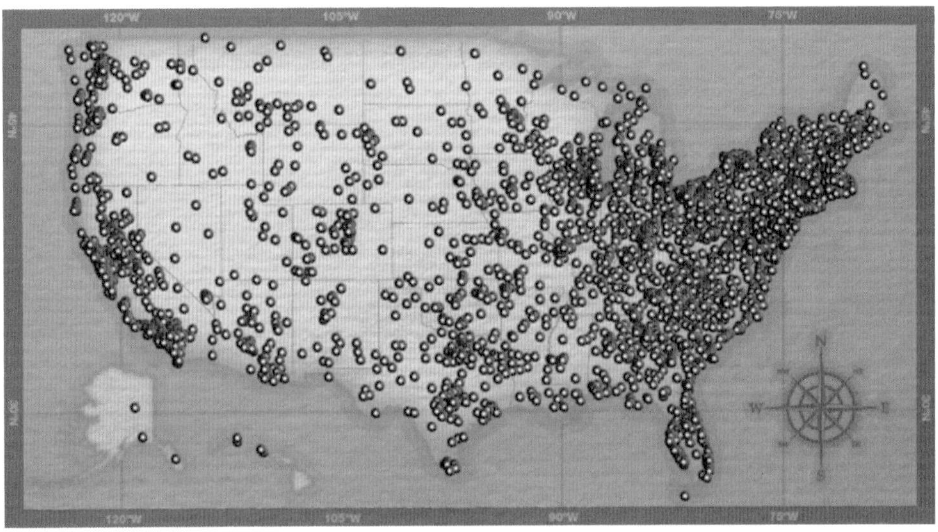